4

THE MASTER ECCENTRIC
The Journals of Rayner Heppenstall, 1969 - 81

Also by Rayner Heppenstall and published by Allison & Busby:
The Blaze of Noon
Two Moons
The Pier

The Master Eccentric

THE JOURNALS OF
RAYNER HEPPENSTALL
1969–81

Edited by Jonathan Goodman

ALLISON & BUSBY
LONDON · NEW YORK

First published in Great Britain 1986 by
Allison and Busby Limited,
6a Noel Street, London W1V 3RB,
and distributed in the USA by
Schocken Brooks Inc.,
62 Cooper Square, New York, NY 10003.

British Library Cataloguing in Publication Data:
Heppenstall, Rayner
The master eccentric: the diaries of Rayner Heppenstall 1969-1981.
1. Heppenstall, Rayner — Biography 2. Authors, English — 20th
Century — Biography
I. Title   II. Goodman, Jonathan
823'.912   PR6015.E56Z/
ISBN 0-85031-536-0

The complete journals of Rayner Heppenstall are now part of the
Brotherton Collection at the Brotherton Library, University of Leeds,
England.

Set in 11/13 Bembo by All Print Services, Lewes Road, Bromley, Kent,
and printed and bound in Great Britain by
Billings & Sons Ltd, Hylton Road, Worcester.

Contents

Introduction

I remember the day (it was a day in spring, a Saturday, the day of some Cup Final or other) when I first met Rayner Heppenstall, not only because of that meeting but because, an hour or so before it, I, without much choice in the matter, lugged an unconscious and inconveniently lanky woman from her flat, which was going up in flames. I have no idea how many steps there were from that flat to the ground; but they were considerably fewer than those rising to Rayner's flat on the fourth floor of 14 Ladbroke Terrace, in the Notting Hill district of West London. I have since learned, from an entry in his journals, that there were ninety-two of those steps; being an obsessional collector of data relating to his milieu (a Gallicism that he would certainly have underlined), he had, of course, counted them, then counted them again, just to make sure.

I was not feeling very well by the time I scaled the ninety-second step. My lungs ached and I was having a job to breathe, for I had swallowed a lot of soot; some of this kept leaking into my nostrils, so that, when I spoke, I sounded as if I had a cleft palate. And I must have looked strange about the eyes, having lost my brows and lashes.

But during the couple of hours of my visit, Rayner made no comment on my appearance or voice. We — he dominantly, though never domineeringly — talked about literature, crime (mostly French crime, the case of La Roncière in particular), the good white wine that his wife Margaret kept popping into the room to pour, actors we admired, politicians we despised, Constable and his country, ways of reducing over-population. Not until I was leaving did he ask if my speech impediment was congenital. I explained the cause of my nasal tones, and he murmured something about the student in the Ghost Sonata, an allusion that escaped me.

Some weeks later, I received a letter from a book-dealer, Basil Donne-Smith (whose name crops up in the journals — and who, now I come to think of it, must have brought about my first meeting with Rayner). He wondered what had possessed me to join the

London Fire Brigade.

I wrote back, asking what he was talking about.

He replied that I knew perfectly well, mentioned that Rayner had told him all about my new career, and said that, though he had to admit that he had never envisaged my sliding down poles and climbing ladders for a living, I had no reason to feel ashamed of what I was doing.

After further notes had gone to or fro, the exchange ended with Donne-Smith's conceding that I was not a fireman . . . but still, he failed to see how Rayner could have misunderstood unless I had given ample reason for misunderstanding.

I failed as well. Much later, however, I realised that my brief reply to Rayner's parting question became an irresistible, fast-growing seed in his mind; but it was as if the seed of a carnation, say, flowered as a gladiolus.

For one thing, he was enchanted by fire. The English criminal case that most intrigued him was the burning of Evelyn Foster, which he thought of twisting into a novel and which he actually used as the basis of a play for television. He was more interested in the fact that Barbara Hepworth and James Laver had died in fires than in the fact that they had died. When, seeking a bolt-hole from the smells and shudderings of a launderama, he moved to Coach Cottage, in the Kent seaside town of Deal, he was delighted that for the first time in his life he had a garden where he could light bonfires — noxious ones, he hoped, vexing the family that lived next door. (As Alan Sillitoe had found out, Rayner needed no reason other than propinquity for dislike of neighbours.)

And, as he was between novels when I first met him, he used my reply to give an outing, a practice run, to his skill at turning fact into fiction.

He was, you see, dichotomous in his treatment of truth. Unmindful of consequences — or rather, determined not to fear them — he was tactlessly honest about what he knew or believed: yet nearly all his novels contain embroideries of happenings that had affected his own life or the lives of people he loved, liked or loathed. Writing in his journal on May 31st, 1970, he notes that entries made before 1969 were casualties of one of his "holocausts"

vii

— burnt, with other writings, because he had used the incidents, his telling of them ("The manner of telling remains, with me, more important than the thing told"), in novels. At least one of the lacunae in the existing journals is an indirect result of "self-plagiarism".

Fortunately, some fragments of autobiography survived the holocausts. Whenever it has seemed appropriate, I have gone to these for footnotes, thus letting Rayner give his own explanations. Information for other notes has come from his published memoirs: *The Intellectual Part,* in which he traces influences on his thinking, ranging back to schooldays in Huddersfield, Yorkshire, where he was born on July 27th, 1911; *Four Absentees,* his reminiscences of his friendships, founded in the 1930s, with the artist, Eric Gill, and the writers, J. Middleton Murry, George Orwell and Dylan Thomas; *Portrait of the Artist as a Professional Man,* his account of his career as a producer and writer for BBC radio from 1945, soon after his release from the army on psychiatric grounds, until 1967. I have also had information and help from, among others, Margaret Heppenstall ("M." in the journals), Adam Heppenstall, and Lindy and Donald Foord; Josephine Falk of the Arts Council, Linda Holman of the National Book League, Felix Hope-Nicholson, Michael Hosking, proprietor of the Golden Hind bookshop in Deal, Sylvie Lyons of the French Institute, and Richard Whittington-Egan.

My aim has been to footnote sparingly but just sufficiently. With few exceptions, nearly all to do with books not yet published when they were spoken of, the notes do not refer to post-entry happenings. I felt that it would be a disservice both to Rayner and to his readers to clutter the pages and deflect attention with details that were widely known, that were implicit, or that were revealed in subsequent entries. Occasionally, when it has seemed to me that just one or two words of explanation were needed, I have inserted these, italicised within square brackets. There are no other additions.

Though I have not tampered with sentences — and, in footnotes, have tried to follow Rayner's way of punctuating, designating, and expressing dates — I have shortened many entries, usually by deleting entire paragraphs. I am sure that if Rayner had edited someone else's journals, he would not have started to select until he had counted every word; and, having made the selection, he would have counted the chosen words: then he would have done some arithmetic. As I am not that methodical, I can only guess that I have whittled away about two-thirds of what he wrote.

In this introduction, I have tried to say very little about Rayner. Even so, I am worried that perhaps I have said too much, spoiling a few of his surprises, anticipating the moments that he felt were right for admitting or proclaiming the components of himself. I want readers to find out about him, as I did, in dribs and drabs, the details cued, as it were, by talk of other things.

Only in a biography is the architecture of a man's life revealed storey by storey. Otherwise, in getting to know someone, or believing so, the particles of knowledge come to light haphazardly, in no apparent order. And that is best. After all, a man's life is what he conceives it to be. He will not have given much thought to chronology in reaching conclusions about himself; the fact that he keeps a dairy is immaterial, for a day is as likely to be made important by a memory jogged by an event as by the event itself.

In his journals, Rayner Heppenstall did not merely let his mind wander: he caused it to. In so doing, he was self-revealing to an extent that few men dare to be. He told a truth. Still, I don't think he would complain at my saying that what follows can, perhaps should, be read as if it were his last novel, because, as he himself said, "We are largely fictitious, even to ourselves."

19 January

Almost six months ahead of the contractual date, I have finished translating Balzac's *Splendeurs et Misères des Courtisanes*. Unless Penguin find some objection to the title, I am calling it *A Harlot High and Low*.[1]

Finishing the translation means also that I have finished reading the book, for, as I found to be a good principle with Chateaubriand's *Atala* and *René*,[2] I made a point of no more than occasionally glancing ahead. This sustained my interest. I had to go on translating in order to find out what happened next. As I translated straight on to the typewriter, with two carbons, I already have a typescript which a Miss Cookman from Penguin will collect in duplicate on Wednesday.

A clear day, yet mild for the time of year. The two one-act Jules Renard plays are to be staged during the summer at a little theatre on the island of Mull.[3] No money to speak of in that, but it would be nice to stay on Mull.

1. Published as a Penguin *Classic* in 1970, and still in print.
2. RH's translations of the two works were published, with an introduction by Robert Baldick, as one volume of the Oxford Library of French Classics by the Oxford University Press in 1963. He wrote the introduction to another title in the series, *The Wayward Head and Heart* by Crébillon Fils, translated by Barbara Bray, also published in 1963.
3. RH's translations, under the titles of *A Clean Break* and *Daily Bread*, were first performed in 1968, on the BBC Third (radio) Programme, by Geraldine McEwan and Robert Stephens. Their first stage performance was as a double-bill in the summer season at the Little Theatre, Dervaig, on the Hebridean island of Mull. Advertised as being the "smallest professional theatre in the British Isles", the Little Theatre had no actors or staff other than the couple who ran it, Barrie and Marianne Hesketh (whose most ambitious and novel production was of Shakespeare's *The Tempest*).

1

22 January

M.[1] is in bed with 'flu and could not go to the French Embassy luncheon. This aggravated a shortage of ladies and caused me to be seated between Boisdeffre[2] and a modestly pleasant man called Felix Hope-Nicholson, who is somehow connected with the Hugo family.[3] We talked about Hauteville House[4] in Guernsey, which I remember with pleasure from fifteen years ago.[5] In addition to the rather unprepossessing couple who herded visitors around at that time, there is a curator, living in Paris, who visits the place occasionally, using a flat in the house which is kept for him. If I were writing a book on Victor Hugo, I could stay in that flat almost indefinitely. The idea appeals to me. The seascape from that top floor is splendid in the extreme, and I find Hugo,

1. RH's wife. In 1935, John Middleton Murry, the literary and social critic, the subject of RH's first book, acquired a derelict mansion at Langham, near Colchester, Essex, on the edge of the Constable country, with the hope of turning it into a "socialist university". RH: "The following year, I was invited to go and live at the Adelphi Centre as one of the permanent nucleus and, rather oddly, as cook.... I went to Langham on July 18th, a date I remember without difficulty, since it was also the day on which the Spanish civil war broke out and the birthday of a young woman, Margaret Edwards, whom I met that evening, not at the Centre but at the house of a local farmer who was giving a party....
    "She was, it appeared, the resident secretary of S.L. Bensusan, a Spanish-Jewish writer of Essex dialect stories... and she came from Monmouthshire. For me, this was the *coup de foudre*. It was never seriously in doubt that I should, in due course, marry this young woman....
    "I do not propose to describe her, beyond saying that she is fairly tall and fair in colouring and that she has always or nearly always looked the picture of health, despite an unfortunate medical history."
2. Pierre de Boisdeffre, author and diplomat, who in 1969 was cultural attaché at the French Embassy in London.
3. His elder sister had married Victor Hugo's great-grandson and heir.
4. No. 38 Hauteville Street, which Hugo bought from the profits of *Les Contemplations*, was his home from October 1856.
5. In 1954, RH, with his daughter Lindy, then aged fourteen, had spent a holiday in the Channel Islands.

especially Hugo in exile, a compelling figure, undoubtedly the greatest French poet of the nineteenth century, a great novelist into the bargain, and at least an intriguing playwright. I already have a chapter towards a book in my essay on the table-turning in Jersey,[1] first done as a radio script, and there will be a lot about Hugo the penal reformer when I get down to *French Crime in the Romantic Age*. It would be nicer to stay at Hauteville House than on Mull.

28 January

Rain. In Iraq this morning, mass hanging of persons implausibly convicted of spying for Israel. At the French Institute, Roland Barthes, a good-looking man, alert and conversable. The trouble with these structuralists is that, having discovered a new way of looking at language, they believe that language now IS what they say about it and nothing else, whereas it is that in addition to everything it has been thought to be in the past.[2]

6 February

My mother's funeral. Lindy and I took the afternoon train back from Preston. This evening, M. and I went to a PEN[3] party for younger novelists. Those whom I met for the first time were Maggie Ross, Paul Bailey and Adam Ferguson.

1. In 1853, Hugo was persuaded to take part in a seance at his home in Marine Terrace, St Helier, Jersey; his scepticism changed to ardent belief when the turning of the three-legged table seemed to suggest that his dead daughter, Léopoldine, was trying to communicate with him.
2. Writing of Barthes after his death in 1980, Susan Sontag argued that if people would stop thinking of him as a semiologist or structuralist, he would appear as "a rather traditional *promeneur solitaire*, and a greater writer than even his more fervent admirers now claim".
3. Founded in 1921 to promote friendship and understanding between writers and to defend freedom of expression within and between nations. The initials stand for Poets, Playwrights, Editors, Essayists, Novelists.

Angus Stewart,[1] invited at my suggestion, I had not, I think, seen as a baby in Leeds, but only his two older brothers. I had yet been aware of his birth before the Innes Stewarts went to Australia. I suppose that I first saw him, therefore, a boy on holiday from Oundle, in Oxford twenty years ago.

Mature novelists also there were Elizabeth Taylor and Nina Bawden, both fellow-members of the PEN English executive committee. Also, decidedly older, dear Leslie Hartley,[2] who told me how broken up he had been by his mother's death.

The fact is, although I can always weep at funerals, that I was far less affected by my mother's death than by that of my father.[3] I shall inherit nothing from my mother, unless it be a

1. Son of John Innes Mackintosh Stewart, the writer (as Michael Innes) of novels of detection and (as J.I.M. Stewart) of general novels and books on, among other things, character and motive in Shakespeare. In October 1930, when RH was starting his second year as an undergraduate at Leeds University, Stewart, who was five years older than RH, joined the university as a junior lecturer in English. Some forty years later, RH recalled that Stewart "was small, fair in colouring and of a pale complexion, wore green tweeds and a wispy moustache, smoked an unconvincing pipe, walked along polished corridors with practised speed and spoke in a mannered voice of light pitch". The two men became friends, and the friendship lasted, kept alive by correspondence between 1935 and 1945, during which time Stewart was Jury Professor of English Literature at Adelaide University, Australia. (His first card to RH merely said, "O God! O Adelaide!") From 1948, he was a tutor at Christ Church, Oxford.
2. L.P. Hartley.
3. RH: "Brought up in a crowded back-to-back house with two younger sisters and a brother, my mother, Lizzie Rayner, was the daughter of a jobbing gardener and a domestic servant who continued to take in washing or go out to help with the wash in big houses after her marriage. The man Lizzie Rayner married when she was twenty-six and he twenty-eight worked in a collar and tie but was the first man on either side of the family to do so. He did it in a modest capacity, as drapery manager at a small branch of the Huddersfield Industrial Society. His father was a teamer, which meant that he drove and groomed carthorses....

    "Both my parents had left school when they were twelve. At that

certain tenacity. From my father I inherited fair colouring, an umbrella, a box of tools, an overcoat, a suit which fitted me almost to perfection, my Y-chromosome and a surname. Like his, the sun readily burns but does not bronze my skin. At sixty-five, he still had more hair than I have at fifty-seven, but it was the same kind of hair. He, on the other hand, had had his last tooth pulled out by forty. A doctor who treated me in the aftermath of my sub-arachnoid haemorrhage[1] described that as hereditary, though I have always supposed that the stroke of which my father died was of the more usual kind. In distinction from my mother, he was of no great longevity, and I expect to take after him in that respect. His features were better than either mine or my sister's, though we both favoured rather him than our mother. He was, in fact, rather a good-looking man, which I am not. He lacked combativeness. Whether I do is a moot point. I do not know whether he was as fanatically truthful as I am, since his circumstances contained less temptation to tell lies than mine have done almost since I first went to live in London, and I never detected him in any form of moral obliquity. He smoked too much, though not as much as I do. He drank little, while I just manage to avoid the abyss of alcoholism. He was of an affectionate disposition,

---

age, I went with a scholarship, available to anyone not hopelessly retarded, to Huddersfield College. The normal school-leaving age then was fourteen. That I stayed on so long thereafter was due in the main to the Huddersfield Education Committee which, twenty years before the Welfare State, ran a little welfare state of its own. As an inducement to my parents to keep me on at school after the age of fourteen, it paid them a maintenance grant of ten shillings a week.

"By some miracle of economy, they paid for me to go on a school trip to Brittany when I was fifteen and to attend *cours de vacances* at a school in Calais two years later. The year after that, living at home and travelling up by train daily, I went to Leeds University as a recognised student in training for the teaching profession. I was reading English and French equally for a degree in what was known as Modern Languages. At Easter in my second year, I went to Strasbourg, a *semestre* at a French university being obligatory for those pursuing honours in French."

1. In April 1955.

more so than his wife. I have a wife of so affectionate a disposition that I have stopped trying to compete with her.

His funeral took place a month before that stay in Oxford during which I am calculating I first met Angus Stewart. We haven't seen Innes so often these last few vacations, if indeed at all since M. and I stayed at their new house out in the country, two and a half years ago. The entirely credible explanation is that both the Stewart daughters now live in London. On his trips up, Innes lunches or dines and perhaps stays the night with one or other of them instead of coming to us.

13 February

I don't know whether professional historians do this early in their careers, but, with the idea of a general history of French crime in mind, I have, during the past year or so, set out, in four red exercise books, with two facing pages to a year and four lines to a month, an exact chronology of events in French criminal history from a few years before the Revolution to the present day. As the desk diary M. got me for this year is exceptionally large, with a foolscap page to each day, I have been entering at the bottoms of pages all the anniversary dates my four red exercise books gave me and am further adding any I come across in my reading also in British and American criminal history.

Thus, on today's date in 1820 occurred the assassination of the Duc de Berri, while on the same date in 1917 Mata Hari was arrested, and in 1953 a franc millionaire, Marcel Hilaire, was awarded a life sentence for the murder of his mistress. It was also on this date in 1946 that, at the Old Bailey, two Polish deserters, Malinowski and Grandkowski, were sentenced to death for the murder of an underworld figure known as Russian Robert, found in Chepstow Place not far from here, and, two years later, that P.C. Edgar was shot dead by an English deserter, Donald Thomas. Classic British anniversaries for today are February 13th, 1891, last of the

"Jack the Ripper" murders, and, 1901, death by poisoning of the second Mrs George Chapman, "Chapman" himself, a Pole under an assumed name, being one of many candidates for the Ripper's identity.

What I should like to do is compile a *Criminal Calendar*, perhaps to be reissued annually. It would be nice to provide each date with A Criminal Thought for the Day, though I have failed to find many with the same depth and resonance as Ravachol's[1] "There are no innocent *bourgeois*." With at least one of each day's anniversaries ought also to appear a relevant passage from some contemporary or classic source. That would mean not less than five hundred words a day, the whole adding up to a volume of, say, two hundred thoughts, whereas it is said that the commonly most advantageous length now is a mere seventy thousand. The undertaking would have to be painfully cramped. I shall persist, though I fear that in the end I shall have no more than the makings of a parlour game, in which people tell me their birthdays and I tell them what those dates mean in criminal history.

20 February

In *The Listener*, a poem by John Hewitt on the death of W.R. Rodgers.[2] Bertie became my immediate colleague at the BBC the year after the war and was inconspicuously around until 1952, when (known thereafter as "Rodgers the lodger") he went off with or at any rate presently married

1. The French murderer and anarchist, Claudius-François Koenigstein, known by his mother's maiden name of "Ravachol", who was executed in 1892.
2. RH: "The first sixteen months of my undistinguished military career [starting in the late summer of 1940] were spent in Nothern Ireland. At the weekend, I commonly got to Belfast and was put up on Saturday nights by John Hewitt, assistant curator of the municipal art gallery, a very nice man and a poet. It was with him that I first met W.R. Rodgers, at the Brown Horse, a public house near the *Belfast Telegraph* building. Bertie Rodgers's first (indeed, to all intents and purposes, his only) volume, *Awake! and Other Poems*, had received a lot

Laurence Gilliam's[1] wife, the splendid Marianne. He was a spellbinding talker, which was surprising in view of the way he spoke, slowly and almost inaudibly. He was a man of strong dislikes, of whom I became one.

9 March

In her posthumous memoirs,[2] Harriet Cohen describes a "new concert dress, ... a medieval type one in red velvet with long sleeves," made for the first performance of Arnold Bax's *Winter Legends* in early 1932. It springs to life as that in which, shortly afterwards, the slim, sheathed figure wowed a largely undergraduate audience in Leeds.

It is, I suppose, a non-book, which could have been ghosted but apparently was not. To what is supplied by letters, programmes and engagement books, little is added but affectionate or merely charitable gush and such general observations as: "The *Majestic* was the first and almost the dearest of a series of magical ships that I gave my heart to, as I did to my series of cats," or: "He was a great joker, as most pianists are." And yet one reads on, not really bored, never seriously irritated, moved most when one can oneself supply background material, as I can at two points.

How good a pianist Harriet Cohen was, better judges than I must say. I fancy that she was very good indeed and that both her heyday acclaim and her posthumous reputation seem insubstantial because she did not concentrate on, say,

---

of attention during the first year of the war, and its publisher was the one who had done my first novel, *The Blaze of Noon*, which saved him from bankruptcy. Bertie (known in the Hewitt circle as 'dirty Bertie') was a Presbyterian minister at Loughgall, in Co. Tyrone. He was a small, brown-eyed, faunlike man, well-dressed in Donegal tweeds, with powerful false teeth clenched less often in those days than they were to be later on a large pipe."

1. Head of BBC Radio Features from 1947 until his death in 1964; responsible for the world-wide Christmas Day programme from 1933.
2. *A Bundle of Time*, London, 1969.

Bach, but championed a contemporary British music now almost forgotten. As the book (with no display of bitterness) makes plain, concert managers, recording companies and the BBC fought shy of her programmes.

There were letters from G.B. Shaw, Arnold Bennett and Ramsay Macdonald. There are glimpses of D.H. Lawrence and the Spanish poet Lorca, who, it appears, was a fine amateur pianist, like Gide. To those old men, the kindly young pianist was a bright and beautiful, reviving presence, Daddy's gifted girl. Though also charmed, her juniors noted those oddly plucked eyebrows, a general air of the 'twenties, a touch of the screen vamp. There are good photographs, but none of the pianist's hands. The later Cohen of scholarships and funds and Zionism comes over as the worthily serious last avatar of an extremely nice woman, not a great joker, unlike most pianists. She does not even repeat the joke she made to me at Lady Margaret Hall, about being known as Mistress of the King's Musick.[1]

19 March

Nice little tea party at Lindy and Donald's,[2] for Charles and Pamela Snow[3] to see Andrew, my grandson, now walking, with what Charles calls determined inefficiency, but I should have thought with some intelligence. Not yet ready to embark unsupported on great distances, he feels his way along the wall, every now and then turning his head to see whether the piece of furniture he means to go to next is yet within the shortest possible distance.

Apropos something or other, Charles says that he is not a theologian. I suggest that, in so far as he might be said to be

1. Her friend, Sir Arnold Bax, was, inconspicuously, Master of the King's (latterly Queen's) Musick from 1942 until his death in 1953.
2. Donald Foord, whom Lindy had married in 1964.
3. The writers, (Lord) C.P. Snow and his wife, Pamela Hansford Johnson. RH: "It was in 1947, at a PEN dinner, the first I had attended, that I struck up an immediate friendship with Pamela, next to whom

a theologian, *The Sleep of Reason* indicates something of a breakdown of faith. With this Charles agrees.

22 March

In the flat below used to be two old ladies, a borough councillor and her former governess. They were Catholics and attended mass daily in the chapel of the St Vincent's clinic across the road. Of the two sisters in their thirties who replaced them when they went to live in the country (both have since died), the elder is away. This evening, the younger had us to dinner with Piers Paul and Emily Read, they first coming up here for drinks.

Piers, known in the family as Jiminy, is another younger novelist whom I knew when he was small. Physically, Piers resembles his father[1] in build and in the shape of his head, but is fairer, has straight hair and more conventionally regular

---

the luckof the *placement* had seated me . . . a small, precise woman, dark-haired but with eyes of a startling blue, not perhaps as large as one might have wished them or set as widely apart, lidded, it might be, orientally. She was then still married to the colonial husband by whom she had two children, a boy and a girl, and they lived with Pamela's mother in Chelsea. To C.P. Snow, whom she was later to marry [in 1950], I was briefly introduced by Jacob Bronowski, one afternoon, at a small club frequented by scientists, just whereabouts in the West End I can no longer recall or what I was doing with Bronowski.... At the time, Charles can hardly have been fifty, but looked more. His apparent age was not to change appreciably in twenty years...a big, shambling man, bald, with spectacles and a slow, deliberate manner of speaking.''

1. Sir Herbert Read, authority on art and literature, himself a novelist and poet.

    RH: "Herbert Read had spent two years at Leeds University before the Great War. In 1933, he returned to receive an honorary Lit.D., in the course of a ceremony which involved a decayed and rheumy Duke of Devonshire in also handing me my unwanted Dip.Ed. Tall, erect, with dark hair waving thickly over his right temple, Read at forty was an attractive figure. At the dance in the university great hall that evening, I was introduced to him just as I was dashing off to catch the last train back to my native town. I'd had one poem in *New Verse* and several in *The Adelphi*, and Read had gratifyingly noted my name.

"[The following year,] my little book on Middleton Murry coming out, Herbert Read wrote to me kindly about it. As it was also favourably reviewed, I ventured back to London. On the evening of my arrival, he took me to a *Criterion* party, at which I met T.S. Eliot and some others who wrote regularly for that opulently produced quarterly. I had seen and to some extent heard T.S. Eliot previously, early that October, when he lectured in Leeds. The effect of the lecture had been spoilt by the repeated detonation of air locks in the radiator system....

"In the summer of 1935, Herbert Read took a lease on the famous Bloomsbury house, Charleston, at Firle in Sussex, from Duncan Grant and Vanessa Bell, while Ludo, his wife, played her viola in the orchestra at Glyndebourne.... Finding me broke and ill-housed, he took me down there.... I stayed there for a week or so....

"At that time, he toyed, like Eliot, with Social Credit. I never tried to understand that, but he remained my favourite uncle-figure, the one it was pleasantest to be with, both before and after Middleton Murry as counselling uncle was replaced by Fr. D'Arcy and Eric Gill, and elder brother George Orwell left home....

"Then another war. I, who had been a pacifist, enlisted. Herbert, with his admirable military record, became a rallying point for all the pacifist-anarchist poets. We corresponded. We met once or twice when I was on leave in London....

"For me at the BBC, Herbert Read wrote three 'Imaginary Conversations' (a Hamlet and the pirates, an Aristotle's mother, a Stendhal and Byron) and also *Moon's Farm* — in prose. I stayed once at his manor house in Yorkshire. I remember Herbert complaining that musical Benedictines from Ampleforth drank all his gin. Then only three meetings in ten years, two of these brief and unpremeditated. Three exchanges of letters, in one of which I was told of a cancer on the tongue, then quiescent....

"In November 1955, I received a copy of *Moon's Farm*, inscribed to me as 'the onlie begetter'. When I begot the piece some years before, it had been in admirable prose. I did not compare the two texts line by line, but my impression was that its translation into verse had been effected simply by dividing up and retyping....

"I am not blind, but know little about contemporary art, most of that little rubbed off in contact with a man I always heard much criticised by artists and those in the art world, a man who yet gained the public ear when they could not. In literary achievement, I put that

11

features. He talks more easily and without northern accent, but has a lot of the same quiet charm. I asked Piers whether he was still both *pratiquant* and *croyant*. He asked me whether I could imagine anyone not being, with Ludo for a mother. That, I thought, answered only the *pratiquant* part of my question, but did not press the point.

29 March

Jean de Beer,[1] due in London for the PEN party and dinner on Wednesday and Thursday, rang on Monday from Paris, inviting me to take part today, Saturday, in a two hours' two-way discussion programme, to be broadcast live, on French Culture. For seven years past, my spoken French has rarely had any practice except at Institute cocktail parties and a very few Embassy luncheons. My ability to speak French correctly and fluently has thus become a bit intermittent and, if I am tired or preoccupied, may lapse altogether. To be adequate for two hours seemed no small undertaking, and during the week I went into a kind of silent training, whenever possible thinking my thoughts in French. In the upshot, I somewhat dominated this morning's proceedings, at moments too much so, with the result that the umpire in Paris, a journalist on *L'Humanité*, ventured a crack about the supposed taciturnity of the English. Knowing that the transmission was "live" and could not

---

strange novel, *The Green Child* (based on a Yorkshire folk-tale) top, closely followed by parts of *The Innocent Eye* and the trench-warfare reporting first published as two little Faber pamphlets, thereafter incorporated in an autobiography not good as a whole, *Annals of Innocence and Experience*.

"I am quite sure I never met a man of sharper or more durable personal charm or, really, a more personable man. The shyness and reserve were genuine but also regional. Herbert Read was a strong regionalist, retiring to the Plain of York not without intellectual calculation. I can't think of any survivor at all like him."

1. French dramatist; administrator of organisations concerned with the arts.

therefore be edited before transmission, I was determined to bring the talk round to the Middle East, where French policy repels me and, I claimed, astonished the British people generally. I got in one observation which pleased me. This was that, after all, the Jews are a civilised people, whereas the Arabs are only savages. No doubt many Frenchmen also think this, but it is not the kind of statement which may be heard on French radio and might well, I thought, lead to ministerial complaint.

20 April

There was rain on Tuesday, but it has brightened up again. M. has a touch of bronchitis, and the sprained feeling in her foot is described as a "march fracture". Income tax forms are out in good time this year. A quick casting out of entries in the little black book shows that my free-lance earnings are only a hundred pounds or so down on last year's, so that with my pension I am not so very much poorer than I was, quite apart from the Arts Council's little subsidy.[1] This is heartening.

28 April

Advance copies of *Portrait of the Artist as a Professional Man.* The before-and-after effect is weakened by the fact that in the frontispiece, young, I look both less well and less cheerful than, old, on the back of the jacket. There are misprints, and there are semi-colons introduced since I passed proofs.[2]

1. A "writer's grant" of £2,000. In 1966, the Arts Council had awarded RH a prize of £1,000 for his first novel, *The Blaze of Noon* (1939), "which showed real merit but had possibly not had the success it deserved".
2. Though RH was open-minded about the use of the semi-colon and the dash by other writers, he avoided these marks in his own work.

29 April

I looked through *Portrait* again in the evening, wondering how it would affect people, wondering how justly I had achieved the various effects I wanted, wondering whether I could have stayed on at the BBC comfortably if I had only played my cards better, musing upon those twenty-two lost years, thinking thoughts, in general charitable, about the many people with whom work in radio had brought me into contact. I missed the company of actors (was very pleased last Saturday to see Stephen Murray again). I missed certain technicians, one or two delightful secretaries, and the studio excitement. I was glad to have no more to do with BBC administrators, but then administrators are frightful all the world over, and those at the BBC had been honourable men in a limited way, with good manners. If they had done me harm, it had been out of stupidity and worry.

With the head of Drama Department, Martin Esslin, I remained on excellent terms, and he was keeping a promise that, after my departure, I should have as much free-lance work as I wanted for the Department. In the past two years, my total income had barely dropped at all and, from BBC free-lance work alone, included sums of, respectively, £1,100 and £950. My view of my former colleagues was therefore rosy, and *Portrait* erred on the side of indulgence to everyone but myself.

Last evening, towards midnight, sitting in my usual chair for a while, perfectly relaxed, before going to bed, I thought these thoughts. I forgave all the administrators, even Michael Standing.[1] So far as I knew, none of them had done me deliberate and malicious harm. The one man who had at least tried to was Joe Burroughs.[2] Moreover, he probably

1. Controller of BBC Programme Organisation (Sound) since 1957.
2. A.J. Burroughs was, like RH, a producer in Features Department; when that department was dissolved at the end of February 1965, he, RH and six other features producers became members of Drama Department.
    RH: "I was not happy in Drama. Indeed, I was tired of radio and the

14

BBC altogether. My preoccupation was to leave without forfeiting my pension rights, as I should if I simply resigned....

"Joe Burroughs was thin, with features of extreme aquilinity and dark hair worn Hitler style, his eyes of indeterminate colour, somewhat exophthalmic or at any rate markedly *à fleur de tête*, but inexpressive, curiously jellied, not mirrors of his soul unless this had at one time turned rigid with horror. His thin lips were stretched over large, uneven teeth, later replaced. His hands were filleted, sensitive and reluctant to feel in his pockets for small change. He walked flat-footedly, his toes turned in....

"Although he was good at his job, Joe Burroughs's most marked characteristic was persistent mendacity on a clinical scale. In general, this was harmless in its effects and sometimes amusing, for most of Joe's immediate colleagues were persons of higher intelligence and better education than himself, who soon learned to discount a great part of what he said and either to avoid his company or to be careful about what they said when he was present. He told lies for all the usual reasons, including self-aggrandisement, or for no apparent reason. His purpose was sometimes malicious. His easiest successes were then, of course, gained against modest and vulnerable persons, notably young actresses, but he must certainly be credited with the departure in disgrace of one of his less gifted colleagues. Among some actors, technicians, secretaries and other simple, hopeful souls, he enjoyed a positive reputation for kindness, while even those who saw through him were often amused, the actor's picture of life, in particular, being so very largely anecdotal....

"Towards the end of 1965, Joe started a campaign against me. This arose from the fact that I had frustrated an attempt by him to sell as his a very promising idea of mine, which he had heard me discussing with Terence [Tiller, another producer], whom also, at much the same time, he estranged by putting about a damagingly untrue account of the latter's behaviour after their joint departure with their wives from my daughter's wedding reception.

"That Joe had embarked on a campaign against me I quickly saw for myself, though it was Carleton Hobbs, perhaps the best radio actor of all time, who came and told me one line Joe was plugging, *viz*, that it was I who had stolen his idea....

"Within the next year and a half, I was to manage my departure the way I wanted it, so that Joe's campaign against me bore no important fruit, and I took no measures against it, but simply ceased to have anything to do with him."

thought he had done me more harm than he had, so that my departure had seemed to him an achievement of his own.

Thinking thus, I became, for a few moments, incandescent with hatred of Joe. The phenomenon appeared to be one not of heat but of intense light. There was none of that rush of blood to the head which might have produced a headache, nothing like that bursting of an artery just outside the brain which, in the same chair fourteen years previously, had been medically described as a sub-arachnoid haemorrhage. I might have imagined that I was emitting a laser beam directed accurately towards a small house I knew in a Kensington mews.

The phenomenon passed, and I went to bed. At ten o'clock this morning, I answered the telephone to Administrative Assistant, Drama (Sound), a nice woman called Marie. With the idea, no doubt, of sparing them the possible shock of hearing about the matter in a roundabout way and perhaps also of alerting them to a funeral they might feel they should attend, she was ringing round to those who had been closely associated with Joe Burroughs to inform them that he had died suddenly as the result of a heart attack last evening, towards midnight.

I experienced no guilt, though I examined myself to see whether I ought to experience guilt. From a legal point of view, I hadn't intended to kill the late A.J. Burroughs or even to do him grievous bodily harm, so it was neither murder nor manslaughter, at worst culpable negligence. Joe was no loss to the world. I did not even feel particularly sorry for his widow, though I had always liked her. No doubt she would be miserable for a while, and it would have been better for her to be rid of Joe earlier, while she was young enough to marry again and be cured of childlessness. She would not be hard up.

From a literary point of view, it would have been a good thing if I had known, while writing my reminiscent volume, that Joe Burroughs would be dead before it came out. An account of some of his more spectacular villainies and discomfitures (the results of him being caught out in reckless mendacity) would have enlivened the book. On the other hand, if I had put them in, I might not have found myself thinking of him with such hatred last night, and so he would still be alive.

6 May

This morning a young man from *The Times*, this afternoon one from the *Evening Standard*, were brought round by the publisher of *Portrait*.[1] In the course of these interviews, he learned that I have a novel on its way out with another publisher. This fact had to transpire some time, and perhaps that was the best way. A little party at his house tomorrow, the day before publication. He has been very good. On Thursday, also by his doing, I am to appear on "Late Night Line-Up". I have never seen this, but my son says it is respectable. They fetch and return me by taxi.

7 May

A piece in *The Times* this morning. The *Standard* dropped theirs, having supposed it would be exclusive. Yesterday morning, the *Times* young man spent an hour and a half asking me questions and making notes of the answers, sipping gin-and-tonic. As he departed, his notebook put away, we exchanged various flippancies. A version of what I said lightheartedly during this exchange features prominently in the opening paragraph.

RAYNER HEPPENSTALL...has written a tart account of his career as a BBC radio producer, which he would already like to rewrite...."The chap who would have been the making of it — a comic villain, I could have been so funny about him — died recently," he explains. "I've been very careful. The book is really too nice."

1. Peter Owen.

There is other stuff, most of it not too badly garbled, and my photograph from the back of the jacket looks out benignly, but that is the bit that will stick, and I don't care for the thought of Eileen Burroughs reading it at the moment.

Four literary editors at the little party this evening, Michael Ratcliffe of the Saturday *Times* and Peter Grosvenor of the *Express*, whom I had not met before, Arthur Crook of the *TLS*, an old friend,[1] and David Holloway of the *Daily Telegraph*. None of them told me what he plans in the way of reviews, but these can hardly be too awful, or they would not have shown up (unless they are lost to all shame). For the cancellation of dinner afterwards Peter Owen proffered a sufficient excuse, but I fancy that all the same it was his way of showing displeasure at the discovery that my next book is with another publisher.

In conversation with Peter Grosvenor, the next general election somehow arose. He said he would "vote the straight Tory ticket". I said that so in effect should I, but that in my case it would not be from love of the Conservatives but from disgust with Labour.[2] He shortly thereafter departing, I went

1. RH: "A not infrequent dinner guest was Arthur Crook. He had replaced Alan Pryce-Jones, whose assistant he had been, as editor of *The Times Literary Supplement*. I had written most for the *TLS* in the late 'fifties, but continued in the new decade, with fronts and middles which I have often thought I ought to do something about putting together in a book. I had liked Alan. I liked Arthur, whose luncheon guest I sometimes was at the Garrick or Rule's. In appearance, at any rate from a distance and in profile, he resembled Alan Pryce-Jones and was almost as talkative, though perhaps less amusingly so. He had a glass eye. This defect caused him, when pointing to something which lay in one direction, to point in another. He was rather sweet on M., with some implication that I was unworthy of her, which I should not have disputed."

2. RH: "My reaction to the Suez operation [in 1955] was not out of line with a number of my settled attitudes. I had long been pro-French. The French minister who ordered his troops in and who must have felt betrayed by our prompt backing down was Guy Mollet, a socialist, a better one, I felt, than Hugh Gaitskell. I was also strongly pro-Israel and considered that Sinai was properly their territory and that the

across to a plump, wall-eyed man who looked a bit lost. I asked him what he was in, and he said (I think) glass manufacture. I expressed interest and wondered just what part he played in this. He was, it transpired, a trade-union official. I told him, I fear, that in my view our trade unions were the enemies of civilisation. That, he said, was fighting talk. With some little variation, I repeated my statement. He again said that it was fighting talk, but showed no sign of wishing to fight. I left him.

11 May

First reviews. *Daily Telegraph* on Friday, *Sunday Telegraph* and *Sunday Times* today. Not bad in column inches, but niggling in tone. The reviewers clearly know more about it all than I do.

16 May

Letter by the later post from Hallam Tennyson, Assistant Head of Drama (Sound), who had a good reason for reading *The Times* on Wednesday last week, since, unnoticed by me, it contained a letter from him in the obituary column, which, to anyone else's mind quite naturally, had ignored the demise of A.J. Burroughs. I, said Hallam, was the villain, and not a comic one either. There I was, dancing up and down on the grave of a man who had been my friend.

---

east bank of the canal ought to be under their control, if not ours. I had never heard a good word said for the Egyptians and thought Mohammedanism a disgusting religion. The moment seemed opportune, since the Russians were busy committing their outrages in Hungary. Most Americans, I felt sure, would welcome a display of aggressive independence on the part of allies so long subservient.

"What surprised me was the sudden strength of my feeling for the Army. That was quite new. It was the leader of the Opposition's utter indifference to the safety of our troops which decided me that I could never again vote for the Labour Party. This did not make me a Conservative. At the next election, I voted Liberal, feeling even as I did it that this was a futile kind of thing to be doing.

"By stages, I thereafter quite ceased to be a man of the Left."

Not everyone thinks I meant Joe. The London Irish (I have this from another former colleague) think I meant the late W.R. Rodgers, another comic villain, about whom also I might have been amusing if he had died in time.

Reviews in *The Spectator*, by Stuart Hood, and *The New Statesman*, by Arthur Marshall, more space in the former (which I take to be what counts). I once used Marshall as an actor in a programme on werewolves by Paul Dehn. I failed later to get anything out of him as a writer. He was nevertheless interested in broadcasting. At his club, as we sat waiting to go in to lunch, a man entered and looked anxiously about. He wore a cumbrous hearing-aid, connected with a small box which he carried. "There goes a man," said my host, "permanently tuned-in to 'Appointment with Fear'."

He treats the book lightheartedly. Hood doesn't like it, but treats me seriously, allowing me "a sombre power" and lamenting the "hideous conspiracy" by which the public was for so long deprived of my "talent for writing". I am myself, however, principally to blame.

18 May

Maurice Richardson in *The Observer*. Pleasant enough. A painful part of the ordeal by reviewer is what you don't get from people from whom you feel you might expect it. I have met Richardson only twice, had much conversation with him only once, two years ago, when he told me about his best friend, Randall Swingler, suddenly dropping dead before his eyes as they emerged together from a pub. I used to see a good deal of Swingler before the War.[1] He was a nice chap, married to one of a well-known pair of twin pianists.[2] He was

1. Most often, at meetings of the committee of the International Association of Writers for the Defence of Culture — (RH:) "on to which I had been wished by the proletarian novelist, James Hanley, and where, among others I was accustomed to see, were Rosamond Lehmann, Rose Macaulay, Cecil Day Lewis, Edgell Rickword and Montagu Slater."
2. Joan and Valerie Trimble.

not a good poet, and he was abjectly Leftish. According to Constantine Fitzgibbon,[1] Swingler made all his money over to the Communist Party. Richardson described Constantine as "an eccentric character". By this, I took him to mean a man who, though normal in other respects, was politically of the Right. Richardson still seems engaged in that 'thirties intellectual task of seeing a synthesis between Marx and Freud.

26 May

I saw *Les Enfants du Paradis* shortly after the War. I was principally taken, like everyone else, with the miming of Jean-Louis Barrault and an extraordinary comic performance by Pierre Brasseur. I did not then know that most of the characters were based on historical figures or that the book was by Jacques Prévert. I did not know this for some years after meeting both Prévert and the actor, Marcel Herrand, who had played the murderer Lacenaire, of whom at the time I had never heard, but with whom I am now much concerned.[2] I have been watching for a repeat showing of the film and noticed only this morning that it was on at the Academy cinema today, Whit Monday. M. and I went to see it this afternoon. Less good in a number of ways than it seemed when I first saw it, but still very nice.

3 June

The Daily Worker has been renamed *The Morning Star*. I find nothing starry about it. A more informative new title would have been *The Daily Striker*. It belatedly reviews *Portrait of the Artist as a Professional Man*. I am, it says, a typical Eng. Lit. gent.

1. The American writer. The Heppenstalls had been his guests at a house near Dorchester which he rented while working on *The Life of Dylan Thomas* (London, 1965).
2. Pierre-François Lacenaire, man of letters, revolutionary and criminal, was one of the main figures in RH's work in progress, *French Crime in the Romantic Age*.

9 June

Party given at the Playboy Club by Sir Anthony and Lady Glyn, who are going to live on the Ile St Louis in Paris. Their breasts so hoisted up, these seemed among the delicacies handed round by the Bunny Girls. The other principal delicacy was cold chicken legs. The girls smelled perfectly clean.

27 June

Arrival of the solid, extensible oak table which M. found at Whiteley's for £5. What used to be Lindy's room now becomes a separate, though very small, dining-room, which we have never had. I shall no longer have to clear this table for as few as two guests. M. and I can also eat in there when the kitchen table is cluttered or when we are feeling a bit luxurious. Bookwise, that has become the fiction room, both English and French, while poetry and dictionaries live in this one, though Balzac in forty-five small volumes occupies one side of the multi-purpose chair behind me, once notably slept in by George Orwell. I ought to put a plaque on it.[1]

1 July

Investiture of Prince Charles as Prince of Wales at Carnarvon. Shortly after midnight, in Abergele, forty miles

1. One night in 1937, when the Heppenstalls had been married only a short time, Orwell turned up at their sparsely-furnished bed-sitter in Hampstead. The three of them went to Paglionni's, a local Italian restaurant, for a cheap meal of spaghetti, then returned to the bed-sitter, Orwell having decided to stay the night. The "multi-purpose chair" was opened out for him, and the Heppenstalls — M. shyly — undressed and went to bed. Some hours later, M. opened her eyes and saw Orwell, stark naked, wandering about the room. With exquisite politeness but no sign of embarrassment, he apologised for waking her and explained that he was trying to find his way out to the lavatory. M. directed him, then turned on her side so that she was facing the wall when he found his way back.

away, a loud bang got people out of bed. Two men were found dead. "This," said the Secretary of State for Wales, "is a dreadful tragedy." Nothing of the sort. It is a comedy. Nothing is more satisfactory, nothing is funnier, than when people carrying a bomb, with which they mean to damage someone or something else, blow themselves up. The only sad thing about this episode is that a public house fifty yards away was badly damaged.

4 July

The voice over the entryphone announced itself as Brian Easdale, whom I had not seen for several years, though it is not long since I saw his sister. The Brian I presently let in had a black eye, was unshaven and looked as though he had slept, if at all, in his clothes. He was supposed to have been at Marylebone magistrates' court at ten o'clock and was now thinking he should go to the police station down the road to explain why he had not appeared. He didn't expect me to do anything. Passing the house, which he had visited twice, it had occurred to him to look in, perhaps for advice. I gave him what I could of that and coffee. He and his second wife are separating.

He didn't call back. I don't know when I shall see any member of that gifted and disastrous family again.[1] Until two years ago, I could be fairly certain of not too long passing without a word or two with Richard Adeney, playing in some *ad hoc* orchestra, the last time a marvellous score I had from Roberto Gerhard for Zbigniew Herbert's play about Socrates.

1. In the summer of 1935, directly after staying with the Reads at Firle (see footnote to March 22nd, 1969), RH had gone to Caerleon, Wales, "where *The Adelphi* was holding a summer school.... I there first met no small number of people with whom I should have to do later.... Joan Adeney Easdale was a young woman who, at the age of fourteen, had published a volume of verse with Leonard and Virginia Woolf [*A Collection of Poems*, 1931]. Her mother also had published, pseudonymously [as Gladys E. Killin], an autobiography, *Middle Age*

6 July

My daughter, my son-in-law and my first grandchild have moved into their new house in Campden Hill Square. This is conveniently near, a mere five or ten minutes away. Yesterday afternoon, M. and I walked round. The house is very pleasant, though not, of course, huge, like Lady Antonia Fraser's next to the bottom. It was entirely Donald's idea that he and Lindy should live there. M. and I have, indeed, been nervous in case the propinquity should seem to have been sought by us or by Lindy because of us. She, in fact, somewhat opposed the purchase, in part because the address was notoriously smart.

9 July

After a doubtful beginning to the day, heavy rain and thunder in the early afternoon. The day's principal criminal anniversary is of the Mme Fahmy shooting at the Savoy hotel, forty-six years ago, during the thunderstorm of the century.

13 July

Among today's criminal anniversaries are the executions of, in 1955, Ruth Ellis and, four years earlier, Michel Watrin. It is, I suppose, generally assumed that no more women will be hanged in this country. Except under the Vichy government

---

[London, 1935]. She had been much associated with the sage and novelist who went by the name of Mark Rutherford. Her son, Joan's brother, Brian, a composer of music, I was to meet later."

For a few months before their marriage in February 1937, RH and M. occupied Brian Easdale's flat in Hampstead. He wrote his first opera, *Rapunzel*, in 1927, when he was eighteen. After the war, he devoted much of his time to the composition of music for films, notably *Black Narcissus* (1947) and *The Red Shoes* (1948). He wrote incidental music for a number of radio programmes produced by RH.

Richard Adeney, a first-cousin of Brian and Joan Easdale, is a flautist.

during the war, no Frenchwoman has been guillotined since 1887. There was for some years a feeling in France that Watrin would be the last man to be topped, but M. de Gaulle is no indiscriminate repriever, and the head of a young farmer, double child-murderer and rapist, fell only this year. That is now expected to be the last. Also on today's date, in 1912, occurred the first of our "brides in the bath" murders. On this date in 1793, Marat was murdered in his bath by Charlotte Corday, who had not thought of George Joseph Smith's little trick of simply raising the feet.

I had hoped that my calendar would reveal interesting seasonal variations, but it doesn't. Thursday was bright, and the heat has since increased without sign of thunder. This looks as though it might be the annual heatwave. For the moment, one feels nothing but contentment. This Sunday morning, it is difficult to imagine anyone occupied other than innocently.

24 July

The Shearers out.[1] The ordeal by reviewer twice within three months. In *The Listener* I get Stuart ("sombre power") Hood again, in the *Daily Telegraph* Iain Hamilton, in the *Guardian* Robert Nye. I know (though not well) and like Hamilton. He seems not to dislike me. Hood's praise really is praise, since he perceives exactly what I was about. Nye holds evolving views about the world, and into these I am fitted.

The novel is dedicated to Pamela Snow. The ass in *The Times Literary Supplement* knows that she is also Pamela Hansford Johnson and that under this name she published a book on the trial of Ian Brady and Myra Hindley three years ago.[2] My novel is therefore not a novel but a challenge to her theses in *On Iniquity*. This is proved by the fact that both in the novel and in the real-life case a person in dark glasses goes free. And so he continues, at considerable length. I hope the

1. Published by Hamish Hamilton.
2. *On Iniquity*, London, 1967.

ass is a young ass and will learn. If he had turned to the page after the dedication, he might have noticed me explicitly stating that I have transplanted a real-life French case into an English setting. I hadn't, as it happens, read Pamela's book when I wrote *The Shearers*. I have read it since. She and Charles both read *The Shearers* in typescript and were quite clear about what I was up to.

29 July

Party at the Japanese Information Centre for Yasunari Kawabata, the Nobel prizewinner. Two or three elegant and beautiful Japanese women in traditional costume. I enormously liked *Snow Country*, which Kaz Tsushima sent me in French. I now have a presentation copy of *The House of the Sleeping Beauties* in what looks like a good American translation. Surprisingly tall Japanese men. The shortest were all British.

31 July

Avant-garde novelists at the house of one of them, Alan Burns, off Portobello Road. They want to start public readings and discussions, under the name "Writers Reading". I was one of two greybeards invited, the other Stefan Themerson. For some reason, Bryan Johnson seemed bent on needling me, though afterwards he, I and the *Spectator* novel-reviewer went on to Henekey's, where we drank whisky, each carefully standing his round. I don't think I shall go along with them. I don't think it will work.

Curious behaviour at the *Lit. Supp.*, which, the week after its demented review of *The Shearers*, belatedly does *P. of the A. as a P. M.*, which came out in early May. The review itself is curious. Some of what it says was clearly intended to be flattering. It begins, however, by stating that I was never an artist but merely a man in love with the idea of being one, and it goes on to impugn not only my professional status (as a radio producer) but that of the acting profession as a whole, "who earn their livelihood as casual, seasonal, semi-skilled labourers". If anyone at Equity reads the *TLS*, they will no doubt have something to say about that. About me the reviewer goes on:

> The author gives us a blow-by-blow, or clause-by-clause, account of his dismissal by the BBC in 1967. Mr Hèppenstall feels badly about this, though the BBC appears from his account to have treated him generously. It was bad luck for him that, unlike some of his more gifted colleagues, he found that his work as a radio producer inhibited his creative writing.... Many of the established writers he first contracted as contributors left him for other producers. Perhaps some of them were as edgy and sensitive to slights, imagined and real, as he himself.

All this is both untrue and defamatory. Mere ineptitude has perhaps left it uncertain whether those more gifted colleagues are to be understood to have been more gifted than myself or simply among the more gifted of my colleagues. But I hardly see myself as having been "dismissed" by the BBC, and I do not "feel badly" about the circumstances of my departure, while the BBC treated me neither generously nor the reverse but strictly according to the book. There is not, and never has been, at the BBC a writer whose writing was not seriously inhibited by working as a radio producer (it could be thought to have killed perhaps the finest of them, Louis MacNeice). In *Portrait*, I name four (not "many") outside writers (two of them not then "established") as "unfaithful". In only one case of the four may there have been sensitiveness to slights, real or imagined. All four writers are to this day my good friends. I don't in my book present those four changes of producer as a weighty or significant matter. It happened, just as writers change publishers. What in fact was rather amusing about it was the way other producers poached, but I do not go into that.

27

You would think that might be enough, but the reviewer also describes me as "a man demanding, suspicious, vain and concerned with money, especially with the shortage of money". I am no slavish admirer of my own character, but I do not think myself vain, and I have never felt secure enough to be particularly demanding. Those are certainly not the defects with which I have been commonly reproached, and, more to the point, they are not those which a reviewer could reasonably deduce from my book.

25 August

M. is in the Brompton hospital again, after almost forty years. They no longer have records, and the old TB scars will make new X-ray pictures difficult to interpret. She was indeed screened when she became pregnant with Lindy, to make sure that the thing had not "lighted up" again, but I have always supposed that a later recurrence of TB was impossible. This is apparently not so, but we shall have to wait.

27 August

Ivy Compton-Burnett has died. At my only meeting with her, for tea one Saturday afternoon some twenty years ago, she talked about servants as a character in one of her novels might.

29 August

The *Lit. Supp.* will print only what suits it of even the modified version of my letter.[1] The breach with Arthur Crook, a man of whom both M. and I were extremely fond, is complete.

1. About the review of *The Shearers*. The original letter, sent to Arthur Crook before publication of the review of *Portrait of the Artist as a Professional Man*, had arrived while Crook was on holiday, and so RH had written a version of the letter, addressing it to The Editor.

11 September

M. back home. I have finished *French Crime in the Romantic Age* and shall take it in tomorrow, after the first cooked breakfast for some weeks.

22 September

Hamish Hamilton sent Simenon a proof copy of *A Little Pattern of French Crime* and has received from the great man a highly gratifying letter,[1] with permission to use it in publicity. It is apparently the first time he has been known to allow this.

1. Translation by Lindy Foord, née Heppenstall:

September 19, 1969

My dear Hamish,

How grateful I am to you for sending me Rayner Heppenstall's *A Little Pattern of French Crime*. I opened it at once and spent some delightful hours reading it. Its unassuming title surprises me since it contains, in effect, the whole history of la Belle Époque seen through a number of legal trials, beginning with the case of the anarchists of that period, Ravachol, Vaillant and many others, and continuing with the trials of Madame Steinheil and Madame Caillaux.

It is a veritable fresco that the author has painted with little brush-strokes or, rather, like a mosaic, interweaving the most unexpected personalities; it is this, perhaps, which brings his account so vividly to life. We go from Alfred Dreyfus to Zola and Marcel Proust, from President Félix Faure to Jean Jaurès, from Paul Bourget to Clemenceau and Maître Floriot, from Aristide Briand to Bonnot and Raymond-la-Science, and from this last to Landru.

I have the impression at the end of this book that, from 1881 to the declaration of war in 1914, we are not left in ignorance about anything, for the minor characters are so alive and colourful: concierges, members of parliament, police superintendents, chamber-maids and dressmakers, prostitutes, both those on the streets and those in apartments.

I take my hat off to the author. And I thank you again.

Yours,
Georges Simenon

5 October

A brown spider has made a big web in the broad gutter outside our kitchen window. It sits in the middle of this, swayed by a wind which is taking the web to pieces.

6 October

The spider has made a new web.

That window faces west, with a broad, far prospect upon which television aerials and new buildings have intruded during the past few years. The landing window looks north, over the roof of St Vincent's. What may be seen there has varied over the years. The first splendid picture I recall was of three tall Sisters talking in a group, their hands in their sleeves, their butterfly headgear blowing. Later on, one such took my head upon her bosom when I was hurried across to have fingers sewn up. In a much later phase, nurses said to be Spanish and German sunbathed there, but this brought out young men with binoculars on the roofs of the block of RAF Benevolent Fund flats and a house, across the road from these windows, facing east, which has undergraduates in term time and coachloads of German tourists during the holidays. I understand that the sisters are not technically nuns, but they are very like. During the past week, a young one has regularly appeared, in white robe and head-swathing but without the blue outer garment and butterfly, at about 1.00 p.m. and sat very still on the parapet for about three-quarters of an hour. It may be that she has been unwell and is allowed to do this. It may be that she is rebellious or at a difficult stage of her novitiate and is made to do it.

7 October

By noon, the second web was almost gone. Towards 1.00, the spider became active. A bluebottle crossed the remains of the old web without being caught as the spider began to make a new one. The young nun emerged a little after 1.00, but did not sit down. A quarter of an hour later, she had vanished. The spider was still at it, blown about by the wind. At half-past one, the nun was back with a chair. She sat facing east, away from the wind, reading what appeared to be a magazine with blue pages. The kitchen window rattled in its frame, to the bottom of which at least one of the lower support threads was attached. The spider worked from the outside towards the centre, clockwise, its back to us. The third web was turning out less regular than the second, whether because of difficulties caused by the wind or by too great decay of the second.

At a quarter to two, as M. was out, I lay on her bed, what used to be Adam's[1] being piled with sheets and towels. The nun was still there, the spider still at work. At half-past three, the nun had gone, and the top half of the new web was collapsing.

The uppermost supporting thread broke during the evening. At 11.00 p.m., the spider was still clinging on in the dark. To the best of my knowledge, it had not eaten for three days, and during that time it had spun three webs out of itself. This must be taxing.

8 October

The spider works best at night. It had a new web this morning.

A sunny day. This evening, Scott-Moncrieff prize presentation in the library at the French Institute. The ambassador was late, which delayed drinking. The winners, of whom the chief was Terence Kilmartin, literary editor of *The Observer* (for Malraux's *Antimémoires*), made no speech. The effect was oafish. Last year, John Weightman, whose French is more than adequate, replied on behalf of his wife and himself in English, in order, he said when I asked him

1. RH's son, born 1944; an architect, employed by the Greater London Council, he had been married since 1966, his wife's maiden name being Yvonne Grainger.

afterwards why, to show his disapproval of M. de Gaulle. A translator of Malraux could hardly take that view in an even more exaggerated form.

Also present, John Raymond,[1] Sonia Orwell[2] (as she now seems again to be called) and Albert Ehretsmann, an Alsatian business man, worthy, very anxious to support the arts. He lost, I fancy, a good deal over the Apollinaire gallery,[3] upon which Innes's *A Private View* is at least in part based.[4]

10 October

The spider in a very ragged web, restless. Now, at just before bedtime, it has gone.

1. Journalist and literary critic.
2. Eric Blair ("George Orwell") married Sonia Brownell from his bed at University College Hospital, London, on October 13th, 1949. He died on January 21st, 1950, three days after making a new will which named his wife as sole beneficiary. She subsequently married Michael Pitt-Rivers.
3. RH published an article on Apollinaire, some of whose poems he had translated, in the August 1947 issue of *Vogue*. The publication coincided with the opening of the Apollinaire art gallery in Litchfield Street, round the corner from Zwemmer's bookshop in Charing Cross Road, where the first exhibition was devoted to Apollinaire himself, with portraits of him by Picasso, Marcoussis, Delaunay and others.

    Earlier that year, while in Paris, RH had met Daniel-Henry Kahnweiler, an elderly dealer in art. RH: "It appears that he published Apollinaire's first book, *L'Enchanteur pounissant*, illustrated by André Dérain. He showed me a copy of *L'Hérésiarque et Cie*, thus inscribed:

    Vous êtes le premier, Henry, qui m'éditâtes;
    *   Il faut qu'il m'en souvienne, en chantant votre los.*
    *   Que vous célèbrent donc les vers et les tableaux*
    *   Au triple étage habité par les trois Hécates!*

    I failed to ask the precise sense of the last line. I do not, of course, suggest that lines like these have any but a private importance. Yet it is this facility which gives their peculiar quality to Apollinaire's finest poems. He wrote in verse with rather more ease than most of us do in prose."
4. Published under the pseudonym of "Michael Innes", London, 1952.

13 October

This morning, the spider was making yet another web, anti-clockwise.

21 October

Heavy mist, almost fog. By throwing up the kitchen window, I demolished the spider's web and its foundations for other webs. I no longer wish the spider well, though it was a good and persistent maker of webs. It can go and make them elsewhere.

26 October

I suppose I haven't been watching for the young nun, perhaps dismissing her with the spider. It is Sunday. She was there before one o'clock, her lips moving, praying. The sky had clouded after a lovely early morning.

7 November

As announced by telephone from Berkshire on Tuesday, Innes and Margaret Stewart appeared in the late afternoon. With them were their elder daughter, also Margaret, and a quiet, dark young man with spectacles, whom I did not gather for some time to be young Margaret's husband. Adam was there. By arrangement, Lindy and Donald came round with Andrew, now highly mobile and a prattler.

Shown a photograph of Yvonne when Adam was not in the room, Innes exclaimed: "Wow! Fate-laden!"

The conversation was in general exclamatory. Innes was doing his elderly act. There was a bit about royalties on *Three Tales of Hamlet*,[1] which suggested that he continued to receive

1. The texts of three "entertainments", linked by the Hamlet theme, broadcast on the BBC Third Programme: a play, *The Hawk and the Handsaw*, and an essay, "The Mysterious Affair at Elsinore", by Michael Innes, and a play by RH, *The Fool's Saga* (Gollancz, 1950).

a trickle, whereas I did not, as I have since checked.

12 November

M. went back into the Brompton yesterday and today was given to understand that she again has pulmonary tuberculosis, though no great anxiety seems to be felt about this. I went to Lindy's for dinner.

14 November

A Little Pattern of French Crime was published yesterday. No reviews then or today. The review copies went out late. This was due to some days' delay in printing the band with a quotation from Simenon.

16 November

A thunderstorm during the night. A cold Sunday morning. Lunch at Lindy's. She has talked to M.'s registrar. The flare-up is, as it were, purely deduction. There is no open TB and no danger of infection.

Reviews in *The Observer* and *Sunday Telegraph*, in the former Maurice Richardson again, in the latter Michael Gilbert, with a drawing by Osbert Lancaster. The expression "*crime passionnel*" has become so acclimatised in English that it is always spelt here with one *n*.

20 November

PEN awards dinner, for which M. was allowed out of hospital, to return tomorrow. The principal speaker was to be Noël Coward. Unwell, he was replaced by the playwright William Douglas-Home, who, himself facetious, was facetiously heckled from a remote table by Henry Williamson,[1] a bit tipsy. The only sensible speech was made

1.   The writer, then aged seventy-four, who is perhaps best known for his book *Tarka the Otter*, which won the Hawthornden Prize in 1927.

by Pamela Snow. She and Charles have been reading *Little Pattern* and enjoying it. They were bright and cheerful before the dinner. Afterwards, they looked very fed-up. Displeasingly to everyone, receiving his silver pen on behalf of John Fowles (in America?) for *The French Lieutenant's Woman*, dynamic Tom Maschler, now chairman of Cape's, seized a microphone and did a commercial on behalf of the book.

28 November

Inquests on the exiled Kabaka of Uganda, who among black men always seemed an attractive figure, and Howard Marion Crawford, called "Bony" for reasons unconnected, unless by antithesis, with his physique. At his best, he was one of the half-dozen most effective radio actors there have ever been, though an awkward customer to deal with. The producer who made best use of him was Louis MacNeice. I had him as the pig dictator Napoleon in one of three productions I did of *Animal Farm*. It went out live, and he came near to wrecking it by going to the wrong microphone for a crowd scene in the barn. The situation was saved by sharp and concerted agreement between the senior programme engineer at the panel and the spot jeep in the studio below, who looked up and at a wave of the finger herded the docile rest of the cast over to the microphone at which Bony had started yelling. The Kabaka died of acute alcoholic poisoning, Bony not of its chronic equivalent but of some accident in which alcohol played its part.

Innes on *Little Pattern* in the *New Statesman*. A long review, which I always take to be what principally matters, but lacking in liveliness and therefore perhaps suggesting a similar lack in the book.

2 December

Death of Stephen Potter announced on the one o'clock news, with a reminiscence of him by Joyce Grenfell. For a while, we had adjacent offices in Rothwell House.[1] His humour coarsened when he invented gamesmanship and lifemanship. His "How" programmes towards the end of and for a while after the War were very sensitive and fine, and perhaps even more evocative was a bird-watching programme called "The Watchers Watched". He was a cool snob, but essentially good-natured, a friendly man. I occasionally viewed him with suspicion, but never found myself disliking him, except perhaps on my first view of him several years before the War.[2]

5 December

The Berlioz centenary exhibition.[3] Piped music. A sort of grotto at the bottom of which a small figure on film, meant to be Harriet Smithson, declaimed Shakespeare with an Irish accent. In a corner which displayed revolutionary scenes, the recorded sound of a football crowd with gunfire. There was, I suppose, not much of strict relevance to exhibit. More than anything, what I liked visually were a few coloured drawings by Victor Hugo. Since Berlioz was, after all, a composer, piped music was perhaps in order, but I found it ill-chosen, too much of it vocal and dramatic, evocative of no more than present-day singers and gramophone studios. The reel could have been made up wholly of rapt orchestral music in slow *tempi*, so much more characteristic of Berlioz. The gimmicks I found merely numbing. Still, M. (allowed out again *ad hoc*)

1. A building, just across the road from Broadcasting House, which was the headquarters of the BBC Features Department.
2. RH: "[In 1937,] I was taken by Herbert Read to see Joe Ackerley, literary editor of *The Listener*, who gave me books to review. At a party shortly thereafter, I first saw Stephen Potter, rather big, rather good-looking and fair. I was to remember him being, as it seemed to my provincial self, positively obsequious with Robert Lynd over a review the latter had written of *The Muse in Chains*, the book by Potter which put the expression 'Eng. Lit.' into drawing-room and journalistic currency. The coin still passes."
3. At the Victoria & Albert Museum.

and I did not hurry away. I suddenly realised that we were hearing the same sequence of music for the third time.

13 December

M. discharged and home. The whole purpose of this second period of almost five weeks in hospital has been to determine her constitutional response to the swallowing of D-pasinah powders and capsules. She will now swallow two packets of the lime-flavoured powder each day for the next two years. Nine years ago, I had a mere fortnight's experience of swallowing such powders, though in those days they were B-pasinah and not fruit-flavoured. I took them with gin-and-tonic. I was also punctured daily, in alternate flanks, by a district nurse, which M. will not have to put up with.

14 December

The Soul of the Ape[1] by Eugene Marais is an animal book with a splendid difference. Its author was an Afrikaner of Huguenot extraction. Poet, lawyer and journalist, he was studying in London at the outbreak of the Boer War and found himself interned as an enemy alien. Returning to Transvaal, he lived, with one human companion, for three years in the Waterberg in the territory of a large troop of chacma baboons. His later work on white ants was plagiarised by Maurice Maeterlinck, with depressing effect on Marais.

The manuscript of *The Soul of the Ape*, written in 1922, was believed lost at the time of his suicide in 1936. Rediscovered, unfinished, written in English, it has been edited by Robert Ardrey, best known these days as an anthropologist, author of *African Genesis*, so that it is almost a shock to be reminded that he also wrote *Thunder Rock*, a play which, with Michael Redgrave in the lead, was so very successful in the early days of the war.

I found it a most attractive book. The description of the

1. London, 1969.

baboons in a state of "depression" at sunset is wonderfully evocative, and there are intriguing speculations on the interplay of conscious and unconscious memory in the primates.

Freud's discoveries were still new, and Professor Ardrey believes that psychology and related "sciences" have gone astray since, mainly through insistence on man's uniqueness and too much emphasis on the environment. Genes, of course, are nowadays coming back into their own. Charles Snow, for instance, is on their side. Certainly, the twilight consciousness of Marais's baboons is one that we need feel no shame at retrospectively sharing.

16 December

Capital punishment "permanently" abolished. The poor intellectual quality of the discussion in the public prints and [Harold] Wilson's shabby manoeuvre in rushing the bill through so that it would not become an election issue culminated in the spectacle of [Edward] Heath leading his friends into the government lobby, no doubt under the impression that to vote "aye" meant that you were in favour of capital punishment.

This will provoke me to adopt in conversation a "retentionist" (now, of course, a "restorationist") position. I do in fact think it better to keep the death penalty on the statute book, even if it is never applied. If offered voluntary euthanasia, most convicted murderers would accept it. Many have to be forcibly restrained from killing themselves. A fair number succeed. The others might be herded together into a special prison, with every facility for slaying one another, all their conversation being recorded for study by criminal historians and other accredited parties. One of the superfluous new universities might be adapted to this penal purpose.

28 December

The five Israeli gunboats, whipped from under the noses of the French, have reached the Mediterranean and are nearly home.[1] I find this the most heartening news item of the year.

1. Delivery of the vessels, built at Cherbourg for the government of Israel, had been held up by an embargo on arms deliveries to Israel imposed by President de Gaulle in January 1969. Their departure was discovered in the evening of 26th December, when workmen entered the shipyard after the Christmas holiday.

1970

4 January

Last year began bright but not cold, this one cold and dull, but with foreign currency restrictions lifted. In view of a general election, the Wilson government has reduced the voting age to eighteen, at the same time arranging that at that age the young shall be able to marry against the wishes of their parents.

All this kind of thing rests on the belief that, in temperate latitudes, the young of the human species now mature physically at an earlier age. This belief strikes me as being fallacious. That doctors support it is neither here nor there. It has never been the practice for a girl to register her first menstruation with a doctor or elsewhere but only with her mother, if even there. What my parents may have supposed I do not know, but I, certainly, though years were to pass before even the purely mechanical side of the matter was to be put to the test, could have begotten my kind at the age of thirteen. At that age, I lived in a state bordering on satyriasis. I used to carry a raincoat over my arm in fine weather to conceal the erections which sometimes thrust my trousers painfully forward on the way back from school in the afternoon. It was regularly helpful to carry it on Saturday mornings, when two pretty and well-developed young women along the street gossiped while kneeling to scour their front doorsteps, the necks of their frocks falling away to reveal barely credible heavens of blue-veined, white thoracic tissue.

23 January

9.30 a.m. Lindy in labour at St George's hospital. Donald present at the birth, as husbands are now somewhat encouraged to be.

40

25 January

M. and I with Donald to see our second grandchild, a girl. To be called Rachel Lucy.

26 January

Charles Fairfield, of County Kerry, Ireland, had two daughters, Cicily Isabel, born at Christmas in 1892, and Josephine Letitia Denny, born how much earlier *Who's Who* doesn't say,[1] but appreciably, since she was schooled at Richmond in Surrey and then went to university in Edinburgh, where the younger sister was at school. It is not clear where and when Letitia Denny Fairfield pursued her legal studies, but at an unspecified date she was called to the bar as a barrister-at-law of the Middle Temple, qualifying finally as a doctor of medicine in Edinburgh in 1911, in which year she was appointed senior medical officer to the London County Council. It seems in fact more likely that all that legal stuff came much later and that Dr Letitia Fairfield had not yet given much thought to forensic medicine when the Kaiser's war broke out, Isabel (discontented with her name, but at least that bit of it was spelt right, if not to the Scottish taste) having by then embarked on a career of political journalism in London. Towards the end of that war, Letitia served medically with the armed forces and then returned to the LCC, while her sister adopted the name of "Rebecca West" from that of an emancipated Ibsen heroine and published a variety of books, beginning with one on Henry James. In one year, 1954, appeared from Letitia volumes reflecting both her medical and her legal accomplishments, one on epilepsy and the *Notable British Trials* volume on Straffen. She also did the *NBT* volume on the IRA bomb murders in Coventry at the time of the outbreak of Hitler's war, during which she held the rank of lieutenant-colonel in the RAMC. In 1957 and again

1.   March 10th, 1885.

in 1958, she was president of the Medico-Legal Society.

I read and greatly admired Rebecca West's novel, *Harriet Hume*, as an undergraduate. Just after the War, she read something I had published on a French Catholic writer and sent me a letter which, as I recall, was about some unpleasant nun she had known in her schooldays. I am sure I replied, but I did not follow up the correspondence, thinking the letter dotty and supposing that the writer of it must be older than I had imagined (she was in fact then in her early fifties) and quite gaga, a supposition which the work she thereafter published soon dispelled. We did not meet until 1962, in Edinburgh, where both of us were appearing in one of the festival's fringe attractions, a writers' circus. My acquaintance with Rebecca West has not much ripened.

The name of Dr Letitia Fairfield I first met little more than a year ago in a book, *The Scarlett Widow*[1] by Ernest Dudley, dealing with the French murder case of Mme Steinheil, who figures prominently in *Little Pattern*. This afternoon, I took tea with Dr Fairfield in Chelsea. She is now in her eighties, but of alert and well-stored mind, wearing a reddish wig not quite up to her years. About Mme Steinheil she is documented up to the eyes. It is, alas, too late for me to draw on her knowledge, whether of that case or of the earlier case of La Roncière, about which I have a great deal in *Romantic Age* and which equally she has studied in depth. Like every criminologist I have met, she is in favour of capital punishment, though politically attached to the Labour Party. Nor for a single moment would she admit that Timothy Evans was other than guilty as charged, while, in the case of Michael John Davies, she is not sorry for him but for the girl at the front of the bus whose evidence was so maligned.

3 February

Clear, not cold. Death of Lord [Bertrand] Russell, the old

1. London, 1960.

pest. Penguin proofs of *A Harlot High and Low*. Interviewed by Melvyn Bragg for a television programme on George Orwell. This was done in a radio talks studio in Broadcasting House, where also a second-class lunch had been laid on. For some reason, the *TLS* poetry young man, dark, heavy-faced, almost speechless Ian Hamilton, was around as literary adviser on this programme. Nice for him, nothing to do.

4 February

In a court of Queen's Bench this morning, Mr Justice Lawton was hearing evidence in a very interesting libel case when in bounded eight Aberystwyth undergraduates singing the American protest song "We Shall Overcome" in Welsh. In this they were joined by girls in the public gallery and a Welsh MP, who had been waiting at the back of the courtroom. After a brief withdrawal while order was restored, Lawton J. returned and sentenced three of the youths to three months each for contempt in the face of the court, went on with the libel hearing, and in the afternoon sentenced eleven demonstrators more. What they had been demonstrating against was the imprisonment, also for three months, of a Welsh pop singer known as Dafydd Iwan, who had refused to pay a fine imposed on him in Cardiff last month for defacing English road signs and who is in any case to be released tomorrow or the day after, the fine having been subscribed.

There was a time when British governments actively discouraged the use of Welsh, but that is long ago. The language is taught in schools, to the annoyance of many of the Welsh, who promptly forget it on leaving school. As to the road signs, it is not a question of substituting the Welsh for the English form of place-names but of suppressing the English form where this differs from the Welsh, for in all such cases both forms are signposted, while the Welsh for a car park is, for instance, just that, though at *eisteddfodau* an expression meaning an enclosure for chariots may be used.

This is a matter about which I know something. M. being half-Welsh and my children therefore a quarter Welsh, I have sometimes felt that this makes me one-eighth Welsh. I picked up a little of the language in order, by way of one-upmanship, to be able to conduct with my delightful father-in-law bits of conversation which my wife, his daughter, could not follow. I have published translation, made with the help of cribs, of some of the earliest Welsh poems. I also, some nineteen or twenty years ago, compiled an anthology of eighteenth- and nineteenth-century English translations from the Welsh for a publisher who went bust before the anthology could be published.

Among the utterances attributed to this morning's demonstrators, two are: "Is this your British justice that you don't allow people to speak their own language in their own country?" and: "The young people of Wales will not be crushed by British imperialism." Well, of course, an Irishman would be making a sort of sense if he spoke of British justice, British imperialism and so on in this way, but Wales, like Scotland, is part of the island of Britain, and long ago Welsh (which is not a Welsh word) was described as British, to distinguish it from the English (meaning Anglo-Saxon) language, while to British imperialism the Welsh contribution, though possibly less than that of the Scots, has not been small. A basic, structural fact which gets in the way of our various separatist movements making common cause is that while the southern Irish insist that an island must not be divided, Welsh and Scottish nationalists want to divide an island. In the terms of the Irish womb-fantasy, the Isle of Wight has a better claim to home-rule than either the Welsh or the Scots.

5 February

Lunch at the Connaught Rooms with Joe Gaute of Harraps. He is their crime man. After reading *Little Pattern*, he would like me to translate *Les Erreurs Judiciaires* by René Floriot, on which he caused an option to be taken after reading my (anonymous) *TLS* review of the book two years ago. One translator has already had a go and found the legalities too difficult for him. It is a good book, and the terms seem all right, five guineas a thousand words and fifty for the Introduction and Notes.[1]

15 February

An adenoidal youth with wavy hair, Peter Hain, a South African resident here, is much in the news. He is running a campaign to stop a South African cricket team playing here this summer. Today's *Sunday Times* shows carefully drawn plans of the main provincial cricket grounds, under the heading "grounds where Hain could stop play". These will be very useful to him and his followers.

M. is in Hindhead, staying with K. Gill and Kitty Davidson. Billy Wordsworth[2] gave up the house next door some years ago and went to live in Scotland, since when his

1. Published as *When Justice Falters*, 1972.
2. At the *Adelphi* summer school at Caerleon, in the summer of 1935 (see footnote to July 4th, 1969), RH had first met "a gentle, white-haired woman, K. Gill, her companion, Kitty Davidson, and a man very little older than myself, William Wordsworth, a collateral descendant of the poet, who was a composer of music....

   "In the autumn of 1936, soon after meeting M., I took her to stay with Miss Gill. Her house lay outside Hindhead, near the golf course. From the road, it was like any other large suburban residence of the Lutyens period. The grounds were nicely kept, and behind the house sparse woodland planted with pines descended to a quiet road, beyond which rose woodland of more public use. Into the area of gentle terraced garden before the steep descent projected a big music room, designed by Ernst Freud, who was there briefly at the time of our arrival....

   "Miss Gill was always addressed and referred to as 'Kay'. One at first assumed it to be so spelt and to be short perhaps for 'Katharine' or 'Kathleen'. One presently noted, however, that she signed her letters only with the initial 'K' and learned in due course that her Christian name was other, 'Nelly' I fancy. I did not discover what the source of

output and reputation have declined. He has had the most dreadful bad luck with his children. First, his daughter was disfigured in a fire caused by the brother. The latter has since been killed in a road accident.

I was last in Hindhead, with M., in early autumn, three and a half years ago. It was a world always remote from my own, but one I liked to visit from time to time. There, I always felt, was a proper use of riches (music is, on the whole, a rich man's world, but then so are the visual arts). The politics of the place had been pacifist and remained progressive. There was no church religion, but much elevated thought of a pantheistical kind. Oddly, K. and Kitty seem never to have had many

---

her wealth was, but there remained in her speech and manner something of a careful gentility which suggested 'trade' no more than a generation back. Kitty Davidson came of a rich family but was not herself rich, so that she somewhat appeared in the capacity of a paid companion. The money in her family came, I understood, from the manufacture of Kodak cameras, and it was hinted that only skulduggery had prevented more of it sticking to Kitty. Of the two women, Miss Gill was the larger and quite solidly built, but she was also the older, and her health was considered to be delicate. I remember her as always silver-haired and of an almost cloying gentleness of manner. Miss Davidson was small, thin, tweed-clad, flat-heeled and crisply spoken. It was she who read most of the books, and it was at her instigation that I read *The Diary of a Country Priest* by Georges Bernanos. I felt easier with and fonder of her. She had a sense of humour and even permitted herself an occasional slanginess of speech. I imagine that, of the two, she had been at the better school.

"In her music room, Miss Gill organised concerts by professional musicians, at which, for example, John Hunt, a gifted pianist, or the Robert Masters piano quartet would be encouraged to give before an invited audience first performances of works by William Wordsworth. He lived next door with his father, a retired clergyman. He was not there at the time of our visit, having been despatched to Edinburgh to study with Tovey, certainly by Miss Gill's initiative, though whether at her expense I do not know.

"In February 1937, M. and I were married. Herbert Read was one of the witnesses. K. Gill provided the wedding breakfast at her London club, with a visit afterwards to the Wigmore Hall to hear John Hunt play the *Hammerklavier* sonata."

friends. Often enough, some relation would be around, keeping an eye on the financial situation.

1 March

A film company is taking out an option on *The Shearers*. I shall receive a modest cheque, and that will be the last I shall hear about that.

8 March

Peggy was another of the rich *Adelphi* women.[1] She was sexually active and indeed still possessed of a husband until, in mid-war, ferrying aeroplanes, he nose-dived one on to an aerodrome. He was nicer than she was, but M. and I always kept in touch and occasionally stayed with her. In her later years, she suffered rather badly from arthritis and read Ouspensky. She was a competent painter. Her son, whom we have known from his tenderest years, closely resembled his father, who in appearance might quite well have been a second brother of Middleton Murry's, so that the son also resembled Murry.

That Peggy had just died, M. and I knew. It was, however, from the *Mail* on Tuesday we learned about her will. There is a photograph of her son with the very pretty girl he married and their two children. Peggy did her best to stop the marriage. She is doing her best to wreck it posthumously. What her will does not leave to organised charities it leaves to her son on condition that he adopts a black child. If he doesn't, it will go to Oxfam. This is pure wickedness. In her lifetime, Peggy was not at all interested in organised charity, nor did she ever herself think of adopting a black child or contribute largely to

1. RH: "Less rich than K. Gill, though substantially well-off, were John and Peggy Andrews, who lived near Reading. They were younger than Miss Gill and Miss Davidson, and Peggy strode about provocatively."

Oxfam. I am sufficiently appalled. M. is more properly so, since she saw more of Peggy in recent years than I did, knows the son and the wife better, knows, as I do not, a friend left, after years of devotion, only her flat. Seeing M. as another friend of his mother's, the son may falsely assume that M. influenced Peggy and is no friend of his. The condition in the will is to be contested. It may be set aside. I hope it will.[1]

15 March

Lunch on Monday with Granada Publishing's fluffy but high-powered press representative and a *Mail* journalist, at the Epicure in Frith Street. This had to do with *Papillon*, the translation of which Granada are publishing and the *Mail* serialising. The ex-convict author of this phenomenal French best-seller is to be brought to London in May at the time of publication. Before then, the journalist is going to Caracas to interview him. I am a recognised authority on French crime.

At least, I was. Four months after publication, Thursday's *Listener* printed a vicious onslaught on *Little Pattern*. This is by Richard Cobb. I do not suppose the review can do much harm, since it is quite long and makes the book sound funny and outrageous, which might make some people want to read it.

To Cobb, I am appallingly trivial. Him, on the other hand, I find astonishingly ill-informed about French criminal cases, at any rate during *La Belle Époque*. Nor does he seem to have read my book at all thoroughly, since the cases on which he comments so very oddly are not among those with which I deal in detail or even within the years I cover. On his errors of fact and on the evidence of him not having read the book he was reviewing I could, I think, have written an amusing and effective letter to *The Listener*, while simply brushing aside the reviewer's obvious indignation at my triviality. It would have had to be quite a long letter, however, and I don't feel that *The*

1. It was.

Listener would be much inclined to indulge me. I mysteriously ceased to be in favour, first in *The Spectator*, then in *The New Statesman,* when Karl Miller became literary editor first at the one and then at the other. He is now the editor of *The Listener*, and, since the appointment, the literary man there has not again asked me to review anything. That Cobb's review appears so long after the publication of the book suggests that the said literary editor hesitated to print it, but this week found himself short of material and thought why not.

It is Marie Besnard about whom Cobb commits his wildest howler. She was, he evidently thinks, an Italian lodging-house keeper, known as (the title might, I suppose, equally be Italian or French) *la Saponificatrice.* Cobb names both Landru and Petiot, but seems to confuse them, since he says, "Landru's victims came from the occupied departments." None of these three cases or those of Weidmann and the Papin sisters belongs to *La Belle Époque.* Landru occurs briefly in my epilogue. I don't think I mention the others. I suppose Cobb's French must be adequate, but he lards his sentences with French expressions in the manner of somebody who knows only a few. I should, it appears, have done well to deal with those cases that reflected the lives of the working class. The fact is that I devote a fair amount of space to the working-class cases I knew, principally those of Joseph Vacher and Jeanne Weber, and, really, it is not my fault, as Cobb seems to think, that the world of that time was unpleasant, selfish, calculating, vulgar, egotistical and heartless, to borrow a little run of his adjectives from one sentence.

It is perhaps a pity to deprive readers of *The Listener* of these and some other reflections, but they might think me simply annoyed. Perhaps I am annoyed. I am.

I was saddened, yesterday, to hear of the death of Alec Clunes. I remember him, first, as one of a gifted quartet who played small parts in Shakespeare at the Old Vic, when the star was Maurice Evans. The other three were Leo Genn, Cecil Trouncer and Alec Guinness. I used Trouncer several times, and delightedly, in radio. The only thing Clunes played for me was the central figure in Richard Rees's version of Simone Weil's uncompleted *Venise Sauvée*, which might have ended up as a very great play.

27 March

Party with food at Peter Owen's. A small black man spent the evening pawing one of the women after another. The most intelligent of these, free-lance wife of an *Observer* journalist, who had given him no encouragement, nevertheless described his behaviour as "red-blooded". When M. and I left, only he and Eva Figes, the novelist, were left. She looked trapped. We tried mutely to signal that, if she came then with us, we would resolve the situation, but she stayed, looking distractedly this way and that, a thin creature with large eyes and hectic colouring, whom before the War one would have assumed to be tubercular.

25 April

Seaford. Though M. is now back at the Oratory,[1] she had a week's holiday due to her and must take it this term. I was here twice, once to bathe and once in the small hours of the morning after walking over Firle Beacon, thirty-five years ago, while staying with Herbert Read at the Bloomsbury house he had taken for the summer because Ludo was playing her viola in the orchestra at Glyndebourne. The town itself is sheltered, but it is almost impossible to keep one's feet on the sea front.

28 April

Only a length of sagging wire discourages the visitor from approaching the cliff-edge on Seaford Head. The drop from there to the flat limestone far below must be the deadliest in

---

1. The London Oratory School, governed by the Brompton Oratory Fathers, where M. was secretary.

the British Isles. Yet is seems that nobody ever jumps or pushes there. An ideal site for a pop festival.

9 May

The oddest telephone call. I was awakened at one o'clock this morning by a young man who said he was a poet and preferred my verse to my prose. He asked me whether I knew Sir Richard Rees,[1]who, he said, had left me £250 in his will. I ought, I am sure, to have made some attempt to find out whether the young man was a *protégé* of Richard's or someone in a solicitor's office, but all I wanted was to go back to sleep.

1. RH: "Him I first met at the turn of the year[1933], on my way through London to take up a job at a senior boys' elementary school in Dagenham, Essex. Rees was too tall. He walked quickly, but as though his legs were articulated only at the knees. He gesticulated in a corresponding manner, as though his arms were articulated only at the elbow. He also spoke quickly and at a high pitch, though had he sung, it would have been found that nature had intended him for a baritone, whereas Innes Stewart would have turned out as a lyric tenor. Both men, however, were quite unmusical. The *Adelphi* office was Rees's flat over a newsagent's at the corner of Cheyne Walk and Oakley Street, in Chelsea.

    "A second baronet, then aged 33, Rees was of noble birth on his mother's side. She, a sister of the fourteenth Lord Dorner, had married a South Wales coal-owner, awarded his baronetcy for political services to Lloyd George. His son had hated him and viewed his mother with the kind of devotion which commonly produces homosexuals, among whom Richard Rees belonged to the non-practising variety, or so I was to be told by George Orwell. An Etonian, Rees had tried the Foreign Service and publishing before, from socialist conviction, lecturing for the Workers' Educational Association and nursing the parliamentary constituency of Gillingham, Kent, in the Labour interest, as I learned from my oldest friend in London, a woman with a Huddersfield connection, who was Labour Party women's organiser for the Home Counties and who was nursing him.

    "He had taken over editorship (and much of the financial burden) of *The Adelphi* three years before I met him, when its founder, J. Middleton Murry, gave it socialist direction. . . . While he was editor,

14 May

Adam and Yvonne now also have a daughter. To be called
Emma, which I fear will, like Rachel, turn out to be common
in her generation. I had suggested "Emily" not because I was
taken with Emily Read, though I was, but because the name
seemed to me both a pleasant one in itself and unusual
nowadays. The young Reads' first child is Albert, an original
choice in similar vein.

15 May

Papillon press conference, followed by drinks, followed by
lunch at a Chinese restaurant for a dozen or so of us known to
speak French. In his briefcase, Charrière carries various forms
of evidence of the truth of his story and rebuttals of the
statements of his opponents. He is rather a large man, stately
in his deportment, his conversation easy, his manners
excellent, at moments ceremonious, though what he says may
itself be unbuttoned, including, for example, reference to the
belles cuisses of the press representative's secretary, who is
indeed well-endowed in that and other respects and comes

---

he was the first to publish many gifted writers, notably E.A. Blair
('George Orwell'), who became his close friend. If he was not quite
the first to publish Dylan Thomas, he was the first to print a signed
review (by me) of Thomas's earliest volume. [It was through Rees
that RH first met both Orwell and Thomas.]

"In 1936, Murry turned pacifist, and at that point Rees parted
company with the paper and went off to drive an ambulance in Spain.
Two years before the Second World War, he took up painting. In the
war, he served with the RNVR, much of the time as liaison officer
in ships manned by the Free French. After the war, he continued
to paint.

"When George Orwell fell seriously ill in 1948, Rees at first took
charge of his farming interests on Jura, in the Hebrides, and
subsequently settled in Edinburgh, where he remained for several
years. He had become closely interested in the writings of the French-
Jewish writer, Simone Weil, about whom he became the leading
English authority. He was Orwell's literary executor."

from Huddersfield. I have seen not only the other books on the case but also contemporary newspaper reports of the trial in 1931. There seems no shadow of doubt that the young Charrière was simply a ponce, that, on the night of March 26th, 1930, he shot and killed Roland Legrand, another ponce, with some premeditation, and that *Papillon* is largely fiction. If it were presented as a novel, it might reasonably be argued to be a great one. Its claim to documentary truth helps with its sales, but gets in the way of a proper critical evaluation. I am sure that the man is full of duplicity, but I did not find that his personality was one from which I instinctively recoiled.

31 May

This is a Sunday morning. During my last two years at the BBC, while I was in Drama Department (with whose continuing head I again lunched at the Garrick on Wednesday), Sunday mornings acquired a special character for me. No doubt they still have a special character for everyone, even patients in hospitals. In my case at that time, they were the only periods of good writing time during which I felt quite safe from telephone interruption. On Sunday evening already, I began, like a boy unhappy at a day school or a clerk in his office, to dread the coming week. Since I left the BBC, almost three years ago, all mornings are good writing time. I tended for a while, nevertheless, to make a very personal matter of Sunday mornings. As sounds and fragrances from the kitchen indicated my wife's progress towards the week's regular banquet, I commonly found myself at this typewriter on this table composing in some kind of present or retrospective autobiographical vein.

I did not continue as I fancied I might. A fair amount of what I got down, on whatever day it might be, during my last three and a half years at the BBC and some of what was done on Sunday mornings for a year or so thereafter went into *Portrait of the Artist as a Professional Man*. The rest I tore up on Friday. It was not all I tore up. I tore up all my diaries before last year's, and that might have gone, too, but for its criminal anniversaries. I spent the whole day tearing things up, with many a satisfying rip of bindings. I went through and tore up typescripts which had survived previous holocausts (more literally then, since in those days we were not yet in a smokeless zone). I tore up what remained of a novel I wrote in the late forties, called in its first version *The Alibi* and in its second *The Idiot Questioner*. Some of this, it is true, went into another, *The Connecting Door*, and some lingers in a sequel to it which I put aside seven years ago. Less, alas, than I thought, for, having now looked at this, I find that I had retyped only the beginning and end of a passage I certainly meant to keep. But it is nothing new for me soon to regret part of what went, whether in a frenzy of destruction or in a turning out and sale of books.

Still, I am now comparatively uncluttered. My present life, such as it is, may be understood to have started last year. I am a criminal historian and translator, who may yet write further novels and who in the meantime keeps a diary which may or may not do wholly or in part for publication. Its longest entries are still likely to be made or at least typed up on Sunday mornings. The outside world will intrude. So, no doubt, will the past.

1 June

Latterly, the young nun has reappeared on the roof of St Vincent's across the way. At some public meeting, [Harold] Wilson was hit by an egg.

7 June

Death of E.M. Forster, aged 91. I admired him in moderation, as he would have wished.

17 July

M.'s last day at the Oratory, where she has worked for almost twenty years and had three headmasters shot under her, as well as a temporary headmistress who, a fortnight ago, was found wandering with loss of memory.

25 July

At half-past six last evening, a man from *The Times* rang, and at nine o'clock I dictated over the telephone to a night reporter an obituary of Sir Richard Rees, which appeared this morning.

Another death this month was that of Alfred Johnson, committed to Broadmoor in 1935 for killing his mother and father and the family pets. He was encouraged to study electronics and bought pieces of equipment from outside firms. Among the items found when his room was recently cleared was an apparatus of coils, bulbs and wires in a metal box. When an occupational therapy officer put it on a work bench, plugged it in and switched on, a hole appeared in a half-inch-thick sheet of steel six feet away. The home-made laser beam clearly has a great future before it.

12 August

For Pamela's latest,[1] not the usual publisher's party but a small dinner at a round table in a room of the Travellers' club, Harold Macmillan as host. The Binghams,[2] very strong for capital punishment. Pamela being against it, I murmured about Socrates.

1. *The Honours Board* by Pamela Hansford Johnson.
2. Lord Clanmorris (author of crime novels under his name, John Bingham) and his wife.

15 August

Jane Degras[1] to tea, talking about Richard Rees. She is looking after the odds and ends, and M. will collect a picture. I told Jane about the young man who rang late at night in May, two months before Richard's death. As I remembered the call, I thought he had said £250 and was therefore wrong and thus more probably a *protégé* than a solicitor's young man. Looking back, I now see that he was in a sense right, since Richard willed £500 to M. and me.

18 August

A French producer and his secretary, with Boisdeffre and an English camera team, to interview me for an ORTF programme on Dickens, in which Angus Wilson also is to appear. With all the wire and equipment, the flat door could not be closed, but on the other hand a man delivering groceries could not get in. In, nevertheless, halfway through the proceedings, got Miron Grindea, the Rumanian editor of *Adam,* uninvited. When the camera team had packed up, he was leading them off to interview him at home, presumably for the same programme, in which I had thought French viewers were to hear English novelists who had views on Dickens and spoke French.

6 September

Translator, diarist and dormant novelist, I am now also an obituarist in great demand. On Thursday, back from a heavy

1. In 1938, the Heppenstalls had visited Rees at his flat in Parkhill Road, Hampstead. George Orwell was staying there. RH: "With them that evening were an ex-burglar, named Henry Degras but calling himself Mark Benney, who had published a book about his adventures in other people's houses [*Low Company*, London, 1936], and his wife, Jane Degras, about whom I am ashamed to say that for many years I was to remember only that I had found her East End Jewish voice shrill and irritating."

lunch with Joe Gaute at the Connaught Rooms, I was dozing
when the telephone rang. M. being once more in the
Brompton, but briefly for a bronchoscopy, I eventually heard
and answered it to hear the charming East Anglian tones of
Jack Lambert's secretary. It is a year since the *Sunday Times*
asked me to review anything, and I was in hopes that I had
been restored to favour. What, when he came on, Jack
wanted, however, was to pass me on to the Deputy Editor,
Frank Giles, who in his turn wanted me to write an obituary
on François Mauriac[1] for the middle pages, in which, as he put
it, I should have the opportunity to step out stylistically. I
should have thought it a job to which Raymond Mortimer
would apply himself, but perhaps he was away. I was perhaps
thought solider than John Raymond.

I wrote my piece and dictated it over the telephone
between two and three o'clock (it took an hour, what with
spelling all the French names) on Friday afternoon. Then I
dozed again. Soon afterwards, on the telephone was Frank
Giles, who had, he said, dined at the Embassy the previous
evening and (he did not put it this way) been sold a Leftish line
on Mauriac. My piece was, in any case, short. He proposed,
therefore, with my permission, to insert a few lines, which he
would read over to me. They sounded grammatical, and I felt
disinclined to argue, but suggested merely that the Right-
wing enemies might perhaps smart rather from the acid than
from the lash of Mauriac's prose.

The piece I dictated had not in fact been short, though
perhaps it had reached Giles short, in consequence of the
reporter's difficulty with some of the French names. Among
the millions of words I have published, this article is unique
in containing a whole paragraph by somebody else. Apart
from that, it represents with fair accuracy what I now think
and feel about a writer on whom I once wrote differently.

---

1.   One of the French Catholic writers discussed by RH in his book
     The Double Image (Secker & Warburg, 1947).

27 September

I have been seen on French television, comparing Dickens with Balzac. I have not been paid. That astonishing double-act, the Hosein brothers,[1] has ended the second week of its run at the Old Bailey. In Los Angeles, the Manson circus[2] has run fifteen weeks and seems nowhere near closing.

4 October

Deal. A large cottage very near the sea front. We arrived yesterday, in good time for M. to do her weekend shopping and pick up the main local news, for me to lay in liquor and lay on papers.

This means mainly that from Monday a copy of the *Evening Standard* will be kept for me. I have no quality Sundays today, but only the *News of the World*, which has started a series of articles on the background to the Manson case. In a seaside town, Sunday morning, one hopes, may be the only good writing time. Without much to read, it is almost enforcedly good because, on Sundays, one stays indoors, avoiding the crowd which appears even out of season if the weather is good, as it is now. Unfortunately, I decided against bringing my typewriter this time and no longer find handwriting in notebooks natural. The Christian bookseller has extended his premises, but all I found at first glance was an unread Ed McBain.

If people are to be explained by their childhoods, those of Manson himself and the two girls, Susan Atkins and Linda Kasabian, née Byrd, seem as exemplary as any, but of what? The lack all three shared was of affectionate parental firmness. The two who seem totally criminal, Manson and

1. Arthur and Nizamodeen Hosein, Indian immigrants charged with the murder of Mrs Muriel McKay, the wife of an executive of the *News of the World*, whose body was never found.
2. The trial of Charles Manson and three members of his "family" of drop-outs for half a dozen murders on two occasions.

Atkins, never found any authority to stop them. They are still trying. They sing in court. This gains them a little extra attention, but then they are removed, which is a deprivation, though not enough to serve as aversion therapy.

At the Old Bailey, it has been said that Nizamodeen Hosein chopped Mrs McKay up with a billhook. This he denies. A rumour has also been mentioned, that she was fed to the pigs. As a change from foolproof shoulder of lamb, this week we have pork.

11 October

Evening. On Monday, M. had a letter from Kitty's cousin announcing the death, on the Saturday we came here, of K. in hospital at Haslemere. Next day, the McKay verdict was in.[1]

We are unlikely ever to know just how Mrs McKay died, unless we are still around when, in ten years' time, Arthur Hosein comes out of prison and publishes his memoirs. Her death was no doubt disagreeable, but most deaths are, the violent ones as a rule of short duration. In Mrs McKay's case, we do not know that her death was violent. When she first disappeared, her son-in-law stated that she suffered from a condition of health which made certain medicines necessary. As she lacked these, it may be that she died a natural death under illegal restraint, which at one time would have been constructive murder. Her last days were probably somewhat more unpleasant than K.'s in Haslemere, where after what M.'s letter called "exploratory surgery", she was no doubt sedated, analgesicised, carefully attended, able to recognise friends at her bedside. During her own last days, Mrs McKay would see only those two dreadful brown faces.

A natural death may be felt by the bereaved to have been

1. The Hosein brothers were found guilty. Sentences of life imprisonment for murder and other terms for kidnapping and blackmail were passed.

a happy release. Bereavement is nevertheless presumably always painful, and mourning is almost a recognised disease, of known symptoms and predictable duration. The symptoms may be worse in the case of a violent death, whether by murderer or by motorist, though in both cases the numbness will be relieved by a sense of something to be done, a culprit to be sought and punished. For the bereaved as for the victim, there must be something peculiarly unpleasant about the period before a murder which ensues upon kidnapping and before its discovery or presumption. In the bereaved, to offset the sense of purpose, there may be sensations of guilt because of something left undone, as there must or should be after a suicide or death from a neglected illness or in one's absence.

The murderer may also leave a mess, and this may cause shock to those who discover the crime and those who, as a rule in the course of their employment and therefore not altogether without gain, are called upon to clean it up. There is, indeed, one class of murderer who may cause endless pain and misery, *viz*, the political killer or assassin, the idealist, whose crime will certainly reverberate for a long time and is likely to entail countless other deaths and cripplings. On a smaller scale, where the notion of *vendetta* is current, as in family feuds or gangster rivalry, one murder may regularly lead to another.

In general, however, it may be doubted whether a murderer causes more pain than a motorist or a virus. For the victim, this is soon over. In due course, kinsfolk and friends cease to grieve in any disabling way.

18 October

Back from Deal yesterday, in time to receive Jean Tsushima, over for a smart wedding, Hoares and Hoggs, and sleeping here for one night. M. first met Jean before the war, when both were working at Paddington Green child clinic, under Donald Winnicott,[1] our neighbour in Hampstead. Jean married a Japanese journalist, Kaz, then stationed in London, subsequently in New York, Tokyo and Paris. They have a daughter, tall like Jean, in facial appearance more Japanese than English, of intermediate colouring. They live in Rueil-Malmaison. Jean sends me not only crime books but all the new French postage stamps, two copies of each, one inside, one on the envelope to receive a postmark, so that I have them both mint and used.

19 October

It is a fortnight since Cross, our trade commissioner, was kidnapped in Quebec. Laporte, provisional Labour minister, was taken four days later.[2] For the moment, Cross is supposed still safe, but Laporte's body was found in a car near the airport yesterday morning. That would be about noon by our time. We have grown accustomed to this kind of thing in Latin America, but it is a shock when it happens in a predominantly English-speaking country, especially one with which we still have close ties, even though the kidnappers and killers are "culturally French". Kidnapping for monetary ransom is a thing we associate with the United States, though, like our Hoseins, the author of their most famous kidnapping, that of the Lindbergh child, was a foreigner, but they have not yet had this sort of political kidnapping. The Arabs have it already. The next to try it will no doubt be the Irish.

1. Described by RH as "a Freudian pediatrician".
2. James Cross, the British Trade Commissioner in Canada, was kidnapped by terrorists of the Quebec Liberation Front, who demanded a ransom of $500,000 and the release from gaol of twenty-three convicted terrorists. Similar terms were demanded for the safe return of Pierre Laporte.

20 October

It is between eight and nine years since, at St Mary Abbots rheumatism clinic, I was discovered to have osteo-arthritis in the knees, especially the left one. None of the treatment made any perceptible difference. I found it painfully unpleasant to climb our stairs or to stand about in pubs or at parties and bus stops, but on level ground walked really very considerable distances (from Deal to Kingsdown and back, for example) without trouble. The French ambassador's residence is, I suppose, about half a mile from here. The Scott-Moncrieff prize presentation taking place this year there instead of in the Institute library, I walked there. By the time I shook hands with the Courcels,[1] I was in such pain that I could hardly speak. They must have thought me drunk. Since I have enjoyed private jokes with Mme La Baronne, she at least knows that I am not simply an idiot or specifically unable to speak French. I can only hope they have both forgotten my name. The sudden or suddenly revealed deterioration in my means of self-propulsion is even more worrying.

Inside, with a glass in my hand, I was soon all right, particularly as Raymond Mortimer's[2] express dislike of standing led us both to a sofa. I was spotted by my former colleague, Christopher Holme,[3] who did not know Raymond but no doubt wanted to and joined us. The conversation touched on the Middle East. Both are pro-Arab. This was perhaps not surprising in Christopher, who spent his war years among the Cairo *embusqués* and whose views, in any case, have always seemed to me the merest notions. He described Israel, which he does not know, as a white settler state. The

1. Baron Geoffroy Chodron de Courcel was the French ambassador.
2. Literary critic and journalist who, when literary editor of *The New Statesman*, had commissioned reviews and articles from RH. In 1951, at RH's request, he had arranged, for the BBC Third Programme, selections from the work of French Symbolist poets.
3. BBC radio producer. When Features Department was dissolved in 1965, he became one of two Assistant Heads of Drama (Sound), the other being Hallam Tennyson.

reason given by Raymond was that he prefers the *Arabian Nights* to the Old Testament.

3 December

Cross released.[1] The difference between his fate and Laporte's suggests that it is better for the victim of a kidnapping not to be locally known. The kidnappers should be locally inconspicuous, however. The Hosein brothers could not have got away with it anywhere in the United Kingdom.

10 December

By candlelight. Two hours' black-out on Monday morning, an hour (unnoticed) early on Tuesday afternoon and from half-past nine to midnight, three hours yesterday morning.[2] In this weather, even tonic waters keep cold enough in the larder. The lights have come on. This cut started only forty minutes ago, at five o'clock.

25 December

Isolated long clap of thunder at midnight, some snow this morning, so a whitish Christmas. Turkey and presents at Lindy's.

---

1. After a deal between the Canadian government and the terrorists had been made, which allowed the kidnappers to fly to Cuba.
2. Resulting from a "work to rule" imposed by the staff of power stations.

1971

7 February

Three weeks without post have already given this year an air of unreality. It started quite normally, its first disaster occurring at the Rangers *v.* Celtic match in Glasgow on the second day and first Saturday. On the twelfth day, a Tuesday, an Angry Brigade bomb wrecked the small, surburban house of the Minister of Employment and Productivity, Mr Carr. The postal strike began on the 19th. In the United States, Manson and his family were convicted on the 25th.

I have flown a little over Europe, but the only geographical perceptions which result from that have to do with clouds and mountains, rivers and the Channel. I have never crossed the Atlantic. To do that by aeroplane clearly involves one with geography at the point at which it passes into the realm of physics. Yet, in a novel, the flight will be described not even in geocentric terms, but as though the aircraft alone were making it. One ought, I feel, rather to read:

New York was still plunged in darkness. Spinning eastward at a rate of somewhat more than 600mph, it stood briefly in the sun's meridian as the evening rush hour started in London. As the small hands of its ten million watches and clocks crept down from three to four, it approached an aeroplane which had risen into the air from Heathrow shortly after noon by Greenwich time and maintained itself there for eight and a half hours in the teeth of that rush of air ten times gale force which accompanies the earth's turning, forced back by less than four hours from its

64

position *vis-à-vis* the sun. Informed of the imminence of New York, the pilot relaxed the forces at his command and, with a nice judgement, was hovering no more than a few feet above it as the runway at Idlewild raced towards his undercarriage, then touched him with a barely perceptible bump.

There cannot, I imagine, be other perceptions to be made, except the greater ear-fatigue, the feeling that it will be somewhat longer before one's soul catches up with one's body, variations of personal behaviour on the part of one's fellow passengers (in general, after all, no different from such as may be observed in a railway carriage) and possible glimpses of things like Bartholdi's statue of Liberty and the New York skyline, of which one's mind is already stocked with images.

Once landed, of course, the stimuli would be as varied as in any other city one has not entered before, Istanbul, Amsterdam or Aberdeen. I was an early but never much of a traveller. I know two foreign cities, Paris and Strasbourg, and provincial England better than most of my countrymen. It will probably have to do now.

I don't even leave the house much. From up here, with seventeen windows, to go down into the street is to go in, not out. I did it on Thursday morning. At the corner, turning away from the Mercury theatre and the Four Square chapel, I saw waiting in the bus queue my short-sighted son Adam, who had, it appeared, called at the bank on his way from Pimlico to St John's Wood. It is always very strange to see a familar face in an unexpected place, so strange that one may fail to recognise it at all or simply feel that there goes someone who resembles the person one knows and, in this case, dearly loves. I walked on to the tube station, noting that in general the fauna of Notting Hill Gate looked fairly normal, the hippies and so on not appearing till later.

Emerging from Holborn station, I proceeded in an easterly direction along Holborn and turned right into Great

Turnstile. The *New Statesman* building had changed. The last time I had entered it, one reached the literary editor's office by way of the fire escape.

Anthony Thwaite, who is small, was in a small room, built round with books. He had telephoned to ask whether I cared to review a translation of Aragon's *Paysan de Paris*. In view of the postal strike, I had volunteered to go and fetch it, as no doubt he would have asked me to.

He has given up drinking. When he was at the BBC, I thought him abstemious by local standards, but he assures me that there were lost weekends. I only half believe this.

18 February

If the postal strike becomes permanent, I shall once more be a regular contributor to *The New Statesman*. Tony might have asked me to do the Aragon even if it had to be wrapped and sent, but I should not have had this Lytton Strachey book or the one on D.H. Lawrence's debt to Edward Carpenter, suitable as the latter is to a reviewer whose first published essay, thirty-seven years ago in *The Adelphi*, was on Edward Carpenter and led directly to the commissioning of a first book.[1] The strike not only favours reviewers who live in London. It eases the consciences of those like myself to whom visiting literary editors' offices is touting.

There this morning was V.S. Pritchett, a former neighbour in Hampstead, who was recently elected president of the English Centre of PEN, partly my doing, since I am a member of the executive committee. I have latterly tended to cut meetings, but I intended to go this afternoon, as V.S.P. could

1. RH: "I received my Dip. Ed. in June 1933.... There was a scarcity of teaching jobs in those days. I was six months at home, filling in several application forms a week. Sir Richard Rees, the editor and financial backer of *The Adelphi*, put to J. Middleton Murry a suggestion I had made in a letter (I did not yet know Rees personally) that I should write a book on Murry. Murry fixed this with his own publisher, Jonathan Cape. I got a contract without so much as writing a synopsis, Murry having much liked my article on Edward Carpenter."

be expected to be in the chair for the first time and might need moral support. He, however, had another engagement, so I am not there either.

If anything may be thought certain in the noosphere of literary influences, it is that Teilhard de Chardin did not read Carpenter. He just might, I suppose, have read or heard about Murry's *God*. It is all there. The only novelty lay in such a vein of evolutionary optimism being opened by a Jesuit. I could not read Carpenter now.

2 April

At Margaret Drabble's in Hampstead to organise a composite novel which she and B.S. Johnson[1] are editing on behalf of the Greater London Arts Association for next year's

1. Experimental writer; since 1965, poetry editor of *Transatlantic Review*. In his first novel, *Travelling People* (London, 1963), some pages were printed in grey to represent a character's loss of consciousness; in another, the chapters were loose, so that they could be read in any order, and in another, a hole was made through several pages, prematurely revealing the denouement.
   RH: "[In 1962,] I was somewhat regarded as the senior *avant-garde* British novelist, also representing the French *nouveau roman*. It was therefore as to a *chef de file* that B.S. Johnson first sent me a proof copy of his first novel, then telephoned to ask if he could come to see me. It may also have been that he wanted me to say something which could be quoted in advertisements, but in fact the question I remember him asking was whether I thought his book had anything in common with the French new novel. It hadn't. If anything, it was reminiscent of Sterne's *Tristram Shandy*, or so a cursory glance suggested to me, for that was all I had given it. I hate reading books in proof, and I have never cared for the experimentalism which has recourse to typographical oddity. Nor, frankly, did I at first much take to Bryan himself, who was fat, uninterestingly pale, without much facial expression, and who spoke with a Londonish accent in a voice I noted as of rather high pitch without at first perceiving that it was a light tenor which might have repaid training, had its possessor been musical.
   "I liked his second novel, *Albert Angelo* [1964], and I liked his thin, sharp wife, Virginia, who had worked in Paris and who spoke good

Festival of London and to which some twenty novelists are to contribute each a chapter.[1]

Driven home by a talkative young man called Peter Buckman, Alan Burns a fellow passenger most of the way, Eva Figes dropped off in Hampstead, a lift to Bloomsbury being then given to Vincent Brome, whom also I knew but only as a writer of radio scripts. Eva is publishing a Women's Lib. book, having been deserted by the father of her children. She was not at Peter Owen's more splendid party at the House of Lords a fortnight ago to celebrate his twentieth year as a publisher, the host, no doubt explicably, being the young Lord Alexander of Tunis.

11 April

Easter Sunday, a bright day. On Tuesday Stravinsky died. Contracts yesterday from Peter for two books on French crime, which with Harrap would have been one. I prefer two, though I shall have to extend the chapters already written. The first is to deal with French crime between the world wars, the second bringing the tale up to the present day.

The action of the composite novel is to take place on yesterday's date, each of us being allocated either the wife or the husband for an hour and a half. I have the wife in the afternoon. I shall receive three-fifths of the novel from Piers Paul Read on June 7th and on the 12th pass it on to a coloured novelist, Wilson Harris. This sequence will be convenient, in that we three live within walking distance of each other. I must carefully preserve today's and yesterday's papers.

French. They dined us in Islington, and we took a present when they had a baby son. A certain pushingness made Bryan unpopular in certain quarters (in others, it succeeded very well), and it was alarmingly said to me (by Charles Snow, I think) that people were making me responsible for B. S. Johnson. There remained that about him which I increasingly liked. For one thing, he would put himself out for you. In those days, he drove a large van, and with this he would always fetch M. and me as well as taking us home."

1. *London Consequences.*

30 April

Shocked disbelief will no doubt be the reaction at Inland Revenue when they learn that, during the financial year just ended, my literary earnings were £650 less than the year before.

3 May

Isla Cameron, the folksinger, who lives two floors down in this house, recently stayed at his house in Kent with Alan Sillitoe. To my astonishment, this morning I received a packet of foreign stamps, largely Russian, from him. There must have been talk about me, and Isla must have said I collected stamps, she herself being a source of Spanish ones, which result from her correspondence with Robert Graves. The interesting thing is that at the moment I am engaged in reading short stories published over the past three years for the Katharine Mansfield prize, awarded by the municipality of Menton. Among the volumes submitted by publishers is one by him, while there are stories by him in two of the annual *Winter's Tales* compilations. The general standard is so poor that very little might lead me to vote this way or that. I don't in fact much care for those of Sillitoe's stories which I have read. They are, of course, about working-class life in somewhere like Nottingham, but, as it seems to me, it is not at all the "working" class of today but of Sillitoe's childhood or even his parents' childhood, which perhaps was properly a class and, if it merited inverted commas, did so for a different reason. Even in a rich town like Huddersfield, there was real unemployment in those days.

I could have done the proletarian stunt as well as the next man and was somewhat tempted to do it during the pink decade before the War. If I were younger, I might be tempted now, for we seem to be in for another pink decade, and working-class backgrounds are in great demand among writers. My difficulty would be two-fold. On the one hand, I should be hampered by the highbrow French line I am somewhat known for, the Continental impression having been reinforced by the name my parents left me, which equally to southern-English and Scottish eyes and ears looks and sounds vaguely foreign. And people, I have found, simply do not believe that a man partly educated abroad can have come from my sort of backround forty years ago.

8 May

I having lamented that for several springs past I had missed the tulips in Regent's Park, Donald, with Andrew, called and drove me there this morning. He had not previously noticed the opalescence of drakes' tail feathers, so vivid in sunlight when they thrust their beaks into the water.

22 May

Hospitable week. On Tuesday, we had Bryan and Virginia Johnson to dinner. Last evening, we had the Snows. The huge pile of volumes of stories had to be kept out of sight, especially on Tuesday, since one of the *Winter's Tales* volumes contains a story by Bryan which I do not like at all

As things go, Pamela's stroke was a slight one, but her speech is still a bit slurred, and her handwriting still slopes up increasingly to the right (well, of course, it could hardly slope up to the left, and by "increasingly" I mean that each line slopes up a little more than the last). On the other hand, there no longer seems to be much trace of that radical inconsequentiality of mind which I feared I detected when we dined with them last month.

6 June

There was, it seems, a great turn-out for Margaret Drabble's traditional novelists' evening, but we of the *avant-garde* had barely fifty people in the big top.[1] Eva [Figes] was

1. Events in the Bedford Square Bookbang, organised under the auspices of the National Book League with the aim of increasing interest in, and sales of, books.

excellent, though everything she said about novel-writing would have done just as well on the traditionalists' platform. Alan [Burns] looked forward with enthusiasm to the day when novels would be written by computers. He failed to communicate this enthusiasm. I, as an experimental father figure, am out of touch with my juniors and disciples, in that they believe in a sort of progress in the novel, their sort of novel superseding the traditional novel, as socialism or (for Alan) anarchism supersedes capitalism. I spoke a little against this confusion of aesthetics with politics and said that I didn't even believe that time marched on, it merely staggered around. I also tried out a joke I am much keener on, *viz*, that we are witnessing the decline of capitalism . . . into socialism, but this produced no audible response. Either my timing was wrong, or the joke needs a larger audience. That was a pretty earnest audience. Perhaps it will go home and think about the point.

10 June

Leg-bothering walk to Wilson Harris's at Shepherds Bush. His wife a Scotswoman. They live without luxury, but produced sherry. I find miscegenation displeasing, but by his colour Harris must be three parts white, and three parts are better than one, though most of the leaders of black militant movements are also in part white but have chosen to parade themselves as essentially black. Their parents may well have felt that they were compelled to do so, but now black, whether beautiful or not, is smart. Though I found it saddening, I liked what I saw of the Harris household. He is certainly a gifted man.

18 July

M.'s birthday treat, lunch out with Lindy and Donald at a really very good little restaurant in the neighbourhood. My

71

sixtieth, next Tuesday week, is to be celebrated on a larger scale, though of course M. will share the delights, as I have those of hers. I have latterly found and stated that Agatha Christie's latest novels have been her best. Incidentally to this statement, I seemed also to show regret at never having seen *The Mousetrap*, though knowing many actors who at one time or another played in it. Adam is organising (paying for, I imagine) the row of six seats, while afterwards we are all to dine at a favourite restaurant of Lindy and Donald's, the Inigo Jones, just off St Martin's Lane.

27 July

I had seen *The Mousetrap* at last and was pleased to have done so. A happy band, we proceeded to the Inigo Jones. Our table was not ready. There would be some delay. That did not matter. We could sit in comfort downstairs over our *apéritifs*. There would be no further delay. A table had been fitted up for us. That was the fatal mistake, though I did not express myself adequately at the time.

The fashion is, it appears, for dimly lighted restaurants, just as candlelight is in favour at private tables. I had a bad experience of this not long ago at the Zavriews'[1] over the French Institute, where, having carefully avoided monopolising Michel Butor[2] earlier, since we were dining together in company, I found myself not only unable to talk to him but unable to see him, Mme Z serving her dinner at six little tables, each accommodating four persons and lighted by one candle, so that walls of darkness lay between tables. Within living memory was also dinner at the Calders',[3] where, Bettina having served red mullet (which, of all fishes, needs light if you are to free it of bones), her husband insisted on

---

1. André Zavriew became director of the French Institute in 1967.
2. French scholar and writer who had occasionally dined at the Heppenstalls'.
3. The publisher, John Calder, and his wife.

switching off the light and reducing us to a single candle in the middle of a large round table.

I am not in favour of dim lighting in restaurants. The lighting at our improvised table was even worse than elsewhere in the restaurant. I could not with comfort read the menu, which in any case was too long and included too many confections with cods' roe. No doubt I could have got beyond that part of the menu had I carried an electric torch. A sort of hysteria was creeping up on me. This, after all, was my sixtieth-birthday treat. I owed no duty to anyone. The treat for me would be to get out of this restaurant. I wasn't, of course, particularly hungry. I rarely am in the evening.

Donald arranged an *exeunt omnes* with a minimum of fuss and ill-feeling. I felt sorry for Adam, who lacks Donald's social sophistication and had been keen on the evening and, from the observed dealings with waiters, had clearly not been involved solely with the earlier part of it. None of this will leave permanent sores. My behaviour on my sixtieth birthday will simply become part of the family legend, like my curious forgetfulness (although I had been rehearsed in the part all day) on the evening when Donald asked me for Lindy's hand. At sixty, I am perhaps entitled to a little eccentricity. Not too much, though.

1 August

Last evening, Joan Easdale ("Sophie Curly")[1] rang to ask whether she could stay here for the night. Nothing could have appealed to us less, but we agreed. She has settled in Nottingham, a town with which, to the best of my knowledge, she had no previous connection. National Assistance and local welfare have there set her up in a council house. She still does not consider Mrs Easdale to be her mother, but has seen her and gave us her address, which is

1. See footnote to July 4th, 1969. Joan Easdale, who had spent some years in a mental institution, was now calling herself "Sophie Curly", as she had doubts about her parentage.

of a disabled gentlefolk's home in Hampstead. Joan also has some contact with the elder of her own two daughters, of whom she speaks in a manner which suggests that she also does not think they are her daughters. She had no recent news of her brother. All her conversation is intelligible, even at times intelligent. The only room with a spare bed now is the crime room, and there she was put. On retiring, she produced a roll of Sellotape, of which, she said, she always places strips across the door and its frame and the floor of any room she sleeps in, so as to know if anyone enters. There was no suggestion that either M. or I was likely to intrude upon her slumbers. It was simply a thing she did, as she explained without embarrassment or apology. She had a bath.

This morning, we made it clear that we did not expect her to stay a second night, and she was several hours on the telephone, trying to get her daughter. Eventually, she left. M. felt that we ought to try to make some contact with Mrs Easdale, now that we had her address, but failed to discover a telephone number.

4 August

The three PEN judges for the Katharine Mansfield prize are Nicolette Devas, Kathleen Nott and myself. All three of us, with Nicolette's husband, a painter, M., and the general secretary, David Carver, and the lucky prizewinner are to be entertained for a weekend in Menton in early October, with free air travel. I am to make a speech in French, to please our hosts.

This afternoon, with David joining us later, Katie and I went to Nicolette's house in Chelsea. We all lacked enthusiasm for any of the stories we nevertheless thought might do. David and Nicolette, like myself, thought that, this being so, the final choice might not improperly be affected by what we thought rather of the authors than of the stories specifically offered and that we might even allow ourselves to be influenced by such consideration   whether we could expect the chosen author to be agreeable company. Katie, very properly of course, took the view that we must judge the stories themselves on their specific merits. This was not easy, and in practice she was just as opportunist (or whatever the right word would be) as Nicolette or myself. Olivia Manning was thought by David and less emphatically by my fellow judges to be particularly unlikely to be agreeable company, while even my reluctant fondness for her was tainted by the feeling of certainty that if she won she would insist on bringing Reggie,[1] whom none of us wanted. My own chief rooted objection was to picking any of the newer Irish writers, while the one story by Frank O'Connor would be difficult to explain to the French, precisely because it had a French connection. Stonewalling, I batted for the Orcadian George Mackay Brown. He was never in London, and this might be the one way to lure him south, what with the auld alliance and all that. Nicolette didn't mind. Katie did, and my enthusiasm for Brown's story increased. A variety of mark-awarding voting systems was tried, and, by flagrant cheating, I carried the day, which ended with Katie and myself not on speaking terms.

15 August

Harry Thornton Moore, the D.H. Lawrence specialist and copious American critic, is in London, is also going to Paris. He was here to dinner this evening, Lindy and Donald looking in later. On recent visits, he has always stayed with Richard Rees in Chelsea, and as a rule his second wife has been with him. We are now his principal or at any rate his longest-established London contact. He first came to see us in 1937, the

1. Olivia Manning's husband, R.D. Smith, a BBC radio producer. It was through his initiative that A.J. Burroughs joined the BBC (see entry for April 29th, 1969).

year we were married, as a friend, then, of Michael Sayers,[1] by that time established in New York, who two years before had been the generally absent third tenant of the flat I shared in Kentish Town with "George Orwell". Our relations have never been very close, but a lot of exasperated affection hangs loosely about them. We do also accept that we must to some extent take Richard's place at the London end of that American life.

29 August

Alan Sillitoe has bought the flat two floors down. He got it at the kind of reduced price which obtains when a flat is occupied by what is known as a sitting tenant. This, of course, was Isla Cameron. Now that the transaction has been completed, she moves out and is travelling north today to stay with the poet Adrian Mitchell, in what I have always fancied must be an especially attractive part of Yorkshire, round Ingleborough, where it bites deeply into Lancashire and in fact comes within ten miles of the Irish Sea. The nearest point I know is Clitheroe, which is on the Lancashire side of the Ribble and near which I was stationed during the War for a short while.

Just gone are George Reavey[2] and a recent wife, better-looking and less oddly dressed than the one at whose wedding reception, as I record in *Four Absentees*, Dylan Thomas spoke viciously of [the composer] Humphrey Searle's thin lips. The new wife has an interesting medical condition, the

1. Sayers, a Jewish Dubliner who wrote short stories and, in the mid-1930s, was drama critic for *The New English Weekly*, to which RH contributed, emigrated to America and became English play-editor to Norman Bel Geddes, the theatrical producer and designer.
2. An Ulsterman — a "literary dabbler", in RH's view — who occasionally translated from the Russian, occasionally wrote poetry, and occasionally ran a private press (his Europa Press, Paris, published his friend Samuel Beckett's first book, *Echo's Bones*).

antithesis of diabetes, not hyper- but hypo-glycaemia. She seems very nice. They, too, are going to Paris. On their return, he proposes to give a party at his hotel or elsewhere in London, a thing I have known Harry Moore do with remarkable effect.

1 September

Dinner with Harry Thornton Moore at Kettner's. Oysters, then grouse. Excellent. On returning home, I was sick. He is to come to dinner here on Sunday with Jane Degras, both having been friends of Richard Rees.

6 September

The Sillitoes being around, M. asked them up for a drink this evening, and I arranged that Harry Moore should come early. He knew the name of Alan Sillitoe, and the long D.H. Lawrence connection has made him familiar with Nottingham, which is Sillitoe's home town and the scene of most of his writing, while Ruth Sillitoe I understood to be American. The Sillitoes came after tea, bringing their children, a son and a niece, the daughter of Alan's sister, whom they have adopted, of much an age, eight or nine, both attractive and well-behaved to the point of self-effacement. Each had brought a book and was seated by the end window, whereafter neither said a word until, it being understood that he was of a scientific bent, I took the boy, David, along to the crime room and got out copies of *The Criminologist*, which contained highly technical articles on aspects of forensic science. These he then sat and devoured silently. Harry came. After a while, Ruth took the children downstairs for a while and then returned with them. Jane came. Ruth took the children away again, but then again returned with them. Harry began to look hungry and unwell. Finally, when it was well after eight o'clock, M., after going to look at the food, returned and announced that we really must have dinner now.

Alan Sillitoe took it in his stride. Ruth was at first a little uptight, but managed a proper, smiling withdrawal. M. assured me that she had made it quite plain the invitation was to a drink before dinner, for Sillitoe to meet Harry. It was not quite a perfect start to a new set of relations with neighbours.

Sillitoe seems less of a young hypochondriac than he formerly did. His hair, which is dark and not thick, trendily straggles, and he wears a shirt fastened in the specifically Russian or generically Slavonic peasant style but without embroidery. He is quite talkative and rolls his shoulders for emphasis with a sort of doggy sincerity. In his way of producing his voice, the Midlands snuffle still predominates. This of course may be deliberate and political. It is the fashionable accent of the Left, except among orthodox communists, who prefer Cockney. Sillitoe was an orthodox communist, but now speaks of Red Fascism, which I suppose is an encouraging sign. There is a curious opacity about the whites of his eyes, as though these were not jellies but blancmange. They also roll.

25 September

This morning, with Martin Esslin, I recorded my narration for three "Cause Célèbre" programmes, respectively on the murder of Jean Jaurès, Weidmann and Landru, a taxing assignment. Afterwards, Martin invited me up to his office, where, he said, he had a bottle of whisky.

In duplicated copies of the scripts, which I received a fortnight ago, I had noticed a number of errors. I wrote to Martin about these. I took advantage of the occasion to note that, for the four financial years since I left his department, my earnings in respect of work done for it as an outside writer had been, respectively, in the neighbourhood of £1200, £900, £600 and £300, this last figure, moreover, including payment for the scripts we were at the moment belatedly involved with, so that for the current year there had so far been nothing. This, I suggested, looked like evidence of diminishing goodwill. Such wide spacing of programmes in it was also, I suggested, not the best way to run a series. In a note meanwhile, Martin had insisted that there was no question of diminishing goodwill, and I supposed that, in inviting me up to his office to drink whisky with him, he wanted to assure me of his goodwill and to explain to me the practical difficulties standing at the moment in the way of its manifestation.

What there was in the way of whisky turned out to be a drop in the bottom of each of two half-bottles, while the only thing to go with it was a small ginger ale. These being poured, M.E. proceeded, for half an hour or so, to sing me a hymn of hate, with verses contributed by various hands, including that of the late Joe Burroughs, who, said his and my former boss, had, after my departure, nearly jumped out of the window whenever my name was mentioned.

At first I attempted to meet the various criticisms, but presently I just let Martin sing on and, when he seemed to have finished, took my leave of him and presently emerged from Broadcasting House feeling that it had all been very strange. It had. It is.

1 October

The Menton trip is off. I was told this morning by telephone from David Carver's office that the municipality, while it will put wives up, will not pay their fares. As it happens, Katie Nott also has called off, and George Mackay Brown will not leave Orkney.

10 October

There is scaffolding all over the house, which, in view of its height, is a lot of scaffolding. Today, as it is Sunday, there are no workmen on it. We expect to have a daytime population of workmen as additional neighbours at least until Christmas.

To date, they seem not an unpleasant lot. They have, for instance, not yet brought up transistors such as one man always had with him, to the mild annoyance of some of his older colleagues, the last time we had workmen inside the house, painting and distempering the staircase. His transistor was part of the general nastiness of his disposition. He played it to assert himself, not because he enjoyed the sounds which came out of it. This, I fear, is a very common phenomenon. Indeed, I often wonder whether personal enjoyment of the thing heard can have anything to do with Pop, which is only technically a form of music. It undoubtedly displays elements of melody, harmony and rhythm, but these are reduced to a level of simplicity and monotony far below that of, say, Moody & Sankey hymns. Workmen used to hum, whistle and even sing the latest tunes. They don't now. There aren't any latest tunes for them to hum, whistle or sing. All Pop is the same, a sort of expostulation on one note, very occasionally changed, bang, strum, wail and shout as its grimacing and writhing performers may within the hellish circle of their three chords, the tempo as unchanging as the key.

The sound of our new workmen is principally that of the speaking voice of their foreman, Bert. His accent is a sort of rural one and southern, though I am not expert enough to place it longitudinally. The voice is loud and penetrating, though not authoritarian. The language is not foul. In subject matter, Bert covers whatever may have appeared in the newspapers or been heard the previous evening on television. He is a gasbag. The others listen. One does not listen, though he appears to. A big, handsome fellow and perhaps foreign, he is a deaf mute.

4 November

Last evening, a television producer, Tim Aspinall, came here for a drink, brought by Bryan Johnson, who has just written a "Thirty-Minute Theatre" script for him. It was proposed that I also should do such a script. The first idea I had thought of was for the jury's deliberations at a murder trial. (I knew of, but had not seen, the Henry Fonda film, *Twelve Angry*

Men.) A trial jury, however, would mean at least twelve actors, twelve characters to establish, too many for a play lasting only half an hour. For a coroner's jury, there need only be seven.

The case I had on the cuff was a seaside murder, based on one in Worthing three years ago. It was that of an octogenarian Army widow, a familiar sight on the seafront, wearing, even in summer, an old-fashioned imitation musquash coat and known as the Painted Lady because of her heavy make-up and dyed hair. She had often frequented coffee bars where teenagers gathered and was found battered to death by one of these, employed at her hotel, to whom she had been in the habit of giving money and cigarettes. The walls of her room were daubed with lipstick, and the word WHORE was scrawled on her chest and thighs. I imagined my jury meeting in the oak-panelled council chamber of a Tudor shire hall, its mullioned windows overlooking the seafront, the lifeboat visible, drawn up on the shingle as at Walmer. At need, to create a dramatic interruption, the room could shake to the sound of maroons and the lifeboat be launched, the capsized boat in the bay perhaps having contained the guilty youth, who had attended the inquest and thought it certain that he would be named by the jury.

The idea pleased Tim, whom, for our part, M. and I found tremendously engaging. This morning already, I put my starved visual imagination to work and typed two or three pages of script, then decided that such a case wouldn't do. It would have needed culpable concealment or perfect idiocy on the part of a chambermaid, the manageress or a policeman to prevent such a death appearing at once as a murder. There would have been a story in that. The chambermaid might have been a refugee terrified of the police. The manageress might have been obsessed with the good name of her premises. The policeman might have surmised that the guilty youth was his son. But such complexities would have been too much for half an hour, and, once a case is recognised as murder, there is not much for a coroner's jury to do.

Not long after the Painted Lady murder and before it came up for trial at Lewes assizes, the skeleton of a spinster, a former schoolteacher, in her sixties, was discovered, a length of window cord wrapped round its neck, when a large house, her property, which had stood apparently empty for six years past, was entered by the *gendarmerie* at a village inland from Nantes. From a railway ticket in her handbag, it was established that she had returned unobserved from Paris on February 23rd, 1964. The police view and that of the examining magistrate was that she had committed suicide that evening or shortly thereafter. It was, they said, loneliness which had killed her. The people in the village thought otherwise. A devout Catholic, she would never, *they* said, have committed suicide.

I toyed with the idea of transplanting this case to a British setting, perhaps in Monmouthshire, inland from Newport, a region I know well through M.'s family.

15 November

We have become almost fond of Bert, who is now engaged in a labour of love, a work, he clearly feels, of art, which he perilously steps back to admire, leaves, returns to, will accept no collaboration on. This consists in plastering cement about what remains of the chimney breast half-way across the back of the block, some two yards clear of the parapet at a point between our bathroom and that of the flat on the same level next door. The old pots and iron cowls were broken, unsightly and even dangerous. I am nevertheless a bit sorry to have seen the last of the tallest cowl, rusty and jagged, for it was a favourite perch of a long-tailed owl from Ladbroke Square. At night, I would hear hooting which did not change direction and in the dark make out its perched shape, the tail hanging down. From those gardens, once important to Adam, the very centre of his more secret life, have come various birds, jays for instance, stray crows one fancied death-predicting, fat, clean woodpigeons, so different from the gutter variety by which we are infested, yet have never contrived to trap and eat, for no doubt their flesh, though sparse, is as clean and wholesome as any other.

17 November

Party at Douglas Cleverdon's[1] in farthest Canonbury, for Stella [Hiller], Features Department's administrative assistant thoughout all but the last months of the almost twenty years of its separate existence.

Jennifer Hewitt, *nee* Wayne, had been [a producer] in Features when I first arrived at Rothwell House more than twenty-six years ago. I had not seen her for over twenty years until this evening. Now she is notably composed and *soignee*, a very attractive mature woman indeed, very still and quietly attentive, but the smile and the rest all there when you go for them. She has three children. We talked about the pleasure of having grandchildren. Hewitt,[2] a penal reformer for twenty-five years, was before that for twenty-five a policeman. He was helpful about coroners' juries.

If one has read Proust at all, one hardly, on such occasions, avoids recalling the final party at Mme Verdurin's. Jennifer Wayne was in fact much older than when I had last seen her, but she had not aged in any deteriorating sense. It was not much over four years since I had last seen Nesta[3] or Stella, even less since I had seen Anthea Holme.[4] To me, they looked much the same. Though we had once been quite thick, it was longer than that since I had seen Eileen

---

1. BBC radio producer, notably of Dylan Thomas's play, *Under Milk Wood*, the stage version of which he subsequently directed in Edinburgh and London (1955) and New York (1957).
2. C.R. Hewitt, whose pseudonym is C.H. Rolph.
3. Nesta Pain, a producer, had, with some friction, shared a secretary with RH at the BBC.
4. Wife of Christopher Holme (see October 20th, 1970).

Burroughs, but she, a darkly attractive woman of Welsh antecedents, neat, slim, smartly dressed and vivacious, seemed quite unaged.

There might, I feared on first seeing her there, be some awkwardness with Eileen, but not at all. She was obviously delighted to see both M. and myself, after what must have been at least six years. She drove us home after the party, and in the car news and reminiscent chatter went on without break. The late Joe was not mentioned.

25 November

For this year's silver pen awards, no more than a party on the Martini terrace at the top of New Zealand House, itself at the bottom of Haymarket. These splendid premises, with their spectacular views over London, seem to be let free or very cheaply to cultural organisations, by way no doubt of publicity for Martini products, though Italian big business seems to have that kind of conscience, while ours is totally Philistine. The first, to my knowledge, to take advantage of this was John Calder. On his occasion, only sweet and dry Martini and other half-soft *apéritifs* were served. This evening, there was gin if you wanted it. For serious drinkers, the trouble was that, most of the time, you could not get to the bar without seeming rude.

The man invited to present the prizes was Richard Hoggart, currently deputy head of UNESCO in Paris. He made a long speech in a Leeds accent on why UNESCO could not give very much money to PEN. At the termination of this, he was reminded that there were awards to be made. In a mumble, he made them. One of the recipients spoke wittily, but at some length. As we all surged towards the bar, the managing staff flickered the lights and then lowered them decisively. The only place at which I have previously seen a party ended in that way was the American embassy, which in any case no longer has the sort of culture crushes it used to have in the library.

12 December

"Man," solemnly wrote Gigi Rousseau at the age of fifty, in 1762, "was born free."

Had he never seen a baby?

In the course of our lives, most of us say a great many silly things. In general, we may hope that by the following afternoon they will have been forgotten or excused. Those whose observations are published will often glance back with discomfort at statements to which they have directly committed themselves or which have been credibly reported of them in periodicals. A writer can, as a rule, amend or deny them in, or simply omit them from, any book which ensues. Rousseau's howler originally appeared as the first sentence of a book. Although this went into numerous editions, he did not amend it.

"Man was born free. He is everywhere in chains."

It was the second statement which made the first famous. What Gigi meant by "chains" is very complex, and the rest of his book, which explains what he understood to be their nature, still repays study. But it was only those two statements which most people heard of, and they took "chains" in whatever sense best suited them.

That chains of industrial servitude could be said to chafe the limbs of many thousands of workmen had, by 1847, been noted by, among others, young Herren Marx and Engels. If, they perceived, sufficiently large numbers of workmen combined under the direction of persons like themselves, they would constitute a force which could assume political and economic control of any industrialised society. If all workmen throughout the world united, there was no limit to what might be done. Herren Marx and Engels urged them so to unite.

"You have nothing to lose," was the punch-line offered by these two, "apart from the said chains."

It was demonstrably untrue. Many of the workmen had wives and children. All had their lives. They had the languages they spoke and at least so much education as was needed to understand what Marx, Engels and others had written, in many cases to read it for themselves. In general, they had health and strong limbs, nourished for at least twenty years by food which they had not themselves scratched from the earth, sheltered and warmed however inadequately, forming bone and muscle by unimpeded exercise. They would not have been workmen otherwise. They would not have been men.

For, of course, men are not born, free or otherwise. Only babies are born. That, in the course of attaining manhood, the least well-endowed, the worst cared-for of them, acquire far more than chains, Marx and Engels had, respectively, thirty-six and forty-eight more years on which to reflect. They let the statement stand. With that which opens *The Social Contract*, that which closes *The Communist Manifesto* must rank as one of the two silliest statements ever made by fully literate men and left unchanged to the end of their lives, still very widely remembered and quoted without derision even by persons themselves of some education.

Born while its paternal grandparents, two and a half weeks ago, on the Martini terrace of New Zealand House, listened with what patience they could muster to statements just as silly but soon forgotten from the bemused Hoggart, Adam's second child is again a girl. How endowed and wearing what chains Lucy Heppenstall may attain womanhood, nobody can predict, and I shan't be there to see (the common pain of grandparenthood, which has its great pleasures). My fourth grandchild was born singularly unfree. She had a dislocated hip. In consequence of this and its prompt discovery, she was placed in an H-shaped structure in which she is expected to remain for at least three months, her legs positioned frogwise. The sight of her thus is distressing to her parents and to us. What occurs to me by way of comfort is that, not yet having enjoyed the free use of her limbs, she is unlikely to feel this confinement as a deprivation. To her, it will be as though to date she has been only half born, while in February or somewhat later next year, perhaps with a sense of having achieved such a result herself, will first come the bliss of released limbs, the one freedom which is indeed given at birth to the generality of future men and women not born, as in Russia, to swaddling bands.

As pretty as week-old babies can be expected to appear and with no other visible defect, it could be taken as certain that in her colouring Lucy would take after her father and in general the Heppenstalls, to say nothing of the Edwards, who are all fair. At eighteen months, her sister, on the other hand, has firmly adopted her mother's dark hair and grey eyes.

It must have been on the first Sunday of Lucy's life that M. and Lindy went to a concert at which Jacqueline Dupré was playing Dvořák's cello concerto, conducted by her husband, Daniel Barenboim, against whose life threats had been made. It would be next day when Elga Duval first came to tea.

Elga is stone deaf. This makes conversation with her tiring, though otherwise it would be easy, for she is lively and intelligent. She is an American artist who has taken it into her head to write a book on Dylan Thomas, whom she met several times in New York and who called her, she says, Theda Bara. Her current surname was derived from a French husband, her third or fourth, an earlier one having been the George Reavey who recently brought his third or fourth wife to see us, but either never gave his party in London or did not invite us. There are people here who adopt it, but the serial polygamy of the American middle classes still seems, in general, a quaint tribal custom here. Its principal effect on the parties directly involved appears to be a large redistribution of their incomes, though it must be rather unsettling for any children they find time to have.

Last Friday, a man from the Ministry of Defence was here between tea and drinks and took neither. He was a public-school Scot, about forty, good-looking in a severe, preoccupied way, quite humourless but intelligent. He is

conducting a survey of university communism in the 'thirties
and had read something I had published. I had nobody either
to shield or betray. He named the one party member I knew
of among the teaching staff at Leeds thirty-seven years ago.
He already had an appointment to visit the highly agreeable
woman who in my time had been the most politically active
of the student body. I asked to be remembered to her. It was
all painless and, I should have thought, pointless. I was asked
to say nothing about the interview.

I have rarely had men about me that were fat. Although it
seems that I was fat as a child and although I took to putting
on weight between ten and twelve years ago, I have usually
been a thin man, with no weight problem and a feeling that
those who had one were glandularly odd and alien, however
comforting their presence might be. Bryan [Johnson] is a fat
man. There is something about him which I enormously like.
An easy man he is not, but then perhaps neither am I.

1972

2 January

The year's first notable death, that of Maurice Chevalier.

9 January

There are several regions in which, though neither ratepayer nor on the electoral roll, I am known and could be thoroughly vouched for as a "good and lawful" man and so might reasonably be asked to serve on a coroner's jury. One lies not far south of the site of a classic case in which, forty years ago, the *vox populi* of a coroner's jury called murder what the police insisted was a sort of constructive suicide, although, for some weeks after the inquest had been formally adjourned, they had gone on treating it as murder, following up a variety of leads.

This was the case of Evelyn Foster, a garage-proprietor's daughter of Otterburn in Northumberland. On the afternoon of January 6th, 1931, she had driven customers to a village in Redesdale. Returning at tea-time, she told her parents of a customer she had arranged to drive twenty miles over the moors towards Newcastle. Mr Foster also ran a bus service, and at ten o'clock that evening one of his drivers saw a car smouldering on frozen moorland, off the road, and, nearby, Evelyn Foster, horribly burnt. Taken home, she remained intermittently conscious all night and, to her mother, in the hearing of a police constable and a doctor who had at once perceived that her burns must prove fatal, as they did towards six o'clock in the morning, told her story of brutalities of which sexual assault had been the least.

89

At the resumed inquest, the coroner insisted that this story was wholly improbable, that murder was out of the question and that the explanation must lie with Evelyn Foster's having culpably set fire to the car, either for the insurance money or to gain notoriety. The jury would not wear this and brought in a verdict of murder by a person unknown. Their verdict had, of course, to be noted, but the chief constable made a public statement to the effect that it was a wrong verdict.

I decided to base my short play rather on this case than on the French one, which I reserved for possible future treatment. As the time was to be the present, the place could not be too precisely situated, because of possible offence to a living chief constable and a real coroner. In my mind, it was somewhere in the north of the North Riding, Swaledale, Teesdale or Cleveland, whose dialect I could manage and in which I could plausibly lay claim to local roots. For I had also decided on a first-person narrative framework.

Most novels and stories are written in the third person, and more often than not the implied third person is omniscient. It is common to all forms of dramatic presentation that the member of the audience is captive, more or less so in respect of his place, wholly so in time, so that there is no equivalent for him to the reader's turning back in a novel or putting it aside and returning to it later. In a stage play, he sees and hears only what is done and said in a confined space. In the cinema or on television, he sees what the camera shows him. He is identified with the camera, with one camera at a time. The use of several cameras, offering him shots from a variety of angles and distances in rapid alternation, gives him the illusion of omniscience. This is the equivalent of the common sort of third-person narrative. In a television or cinematic equivalent of first-person narrative, this facility has to be suppressed.

In real life, a man may look down at his feet, and he is constantly seeing his own hands, but he never sees his own face except in a mirror. I therefore laid it down that no shot whatever should be taken from any position other than that of my seventh juror's eyes at any given moment. With a tape measure I established that, from a seated to a standing position, my own eyes rose vertically a foot and a half.

On Tuesday, Tim came to dinner, clearly enjoyed his food and again delighted M. and me. I asked him whether the cameras generally in use would thus, as it were, stand up and sit down with reasonable alacrity, also whether they could turn their heads quickly to left and right. There appeared to be no difficulty about this. There might be some difficulty in persuading the same camera to tilt its head so as to gaze up among the rafters or glance at the legs and feet of a girl opposite, let alone of the supposed me. As to mirror shots, they could be faked.

Somewhat to my own surprise, I finished *The 7th Juror* on Thursday, and the script has now gone off in three copies and two packets. Yesterday afternoon, M. went round the corner to Multibroadcast and hired a television set, which a young man installed last evening. Having written a television play, I ought, I feel, to take an interest in television drama. The only set we have had here before was twelve years ago, when the BBC lent me one while I was on sick leave.

22 January

To Lindy's for Rachel's second birthday party. The birthday itself is tomorrow, but today was better for Adam and Yvonne, who brought their two, the jolly, crowing Emma, now a year and two-thirds, who waves her arms with sheer *joie de vivre*, and Lucy, of whom it was my first glimpse, the line of her thighs horizontal and continuous along the brace. She does not seem unhappy, moves the lower part of her legs freely and, of course, has never known greater freedom.

30 January

- - - - is away. The woman occupying his flat, out all
evening, came in at a quarter past one and was still
intermittently active two hours later, when a shout of male
laughter was followed by her cry of "NO! Henry, don't!"
This is really very tiresome. As I am neither a *voyeur* nor an
écouteur, the creature must go.

11 April

Adam to dinner. He is taking out a mortgage on a long
lease of this flat, doing it for a variety of reasons, all of them
good. One of them is to secure his mother and me against
inflated rents. He will acquire the property, and we shall pay
only ground rent and a service charge while we live, though
I am to find a thousand pounds or so, to be regarded as a loan,
by way of meeting the advance on the mortgage. Adam now
earns a decent salary at the GLC architects' office in or near
County Hall. Donald advises him that the investment is
sound, but also he feels attached to these premises for their
own sake, having been brought up here from the age of seven
until he married. This is his thing, and I don't much question
it. He is an utterly good and decent young man, and I could
hardly love him more.

These, I suppose, are the kinds of thing I ought to be
writing about, not murder, too much attention to which
must somewhat have disturbed my serenity of mind during
the past five years, as must daily exposure to the mindless
yawping of trade union leaders, by contrast with which
murder in the private sector often seems, to a free-lance
reactionary like myself, harmless and even charming.

3 May

Into St George's yesterday, early this afternoon Lindy
produced her third child and second daughter, my fifth
grandchild. This was nicely timed. M. and I may now with-

out anxiety go to Lyme Regis on Saturday. We have stayed in Dorset only twice before, once at Waterston Manor when Constantine Fitzgibbon had it, once, on a chilly Easter seven years ago, at a hotel in Swanage. We have long fancied Lyme Regis, and to the literary associations of Jane Austen's *Persuasion* were recently added those of *The French Lieutenant's Woman*, as which neither of us has enjoyed and admired a novel so much for years. Our elegant and charming Norwegian twice-weekly help, Mary, has a sister who runs a vegetarian guest house there. Mary went down to help out at Easter. They found us the cottage. We have always started these rentings on a Saturday, arriving in time for M. to sort out the local shops and buy her joint and vegetables for the next day, I meanwhile laying in liquor. In fact, no joint will have to be bought this week. We are to be taken out to lunch on Sunday by the Donne-Smiths, who will drive over from Crewkerne after their Quaker meeting.

That, unless I wrote again to say that it was impossible, this would happen was the prompt and splendid response of a man I have never met, to whom I had written to say that I should be in his neighbourhood and would like to meet him, but had neither car nor a local telephone number. Basil Donne-Smith is a second-hand bookseller, who conducts a postal business, specialising in criminology. He issues, every two or three months, a catalogue with the title *Naked Villany*, a note explaining that this is how the word was spelt by Shakespeare. Among criminologists, I suppose him to be nationally known. Julian [Symons] once visited him at Crewkerne and praises both him and The Abbey, where he lives and from which he conducts his business. I have found him most engaging by post.

7 *May*

Lyme Regis. The cottage is small but spotless, the kitchen fully equipped, linen provided (a voracious slot meter provides electricity if constantly fed). No traffic passes. We stand along a concrete path beside a stream, the Lym.

M. is back with the papers, and we await the Donne-Smiths. The weather still looks unpromising, but the rain may hold off for a while. This cottage is perhaps a little difficult to locate. I shall walk along the concrete path, which is called Jordan, to the end of Mill Green, where our visitors will have to stop and get out of their car.

8 May

Though uninformed about the limiting effects of the osteo-arthritis in my legs, Mary had warned us how steep the principal streets of Lyme are and discouraged us from one let in the upper part of the town, noticed by M. in *The Lady*.

M., with her splendid legs, climbs uninhibitedly anywhere at any time, despite the far more painful rheumatoid arthritis which has done so much damage around her middle and elsewhere (for her, cortisone injections in the hands really did something). But I also climb on occasion. I have climbed Sherborne Lane, for example. This is comparatively short, though very steep indeed. Its bottom end lies at the point where Mill Green joins Combe Street over the Lym. At the top, Sherborne Lane comes out where Broad Street divides, and across the junction lie the cinema, the Peek chapel (wagonhead ceiling, very attractive) and the entrance to Langmoor Gardens, through which one descends windingly to the Cobb.

M. and I took that way this morning. It rained heavily while we were crossing the gardens. We made for a shelter and stood there until the worst was over. As in *Persuasion*, the wind discouraged walking along the higher level of the Cobb. We failed to decide at what point Louisa had done her jumping. Further rain drove us back.

The buildings at the head of the Cobb seem to constitute a separate village, distinct from Lyme. Among them are a butterfly shop and a shell shop, outside the latter big baskets full respectively of murexes and foxheads, the rarer specimens inside. We shall take back a large shell and a mounted butterfly for each of three grandchildren, and I may buy a few South and Central American butterflies for myself, putting them in the crime room to remind me of the convict settlements in French Guiana, catching the big, blue, shimmering morpho butterflies for costume jewellery being one lucrative activity of the convicts when they were *libérés* or had first escaped to Venezuela.

9 May

This morning, to the Cobb again. This evening, to the cinema, almost empty. Four hours of continual gore. The two main films were *Borsolino*, with Alain Delon and Jean-Paul Belmondo as pre-war gangsters in Marseilles, and *Riot*, with Gene Hackman and Joe Brown leading a prison revolt. Between these were trailers for *Straw Dogs* and for a film in which some place is nightmarishly overrun by rats. There was cheerfulness about *Borsolino*, more especially about the fist fight between Delon and Belmondo near the beginning, but the memorable image is the jerking dance of men being shot up with tommy guns. The closing image of *Riot* was a gaping throat, supposedly Hackman's, slit, as he clung to a wall before dropping to freedom, by a mad fellow-convict. I came out shaking. Never have I witnessed such an orgy of blood-letting, though, now that I come to think of it, the last film I saw before these must have been *The Boston Strangler* in Deal. In London, I never go to the cinema.

11 May

This morning, the Donne-Smiths drove over again and had lunch with us. Though Quakers, they drink in moderation, are what Donne calls BFs ("boozing Friends"). He is on the small side, with one eye wild and a mock-ferocious manner, rather military. His wife, Audrey, is enchanting. Both are in their seventies, but I am sure she still elicits wolf-whistles. On

Sunday, we lunched at Chideock and were then driven to
Crewkerne, where I inspected new stock in a cellar and
bought four books (that, said B. D.-S., paid for our lunch).
The weather was not bad that day. This afternoon, we drove
through blinding rain and walked across wet grass and mud to
a historical nonconformist chapel in a hollow.

A great pleasure, meeting the Donne-Smiths.

12 May

The tide being sufficiently out, M. and I walked to
Charmouth this morning by way of the beach, my legs
performing sterling service. The Black Ven cliffs, where
fossils are found, are very sinister, ugly and curious. The slabs
of stone which lie below them, once they have been washed by
sea or rain, are almost white, but they were lodged in shale
which is like coal dust. In front lies a broad ledge of slippery
sand and clay, where boards warn of quicksands. I walked
over this, while M. skirted it on loose rocks and shingle.

A young second-hand bookseller has just moved down by
the bridge from premises up the hill. He found me a copy of the
volume of De Quincey's essays which contains *On Murder,
considered as one of the Fine Arts*, with its appended account of the
Ratcliffe Highway slaughter, of which it seems that a new
book argues John Williams's innocence.[1] Browsing, I
discovered a copy of the Melville-Marzials parallel-text
edition of Beckford's other Arabian tales, to my mind
wrongly titled *The Episodes of Vathek*. The shop is called
Serendip.

The Beckford acquisition somewhat revived an old project
for translating the other tales in the manner of the Rev.
Samuel Henley's *Vathek* and regrouping all four as I conceive
Beckford may have intended them finally to stand. On the
other hand, I had begun to toy with the notion of a murder

1.   *The Maul and the Pear Tree* by T.A. Critchley and P.D. James (London,
     1971).

mystery set in a renamed Lyme Regis. First calling at the butterfly shop and for the moment simply asking whether they had (they hadn't) a book specifically about South and Central American butterflies, I noticed bottles of killing fluid and also lethal-looking little picks which I supposed to be geological hammers, since clearly they were unsuited to catching butterflies. Black Ven, with its quicksands, has possibilities as a setting, and it might be possible also to work in a basket of foxhead shells (under which a human head might easily lie concealed), perhaps a hoopoe, since one has been reported on Black Ven, or the mantrap in the museum, which the curator got down to demonstrate its working to me and upon which an imprudent other visitor almost placed his foot when it was set.

M. and I went to lunch at the vegetarian guest house with Mary's sister and her husband. What I might be writing arose, and there was mention of a local writer, a Mr Fowl or Fowler, with whom there had been abortive property negotiations. Clearly, it was John Fowles. Despite the evidences in his work of a connection with the place, not till then, towards the end of a fortnight's stay there, had it occurred to me that he might live in Lyme Regis. He lived, it seemed, in a big house at the top of the hill. His telephone was unlisted, but by complicated means (a note left, a call to Mary's sister, her daughter round with a message, a call from us) it has been arranged that M. and I shall go to tea at Belmont tomorrow.

17 May

This was an agreeable occasion. Memorable, beyond the terrace and steep shrubberies, is a view opened through woodland over the Cobb, comparable with that over St Peter Port from Victor Hugo's study at the top of Hauteville House in Guernsey, a comparison which I suppose may have pleased Fowles, whose academic qualifications are in French, which he taught for a living until his success with *The Collector*. I wondered whether this novel was in part inspired by the

97

butterfly shop, but no, its author did not then live in these parts. As a schoolboy, he collected butterflies. In his killing jar, he put laurel leaves. I must find out what the poison is in these.

A matter of shared interest is the La Roncière case at Saumur cavalry school in 1834, about which there are chapters in *The French Lieutenant's Woman* and in my *French Crime in the Romantic Age*, as well as in the Floriot book which he instances and I have translated. I did not know the contemporary Matthaei volume which Fowles quotes. He brought it out. It also contains Maître Chaix d'Est-Ange's concluding speech for the defence at the trial in 1835. I should have liked to borrow the volume, but did not feel able to ask on first acquaintance. As who should know better than I, some of us are neurotically chary of lending books, not without justification.

21 May

On Thursday, M.'s old headmaster at the Oratory drove over from Weymouth. On Friday, we took a late-morning train and arrived home in mid-afternoon. At five o'clock, Tim telephoned. The Director had gone into hospital with his wisdom teeth. So, presumably, all is in doubt.

Yesterday afternoon, I saw my new grandchild and distributed shells and butterflies. This evening, Adam is to appear with the contract for purchase of this flat. We are all to sign it. He will take the remaining cowry and the small copper.

4 June

Pamela Snow's sixtieth birthday fell on Monday. As this was the new spring bank holiday which has replaced the movable feast of Whitsuntide, M. had got her interfloral lilies and carnations off the previous Saturday afternoon. The party at Alexander Macmillan's in Smith Street was on Thursday.

It was not a good party. For one thing, Pamela herself and Charles seemed in poor spirits. While her three grown-up children should indeed have been there, it can have meant little to the young men from Eton and Oxford that either Philip's mother or the novelist Pamela Hansford Johnson had reached the age of sixty. The party could have been more literary or less. Of the few literary persons, three were literary editors. They were Jack Lambert, Tony Curtis and Arthur Crook. The presence of this last caused a slight awkwardness. Also to be carefully avoided was the conspicuous Bishop of Southwark, dressed from neck to boots in rustling pink.

I had not previously met or even seen him, but thought it better to avoid introduction. With him indeed I had not quarrelled, except in my own mind. The quarrel there was bitter, as it was with all those South Bank bishops and some others. I remember, in the 'thirties, parsons who had "lost their faith" and who, in some cases at the cost of great hardship to themselves (I knew one such who was staying, almost destitute, at Middleton Murry's Adelphi Centre), gave up their livings. From what I had read of their writings and from some of their public utterances and exhibitions of themselves, it seemed to me that these new bishops had lost their faith in just the same way, *i.e.*, had found that they could no longer subscribe to more than a few of their church's thirty-nine Articles of Religion or many of those of the Apostles' Creed, let alone that of St Athanasius, but were attracted by socialist principles and the stock progressive causes of their day.

They did not renounce their livings, in both Stockwood's and Robinson's cases curacies at a Bristol parish of which the former had become vicar when his younger Cambridge contemporary first came to him as curate. Fourteen years later, when Stockwood became Southwark and Robinson his Woolwich, with the appropriate residences, salaries and perks, administrative authority, opportunities for dressing up and an assured market for their writings, they must, I suppose,

99

now and then still have had to stand up in church and lead their flocks in reciting the Apostles' Creed and at certain seasons the Athanasian, too. In due course, as older bishops died, Southwark at least would acquire a seat in the House of Lords and there meet Charles Snow, as a result of which I stood in danger of having to shake his hand and speak to him without exhibiting hatred, ridicule or contempt.

He departed. I saw that M. had been cornered by Arthur Crook. I restrained myself from immediately going over and telling him to hop it. Presently, he went.

9 June

Alan[1] is colourful. Among his carefully toned-in separates at our first meeting in Anne's[2] office, orange predominated. When he came to dinner on Wednesday, he wore a violet or, as it is called, aubergine suit, with a watch-chain and bell-bottomed trousers. At the read-through this morning, he wore a pale tweed almost identical with my own, but very differently cut and with a florally patterned shirt. His dark hair is trendily but not absurdly long. It has passed its first thickness.

None of the cast of *The 7th Juror* is or looks or sounds remotely like any of the actors I had in mind when I wrote the script, in three cases with both voice and appearance, in one case with appearance, very strongly present to me as I wrote, so that I might be said to have written the parts for them. Different appearance seemed to me to matter very markedly in two cases, those of the arty-crafty young woman, whom I call FOSSILSHOP, and of FOREMAN, Scottish head gardener at the Hall. This matters. It matters less than the question of dialect accent in three cases, those of FARMER, PUBLICAN and POSTMISTRESS. For a variety of reasons, most actors come from densely populated areas, the

1. Alan Cooke, the director of *The 7th Juror*.
2. Anne Head, series producer.

Yorkshire ones almost exclusively from the industrial West Riding, few even from Middlesbrough, none discoverably from the Dales or Cleveland. The people of the West Riding, let alone those of the rest of the United Kingdom, do not know how people speak in the rural North Riding or that their speech has less in common with that of most of the West Riding than with that of rural Cumberland, Durham and even Northumberland, which areas themselves do not produce many actors. Those playing FARMER and PUBLICAN come respectively from Tyneside and Bradford. POSTMISTRESS has spent a good deal of time up and down Yorkshire but is in fact a Scotswoman. Yet into FARMER's mouth I put lines from *The Cleveland Lykewake Dirge* in its original form, as recorded by John Aubrey in 1686, well over a hundred years before Sir Walter Scott made the version set by Benjamin Britten and chanted in Arnold Wesker's play, *Chips with Everything*, where it is attributed to Burns. All three actors have lines to which they inevitably give wrong intonation and even pronunciation.

After the read-through, during which I made notes on a copy of the script, I was given free rein to talk to the cast, and Anne tells me that they found this helpful.

18 June

Adam comes to see us fairly often, but, because they live so much further away, we do not see his wife and their two little girls as often as we see Lindy's husband and their children, especially their eldest, the son, who with his father climbs the ninety-two steps from street level to the main part of our premises at least once a week, while also at least once a week M. visits our daughter's house in Campden Hill Square. This morning, however, Adam and Yvonne are coming with their two, and that means I cannot write much.

This evening, M. and I are going to Wood Lane for the recording of *The 7th Juror*. I must ask Anne what there has been

in the way of murder mysteries set in television studios. This
in itself suggests a beginning. The Producer and the Writer
are looking at the sets and (mainly the Writer) talking among
the cameras and cables, the studio space being otherwise
empty, Director and cast and technicians having broken for
supper, though presently they will be returning in ones and
twos.

The Producer has stopped listening. She is looking at
something ten yards away.

WRITER: Has anyone ever written a whodunit set in a
television studio?
PRODUCER (*giving him her attention*): I don't know. I
haven't heard of one.
(*Her attention reverts to what she was looking at before.*)
WRITER: All kinds of possibilities, aren't there?
PRODUCER: Yes.
(*She looks worried. He follows the direction of her eyes. Against
the back of a piece of scenery, a man lies prone, a knife in his back.*)

And so on. There are most of the usual possibilities. With so
much money involved, a question bound to arise would be
whether the show could be got in the can before the police
were called. The answer might well depend on whether the
dead man, if he were an actor, could be replaced. This might
involve breaking Equity rules. Much then would depend on
the make-up girl, who of course herself must be one of the
suspects.

But there goes the buzzer. M. answers, presses the button
and goes down eighteen steps to open the flat door. Already I
can hear both childish and adult voices five landings below.

25 June

To the little I wrote last Sunday I ought perhaps to have
added a late-evening postscript, noting my impressions of the
production and recording or video-taping of *The 7th Juror*.

This morning, I feel disinclined to deal with any BBC matter, for, although playing with television and even the watching of much television are new to me, in its background lurks something of that BBC effluvium which, for the past five years, I have tried to avoid.

I found in fact that I was able to see *The 7th Juror* in two distinct ways. As a show to which I happened to have contributed a script, I thought it very good and was only a little worried that the eventual viewer might find it obscure. As a translation into audible and visual terms of my intention, I found it altogether too animated. Alan thought in terms of rapidly changing shots. As, according to the rules of my game, the camera could do little to shift its distance from or angle to the cast, they were encouraged to shift their angles and distances to and from the camera, with the result that those twenty minutes in the jury room, which I had meant to be static and claustrophobic, were a scene of constant bustle. Luckily, while M. and I were in the studio gallery and afterwards when one of the refreshment rooms was unlocked for a small party, I was able to sustain the detached view, so that a pleasant evening of general congratulation was enjoyed by all.

In the canteen with Anne beforehand, we were joined by John Mortimer. "Thirty-Minute Theatre" has been doing a sequence of plays by him, old and new. I found them extremely flimsy, protracted revue sketches, each with a pay-off that could have been reached in five minutes.

Of things seen on telly during the week, sunrise at Stonehenge (presciently photographed the day before, in case it was cloudy on the 21st, as it turned out to be) was pleasing to watch. That same evening, Wednesday, in a retrospective film on its great days, somebody was quoted describing Hollywood as a small town "with a greatly exaggerated reputation for notoriety". This sounded familiar and was perhaps a Goldwynism.

The dreary weather, with sly winds, goes on. We have passed the summer solstice, and in effect there was no spring, though the usual leafings and efflorations took place more or less on time. The papers blame floating icebergs. I blame the mild winter. The splendid summers of 1940, '47, '49, most notably that of 1947, followed winters of exceptional severity. True, something else must have caused the severe or mild winters, but the year's weather equalises out. This is an outward and visible sign of what it would be nice to think is true of the good and evil in the world. The general balance remains unchanged. Liberty, for instance, in one sector will lead to oppression in another, and *vice versa*. One man's, one class's, one nation's, financial good fortune demonstrably causes depression elsewhere. It is indeed possible, individually or as a member of a group, to spend the whole of one's life in a bad pocket. This ought to redound to somebody's advantage.

On August 20th, as the result of a fall, Adam Heppenstall became paralysed. Medical experts concluded that he would spend the rest of his life in a wheeled chair.

If RH made any diary entries during the second half of 1972, he subsequently destroyed them, perhaps because he had used some or all of the material in his novel, Two Moons.

1973

18 January

To the Royal College of Surgeons in Lincoln's Inn Fields, to see the skull of Eugene Aram and the fully articulated skeleton of Jonathan Wild[1] in the Hunterian museum. A large, square glass case contains these, together with the skull of John Thurtell, murderer of the Mr William Weare who lived thereabouts, and the skeleton of William Corder, convicted of and hanged for the murder of Maria Marten in the Red Barn, Polstead, Suffolk. Surgeons having been separated from barbers in (the curator, a tall, fair young woman, thinks) 1747, the royal college was founded in 1800 in that building. Aram's skull was presented to it in 1869, Thurtell's five years later.

Aram's skull is very small, but with long and sharp projections (the mastoid process) at the jaw corners (one broken). Thurtell's is much bigger. Corder must have been a small man, Wild quite a tall one. All their skulls seem "long" (dolicocephalic), but perhaps even a typical Frenchman's does, once it has shed all the trimmings it wore in life. At the entrance to the museum are the skeleton of "the Irish giant" (said, in his own, rather short time in the later eighteenth century, to be well over eight feet tall, but now a mere 7'7") and the pickled foetuses for which the collection is principally famous.

The skulls stand on the narrow floor of the case, the complete skeletons towering above them, Wild's suspended in a way which makes it look as though he had just been hanged.

---

1. The "Thief-Taker General", hanged in 1725 for receiving ten guineas from a shopkeeper for the return of some stolen lace without apprehending or prosecuting the thieves.

20 January

A wet night, during which Max Adrian died. A friendly and amusing man, what he once played for me on radio was M. de Charlus in one of Pamela Snow's Proust reconstructions.[1] This was perfect casting. I also cast him for the central figure in *Hadrian VII*, dramatised by myself, but, as I shortly thereafter coughed blood and as X-rays showed a patch on one lung, another producer had to take rehearsals. It was Douglas Cleverdon, and one thing he could not manage was to drill the cast in church Latin. A pity I did not write a stage version. Peter Luke did, and it made him.

Adam had his operation yesterday morning, with no more than a local anaesthetic, at short notice, which was perhaps a good thing. It seems to have been successful. It puts Adam back in bed for ten days, which is simply a bore. He is very positive, states explicitly that he is not depressed, that he is "adjusted". From exercises between parallel bars, he is confident of being able to walk eventually in calipers. He has already been to the swimming baths and can almost manage the breast stroke without the use of his legs. He was never much of a swimmer, unlike his sister.

24 January

The first sign of the television aerial raid was the sight of a large, fat young man standing on our flat roof, outside the scullery window. I asked him what he was doing there. "Just looking round," he said. I told him to get down, or I should call the police. He shuffled along the parapet and let himself down to Jill and Bridget's flat roof. Presently, an elaborate, three-fold aerial was affixed to the chimney structure which rises from that piece of flat roof, so lovingly plastered by Bert two autumns ago. When she went out to work, Jill had left her door open, and the members of the commando tramped in and out. It was about half-past twelve when, happening to go up

1. The first of these was broadcast on the Third Programme in 1947.

to the attic, I saw a line crossing the skylight. The fat man had slung two white cables over the roof of the house. Nothing of the kind had been agreed at the time of Sillitoe's visits with persons from the firm of television aerial erectors, and I had asumed that a lead would simply be taken down the wall to a back window. The plump wires lay knotted loosely on the parapet outside our bathroom window. I told the fat man to remove them. He moved them to one side. I went down two floors and rang the Sillitoes' bell. Alan Sillitoe came to the door with his mouth full. "Why are you making trouble?" he said. I suggested that it was he who was making trouble, that he was behaving like an imperialist and trying to take the whole house over. I told him that he should get his gang to haul back the wires they had slung over the roof. "I'll try," he said. With this apparently conciliatory expression of willingness, he stepped back into the safety of his own premises and...slammed the door. I poured a drink and ate my sandwiches. When M. came home, she saw that white wire hung all down the front of the house. When Jill came home, she found, as well as muddy floors, the window frame wrenched loose, through which access was gained to her flat roof, and, across this piece of roof and the low wall and railing which enclose it, a profusion of stapled wires.

It does not seem at all clear what can be done in the face of this *fait accompli*, short of cutting the wires.

27 January

A cease-fire in Vietnam. The gangster film star of the 'thirties, Edward G. Robinson, has died. From my sister, a number of family papers, including a certificate, dated July 18th, 1910, about the time of my father's marriage, for two hundred and fifty shares in the Puget Sound, Chelan and Spokane Railway Company, organised under the laws of the state of Washington. These shares turned out to be worthless. At the time, my father was earning two pounds ten a week.

31 January

The new novel, *Christie Malry's Own Double Entry*, by B.S. Johnson, is being read twice in full on Radio London. There is, it seems, almost no money in this, but it is something of a *coup* of the kind in which Bryan has specialised. The first he told me of was getting £1200 advance out of Fred Warburg on each of two novels to be written in three years. He said that he needed, during those three years, the equivalent of, say, Fred's secretary's salary, which was £800 a year. This appealed to Fred's sense of fair play. So it should, but it was a great deal more than a new novelist had ever had before in the United Kingdom.

Jill has seen the Sillitoes, who will pay for her window frame to be mended. For reasons to do with his thinness, his complexion, and, I suppose, the white cables now hanging down the front of the house, we are referring to him as The Tapeworm.

23 February

Death of Elizabeth Bowen. In the late 'thirties, when she published *The Death of the Heart*, she was the most highly regarded novelist in this country. She was at that peak of her reputation when she wrote a foreword to my first novel, *The Blaze of Noon*. I did not meet her at the time and called on her only once, a year or two after the war, at the house in Clarence Terrace from whose first-floor windows, looking over the bridge in Regent's Park, the opening scene of *The Death of the Heart* is witnessed. This novel was understood to be closely autobiographical, its anti-hero based, so I was told, on Goronwy Rees.[1] Him I was accustomed to see at meetings of the executive committee of the Association of Writers for the Defence of Culture, at the Williams-Ellises'[2] house, called

1. Author and journalist.
2. Clough Williams-Ellis (later knighted) designed and built the "model resort" of Portmeirion in north Wales.

Romney's House, in Hampstead. He always arrived in the
wake of another highly regarded woman novelist, Rosamond
Lehmann, a woman of statuesque beauty, who was very nice
to me during and shortly after the war, when the man who
moved in her wake was Cecil Day Lewis.

Elizabeth Bowen, of remoter Welsh extraction, was
Anglo-Irish by upbringing at a great house. She was a fair,
big-boned, handsome woman, with a bad stammer.

27 February

To a cluttered, inelegant office at the top of a building
towards the City to record "Consolation in July"[1] for the
Dial-a-Poem service. One records into a defective telephone
mouthpiece, but, when I dialled the number afterwards from
home, I could be heard, as I shall be, by whoever dials the
number, for a week, after which I shall be replaced by
someone else reading a different poem.

---

1. RH: "[In 1946,] we were living on the second floor of a house at the
    corner of Rosslyn Hill and Pilgrim's Lane [in Hampstead]. I had much
    to be happy about, but also what I took to justify a certain melancholy.
    This I recall experiencing on spring evenings in Pilgrim's Lane,
    despite the flowering cherry and forsythia in front gardens there. I
    thought it wrong. I fancied it might lift when, in July, if it were as it
    had been the year before, the white jasmine on the balcony bloomed
    spectacularly.

    "I wrote the poem in June, when the myriad white stars were only
    beginning to show colour. I gave it to Patric Dickinson, who had it
    read on the wireless by William Devlin and passed it to J.R. Ackerley,
    who printed it in *The Listener*.

    "When, between whiles, it was translated into French, I saw that
    'Fortune' might easily be taken for an abstract noun. I meant in fact
    Robert Fortune, the explorer and plant hunter who introduced
    forsythia to this country.

    "It would turn out to be the last short poem I ever wrote."
    The poem appears on page 268.

18 March

Death of Lauritz Melchior, the Wagnerian tenor, aged 82. People of my own age but different upbringing are astonished, if not downright incredulous, when I tell them how frequently in the 'thirties I heard him and Lotte Lehmann in Wagner on the wireless, relayed from Covent Garden. The only two British singers in leading parts in *The Ring* were Walter Widdop, a tenor from Halifax, and Norman Allin, a bass from Newcastle. Heddle Nash used to sing chief apprentice in *The Mastersingers*. The performances were in German.

22 March

Mine disaster in Yorkshire, seven miners trapped. Today, as every day, three times as many will have been killed on the roads. Mining, which keeps miners off the roads, must now be one of the safest jobs in the world. It cannot be pleasant to die down there, but few deaths are pleasant, certainly not many of those on the roads.

Two deaths in, I hope, fair comfort today, of Binkie Beaumont and Fred Bromwich, both theatre men, Fred manager at the Mercury, a very nice man indeed.[1] Binkie Beaumont was H.M. Tennant's casting manager or something of the kind.[2] Heterosexual actors used to say that they could never get parts in an H.M. Tennant show.

26 March

Another loss to the theatre, Noël Coward in Jamaica. The gas strike is at an end.

1. It appears that RH had first met Bromwich in 1935, while he was writing *Apology for Dancing*. The Mercury Theatre, in Notting Hill Gate, was opened in 1933 by the playwright Ashley Dukes, and was often used for productions by the ballet company run by his wife, Marie Rambert.
2. Actually, he was managing director.

8 April

Death of Picasso, aged 91. Leslie Hartley was more than comfortably off. He leaves £370,000, to whom is not stated, a fair whack to one or another of the *louche* male members of his staff, no doubt.

12 April

Bernard Wall seems really to have "taken to his bed", with just what ailment he did not make clear, not did Barbara.[1] He is depressed about almost everything and worried about Ireland, in both cases with reason. It is island Catholicism which generates secret societies and gangsterism, in Sicily, Corsica, Malta and Ireland. The *mafiosi* monks of post-war Sicily were never summoned to Rome for examination, so that the Vatican shares their guilt, which was perfectly hideous.

24 April

My income tax form filled up and ready to send off to Inland Revenue. My literary earnings for the year are shown as nil. They did not cover the cost of stationery, telephone calls and the other necessary expenses I am allowed. In fact, with one

1. RH: "A durable acquaintance I formed towards the end of 1935 was with Bernard and Barbara Wall, recently married, who from a flat in Garrick Street, behind Charing Cross Road, edited a Catholic quarterly, *Colosseum*, whose files historians of the decade would do well to study. I was, at the time, in the throes of a conversion to Rome, which proved abortive. Barbara wrote novels under her own name, as Barbara Lucas. She was a niece, on the one side, of E.V. Lucas and, on the other, of Francis Meynell, being a granddaughter of Alice and Wilfred Meynell. She and her two sisters and their parents had figured in D.H. Lawrence's cruel story, 'England, my England'.
    "In the winter of 1954, Bernard Wall became editor of *The Twentieth Century*, a monthly revived under the wing of *The Observer*. This provided me with something of a platform. My literary fortunes were nevertheless at a low ebb."

thing and another, most of them consequent upon my son's accident, I am about four thousand pounds poorer than I was a year ago.

26 April

First and perhaps also last attendance at a Foyle's literary luncheon. This was for *The Oxford Book of Twentieth-Century English Verse*, edited by Philip Larkin. It did not seem tactful to invite poets or former poets who had not been included. Another was Laurie Lee,[1] who went round making a fuss, jocularly of course, about his exclusion. I do not mind being left out. Since I stopped writing poems, nobody pays attention to those I once wrote. I am more irritated by some of the poets put in. The fault lies, really, with Oxford doing such a book with the century somewhat less than three-quarters over. If it had been done for the first half of the century, its worst blunders would not have been made, whether by Larkin or another.

I sat between a Russian cultural *attaché* and Michael Hamburger,[2] who had a Chinese cultural *attaché* on his left. I find Michael Hamburger thoroughly agreeable and civilised.

1. RH: "I became acquainted with Laurie Lee towards the end of the war. He was staying in rural Berkshire with Rosamond Lehmann ....

    "[In January 1946, six months after joining the BBC,] I started a series of 'Voyages of Discovery'.... The scripts for all but the Marco Polo were commissioned from outside writers, though one I had to rewrite completely and another to show as a collaboration. The outside writers were Robin Fedden, George Orwell, Anthony Powell, Henry Reed and Laurie Lee. I wrote the Marco Polo script myself. Henry Reed's *Pytheas* and Laurie Lee's *The Voyage of Magellan* outgrew themselves and became self-contained epics in verse, produced later in the Third Programme which had not yet been started....

    "I commissioned incidental music from Brian Easdale for *The Voyage of Magellan*.... I more than once had to do a further recording of his first-rate score for a new production."

2. Authority on German language and literature, translator, poet.

I last saw him at dinner on a very foggy evening in Reading. I failed at first to recognise John Pudney,[1] when he came up to me before we went in. Though unlisted among the guests, Charles Snow was there. On the way out, willing either to take a cab or to walk to the bus stop at Marble Arch (which I eventually did), I spent an eternity negotiating, at my peril, miles of railings designed at once to stop people crossing Park Lane and to facilitate riot control if mobs formed in Hyde Park, as they are very liable to do.[2] I had become a one-man mob. It was lonely and exhausting.

28 April

Death of the philosopher, Jacques Maritain, at the same age as Picasso. He meant a very great deal to me in the 'thirties, far more than Picasso ever did. How vernal French Catholicism seemed in those days, and there was spring in the air even here. There was no high summer or very much autumn. It is all wintry now.

A visit at noon from the young man at W.H. Allen's to whom an agent sold the idea for *Reflections on the Newgate Calendar* which I had not instructed him to offer or even decided that I was ready to write. I shall do it now.

9 May

At the London School of Economics, a gang of "students" (surplus undergraduates) from Birmingham last evening not only prevented Dr H.J. Eysenck from delivering a lecture but further climbed up on to the platform and physically assaulted him. This was because he had been reported in the (capitalist) press as saying that Negroes were of lower intelligence than white men. It is clearly impossible to be of much lower intelligence than most young white men, some

1. Hard-drinking poet.
2. There was industrial unrest, abetted by the Trades Union Congress.

of whom must be of even lower intelligence than the surplus undergraduates, or they would themselves be "students". Some white men are, however, of the very highest intelligence, and so are a few Negroes. It is not permitted to say any of these things. While it is "racist" to say that Negroes are in general of lower intelligence than white men, it is "elitist" to say that anyone is of higher intelligence than somebody else. The holders of racist and elitist views cannot, therefore, be excused on the ground that they are exceptionally unintelligent. The views they hold must be deliberately wicked. They can only be politically wicked, since deliberate wickedness in other fields is a notion progressives do not allow, all criminality being the fault of society.

But the contents of today's papers were unusually nauseating altogether. By contrast and from the most unexpected quarter, television this evening provided us with a consoling spectacle in the Russian gymnasts. The small, fair one, Olga Korbut, who is everybody's favourite, was great fun, but I was quite bowled over by the beauty and the accomplishment of the taller, dark-haired champion, Ludmilla Tuvitsheva. The stultification of the mind under Soviet rule perhaps forces Russian energies into the pursuit of physical goals. On the other hand, music, even musical composition, seems to thrive somewhat in Russia, whereas the visual arts do not, which suggests that there is a greater mindlessness in music. But then nothing thrives here much at the moment, and there is a great deal of mindlessness about.

19 May

At noon, P.J. Stead.[1] At half-past five, Jonathan Goodman. My two best criminologists in one day. I should have liked to bring them together, but it was impossible. I suppose they

1. Authority on French crime and criminals, including Lacenaire (see May 26th, 1969); he translated and edited *The Memoirs of Lacenaire*, London, 1952.

would prefer the title of criminal historian, as I do.

Jonathan spent last evening with the forensic medical expert who was reported as proclaiming his belief in the guilt of Jeremy Cartland,[1] but then denied that he had said anything of the kind. It appears that the body of Cartland senior is not in France, where it might be expected to be, but at the London Hospital, having been smuggled over in a cloak-and-dagger operation. The learned specialist was taking Jon along to see it, but some encounter diverted them from their purpose. The popular view of this matter is that, since Jeremy Cartland is an Englishman and the French police are frightful, his innocence is simply not open to question.

2 June

Back from a few days in Sandwich yesterday, M. and I dined this evening at our daughter's and afterwards discussed with her and Donald, mainly the latter, what we felt about living either in High Street or at Centuries.[2] I came out against it. Neither house is at present without its great disadvantages. I do not greatly care for Sandwich itself, and it is a little too far from London, that much further even than Deal. Of those south-east coast towns, only Folkestone, in itself the pleasantest, seems close enough by rail. M. might find herself a part-time job as school secretary in Sandwich, but is a little inclined to hang on at the Bousfield[3] while it lasts. There is also the important question of proximity to our son. Him it is possible to imagine as borough architect in a seaside town, bowling along the promenade in his wheeled chair, but that could not be fixed up at the drop of a hat.

1. Whose father was axed to death outside their caravan, parked near Salon-de-Provence in the south of France. Jeremy Cartland told his side of the story in *The Cartland File*, Brighton, 1978.
2. Houses in Sandwich owned by Donald Foord.
3. The Bousfield School in Little Boltons, Kensington, where M. had a part-time job as a secretary.

The flat or maisonette he and Yvonne have vacated over the Launderama Donald proposes to rewire, redecorate and let furnished. That M. and I could then move into that and leave this flat to be let clearly exists, but was not discussed.

24 June

A week of dining in and out. This is always a trial. I eat a cooked breakfast, enjoy quantities of cold food at midday and have very little appetite in the evening, largely no doubt because of the alcohol consumed between noon and half-past one or two and then again between half-past six and eight, while from ten o'clock in the evening I consume none till noon next day. That interval is three times as long as the afternoon one. The nocturnal period of not smoking, moreover, is some eight or nine hours compared with a mere two.

Two American academics have been around for a fortnight. First, Harry Thornton Moore appeared again, pursuing his incomprehensible but certainly literary aims, centred now as much upon Henry James as D.H. Lawrence. He was first here to dinner ten days ago. Next day, but not to eat, came someone new, Gordon Beadle, a younger man on the Orwell beat. He had taken a short lease of a flat in Elgin Crescent and invited M. and me to dinner there last Wednesday. Meanwhile, at the close of a bright week, the temperature had just achieved the eighties, and we had again eaten with Harry at Kettner's, where I chose my food with care and enjoyed it more than last year or, at any rate, kept it down. The weather broke before we went to Elgin Crescent, where a good-looking and very charming Mrs Beadle did us well. As I guessed from her legs, she used to do ballet. As one would not have guessed, she is Jewish.

On Thursday, Harry dined with us again. On Friday, our company was French, with several dashes of Italian and Russian in the ancestry, Madame Zavriew giving a farewell dinner for the Antoninis. Again, she had us at several tables, but luckily, as it is summer, we were spared the candlelight. It is Nadia Antonini whom we particularly dote on, the two of them having somewhat taken the place of Jean and Madge Mouton since they went back to Paris.[1] Now we are to lose the deliciously modest, sensitive, smiling, kind, petal-skinned Nadia, too, to say nothing of her nice if rather angry and unintelligible Antoine.

The Beadles came to dinner last evening. There are a whole race, the Arabs, and a mongrel people, the Irish, upon whom, if it were possible merely by pressing a button, I would happily commit total genocide. I'm afraid I said as much. In the case of the Arabs, Carol Beadle was, of course, predisposed to go along with me, though she is naturally opposed to genocide. I am sure I could love Ireland were its towns and villages not full of professional Irishmen, did it not crawl with priests like black beetles and bad character actors.

Gordon told me a little about Abe and Stansky and has undertaken to convey to them that my opinion of their book[2] is more favourable than might have appeared from my review as published, while I am in no sense an ally of the lady who was briefly Mrs Orwell or, more properly, Blair.

8 July

A small heat wave foundered in rain and thunder on Thursday night. Three very different glamour girls died during the week, Nancy Mitford on Monday, Betty Grable on Tuesday (of lung cancer), Veronica Lake yesterday. Otto Klemperer also yesterday. Betty Grable was famous for her legs, Veronica Lake for her peek-a-boo hair style. I saw her with Alan Ladd in *This Gun for Hire*, based on Graham

1. Jean Mouton taught at the French Institute, and for a few months before he left, in the summer of 1967, was the director. He was replaced by André Zavriew. The Antoninis were also associated with the Institute.
2. *The Unknown George Orwell,* by Peter Stansky and William Abrahams, London, 1973.

Greene's "entertainment", *Gun for Sale*, at Northfield military (psychiatric) hospital, on the outskirts of Birmingham, thirty years ago. At the time of the U and non-U excitement eighteen years ago, Nancy Mitford told a lie. She said that if anyone addressed her, beginning a letter, "Dear Nancy Mitford," she never replied. Not long before, I had written to her, from the BBC, beginning "Dear Nancy Mitford," and she had replied, addressing me, I fancy, in the same way. Brought up in a part of the country where the speech is free of Cockney-suburban genteelisms, I felt unscathed by U and non-U and only mildly interested in the game by the hurt I saw caused to the self-esteem of pleasant, modest people and by the fact that I remembered Alan S.C. Ross, who started it all, as a junior lecturer in English at Leeds. I remember Klemperer best not for Beethoven but for *The Mastersingers*, more especially the transition from the first to the concluding scene of the last act, which I discovered to be the most highly organised piece of lucid musical thought in the world. There was nothing wrong with Betty Grable's legs.

18 July

Jack Hawkins died. Him I first remember as Orlando in *As You Like It* at the open-air theatre in Regent's Park, my first summer in London, thirty-nine years ago.

8 August

Abe and Stansky are in London. I am to lunch with them at Bertorelli's on Monday. That is because it was at Bertorelli's that I first met Orwell, he with Richard Rees, I with Dylan Thomas.

The Sillitoes are presumably away at their house in Kent till the end of the school holidays. Not that I am nowadays ever aware of their presence in the house. I used now and then to meet one or another of them on the staircase, but since the day of the television aerial I have seen neither. They have perhaps installed some electronic device which tells them when I am on the staircase, warning them not to emerge until the all-clear is given.

13 August

Bright, hot day. Excellent lunch in Charlotte Street with William Abrahams and Peter Stansky. Not only were they forbidden the use of all copyright material, which means that they could not quote from Orwell's writings at all, but also Ian Angus has instructions to deny them access to the archive at University College.[1] The quarrel took place at a restaurant in Paris. They were going to Argyllshire to see Avril,[2] but Sonia said it was unnecessary, since she herself could tell them anything that Avril could have told them. This would not include Avril's views on Sonia. These would be expressed gently. Not so Bill Dunn's.[3]

31 August

Just back from Long Crendon, where M. and I spent eight days and where last year we stayed somewhat longer, largely because it was within reach by bus of Stoke Mandeville hospital.[4] We again occupied the cottage owned by Bridget.

This time, I was there for two reasons. One was that I have been commissioned to write a short television play centred on the real-life case of a gifted bellringer who was killed by a lorry, on the main road between Aylesbury and Oxford, within a few days of my son's accident. His father is the captain of the band who ring the bells in Long Crendon tower, and from him I hoped to learn as much about bellringing as I

1. Ian Angus, then deputy librarian of University College, was in charge of the Orwell Archive.
2. Orwell's sister, Avril Dunn.
3. Avril's husband.
4. Where Adam was a patient.

needed to know for the purposes of my play.

The other reason was that Bridget hoards newspapers, those she takes being *The Times*, *The Observer, Radio Times* and the *Bucks Herald*.

From this last what I principally wanted was an account of the young bellringer's accident, with photographs of him and of the two friends killed with him. From the four papers I proposed to compile a documentary background of international, national and local events, of the weather, the phases of the moon, the times of sunrise and sunset and even of what was being broadcast at any specific moment during the months of August and September last year. Against this I mean to set what I understand of the two accidents and out of it all to make a novel. The present tense of the novel will be last week in Long Crendon, during which I sat in on ringing practice, Sunday morning touches and a quarter peal at another tower.

1 September

It was at our flat that the two young novelists, B.S. Johnson and Ann Quin,[1] first met. This morning, from Bryan on the telephone, the news that Ann Quin has committed suicide, swimming out to sea from the beach at Brighton, her home town.

---

1. RH: "I first met Ann Quin in the early 1960s. She was a splendid hunk of young womanhood, with a face almost to match, her hair cut short and scrupulously clean, unlike those of her friends whom M. and I met at a party she invited us to....

    "Henry Williamson, a talkative and engaging old man of remarkable vitality, had fallen heavily for Ann and did a great deal for her, arranging, for instance, an American tour for which she was not yet ready, intellectually or temperamentally. Her first novel, *Berg*, appeared in 1964. She first met B.S. Johnson at our flat, over a light, early dinner, after which Bryan drove us all to the shop called Better Books in Charing Cross Road, where Nathalie Sarraute was lecturing, with me as her chairman."

19 September

Isla Cameron called to collect some of the pictures we have been keeping for her. With her was a handsome colonial girl, Shirley Abicair, whose name, as it happened, I knew, as also the fact that she accompanies her singing on the zither, which ought to make a nice change from guitars. She found our flat chilly and said so, but indeed the weather has broken.

29 September

Jill in the flat below is friendly with Richard Hughes's daughters and is putting him up while his wife is in hospital in London. She had us down to dinner with him this evening. It is over a quarter of a century since Richard Hughes dined me at, I think, the Savage and later ate with us in Hampstead. It is almost fifty years since I heard on the wireless a play he had written about people lost in a coal mine.

27 October

M. and I spent last night out of London at an excellent hotel in Dedham, Essex. The excursion had been planned by Donald, who knew that I wanted to look round Polstead, in Suffolk, the scene of the Red Barn murder of Maria Marten in 1828, and who knew also that his mother-in-law and I had first met at Langham, on the Essex side of the Stour.

It was a highly successful excursion, the weather uncertain but never bad, the view of Stoke-by-Nayland church wonderful in cloud and sunlight as we approached it, Polstead itself rewarding, neither Flatford Mill nor the bell-cage at East Bergholt quite as I recalled them, alas. The remembered figure in East Bergholt was no longer the nun who had escaped from a convent there and written a book about it, but that abominable if well-connected oaf, Randolph Churchill. The Oaks, Langham, which I had known first as the Adelphi Centre and then as Basque House, seemed smaller. The Shepherd & Dog was not even open.

12 November

PEN party, to do with the publication of an annual anthology of new verse. I talked mainly to Vernon Scannell and Danny Abse, whom I have found less dreary than the other poets to be seen around nowadays.

15 November

I did not particularly note the absence of B.S. Johnson, whom I have never thought of as primarily a poet and whom I knew not to be on good terms with David Carver, the general secretary of PEN. I have only just heard, from Lindy and Donald, who were round, that he must, on the night of the party, have taken an overdose of barbiturates and was found dead in the morning, at a house I know quite well in Islington.

I am more shocked by this death than I have been by any for a very long time. For one thing, Bryan was the last person I should have expected to commit suicide. For another, as I have suddenly realised, he was my only friend of his generation. Indeed, I wonder whether, outside the family, he was not my only friend.[1]

16 November

M. rang Carol Burns last evening. This morning, Diana Tyler rang me. Carol is the wife of Alan Burns, an *avant-garde* novelist of that generation. Diana I first knew as Hallam Tennyson's secretary at the BBC. She had left to join Michael Bakewell, who was starting a literary agency, with Bryan very much on his list. She told me about the funeral arrangements and a party in Ennismore Gardens afterwards. She had been with Bryan on his last day.

I wonder how she feels about that. When a person you have

---

1. His last book, a collection of essays and occasional pieces, had been called *Aren't You Rather Young to be Writing Your Memoirs?* (London, 1973).

been seeing lately commits suicide, it has long seemed to me that you must have some sense of guilt, if only because you failed to see how things were shaping. On the other hand, perhaps I am guilty because I have not seen Bryan lately.

It is not much over two months since Ann Quin committed suicide. Ann was beautiful, though highly neurotic. It has crossed my mind to wonder whether there was any love affair between them. I conclude that it is unlikely. On the other hand, I feel quite sure that Ann's suicide continued to affect Bryan, from whom I first heard of it.

I last saw Bryan on television, in an embarrassing film, *Fat Man on a Beach*, in which, directed by Michael Bakewell, he was the only performer. It was also on television that I last saw Alan Sillitoe. He was discussing D.H. Lawrence with a short but strongly built, clean and attractive she-don, Barbara Hardy. He writhed as usual with sincerity, the marbles of his eyes spinning. The discussion, guided by Barbara Hardy, was entirely about whether D.H. Lawrence liked women. It is remarkable not that I should last have seen Sillitoe on television, since that was only ten days ago, but that I had not seen him in the flesh for ten months, apart from one glimpse of the top of his head as he was nipping into his flat when I was emerging from ours, since he lives only one flight down from our landing and I am up and down the stairs whenever M., on her way out in the morning, rings the street door bell to indicate that there is post for me. He might, I suppose, be fully visible at Bryan's funeral and wake, but to these I do not think I shall go, only writing to Virginia to say how sorry we are and that she will still be welcome whenever she chooses to come and see us.

6 December

After six uncomfortable years in Hampstead, we moved into this flat in the early part of [1951,] the year of the Festival of Britain, the last year of the Attlee government, when Labour was still comparatively decent and few of us saw what the Welfare State would lead to. I was not quite forty. I had been six years at the BBC. I was to be there sixteen years more.

Precisely how long Mary was with us, I cannot be sure, any more than I could say with certainty just when Miss Rose-Innes and Miss Stratton left the flat immediately below and were replaced by Bridget and Jill. Bridget and Jill were there when Lindy got married in 1964. I remember that we met Bridget coming upstairs as we were off to the wedding. We told her what was afoot, confident that she would be interested, but not feeling that we yet knew the sisters well enough to invite them to the wedding or to the reception afterwards.

We got Mary at about that time. She answered a card M. had put in a stationer's window. Handsome, though unduly elongated, Mary, a Norwegian, whose name we anglicised by her choice, had no work permit and could only go out charring or help with meals in a school, yet was always well-dressed and lived, we had gathered, at any rate in a flat with wall-to-wall carpets, which we did not have. Totally conscientious, she also had beautiful manners and was eminently conversable, though she herself never started or sought to prolong conversation. We regarded her as a friend, and I think she was fond of us to the point of serious concern. There had never arisen the shadow of a dispute between us.

Mary's younger sister lived in Lyme Regis, married to a vegetarian and keeping a vegetarian guest house. Mary had regularly gone to help her sister with this at holiday seasons. Eventually, the boy had gone to live with his aunt and was at school in Lyme. He had got into bad company, and recently his headmaster had stated that he would only keep the boy if his mother lived in the town. So, with much regret on both sides, Mary gave us notice and left in early December.

The flat had really been too big for us ever since the children left home, but with Mary's twice-weekly help M. had managed, despite the fact that she still went out to work. There were other factors. The ninety-two steps had become too many even for M.'s legs, to say nothing of her breathing apparatus. The journeys by bus to and from the Bousfield had become increasingly burdensome, mainly because of the waiting at bus stops in cold weather. We should have liked to be nearer our disabled son, who was heavily engaged with mortgage payments on a flat he would never be able to visit again.

The Pimlico maisonette he had been living in at the time of his accident was the property of his brother-in-law, Donald, who had been living as a tenant on the top floor when he married. Lindy had spent the first two years of her married life on that second floor, Donald then buying the whole house from a departing butcher who had, however, already let the ground floor and basement for use as a launderette and dry-cleaning establishment. Once the GLC had found Adam and Yvonne a ground-floor flat in Lambeth, the first and second floors in Churton Street stood empty, though latterly Donald had had the place rewired and was engaged in redecorating it.

At Churton Street, there are four rooms instead of six, two on the first and two on the second floor. M. thought we should move there. Her journey to and from school would be quicker. We should be much nearer Adam. I went to look at the place on Saturday morning.

The door was round the corner, in Charlwood Place, that in Churton Street being the entrance to the launderette or, as it called itself, Launderama.

Across the road was a Henekey's pub, the Constitution. It might be dangerous for me to have a regular pub just across a road along which there was always some traffic. Not for some twelve years past had I much used public houses in London. When we stayed elsewhere, M. and I, though also buying drinks in, had commonly settled for one of the pubs nearby, and we somewhat proposed to do this in Churton Street. For I supposed that we should move there. I might yet change my mind, but my verdict that morning was a *nihil obstat*.

1974

RH linked some entries for this year and the following one into continuous narratives. Such passages are signalled by the printing of the first few words in capitals, thus:

ON JANUARY 4TH, A FRIDAY, Donald appeared after dinner and stayed until one o'clock in the morning, discussing Churton Street. He wanted Adam to hear from me personally and convincingly that I should be moving there by choice. Adam would himself be my landlord, since he had the lease from Donald. M. and I would live there rent-free, paying only the rates and so on, but Adam would continue to receive the few hundred pounds' rent paid by the proprietor of the Launderama. Adam and Yvonne were going to lunch in Campden Hill Square that Saturday, and I was to go round for a drink before lunch to assure Adam that I really wanted to move to Churton Street. This I did.

On Friday the 25th, in the morning, at the house with the yellow door at the far end of Ladbroke Grove, just opposite the police station, James Pope-Hennessy, biographer of royalty and Trollope, was beaten to death by an Irish homosexual, a former boy-friend. Little more than a hundred yards away, I was unaware of anything untoward.

On the last day of the month, in his ninety-second year, the infinitely amusing Sam Goldwyn died.

Alexander Solzhenitsyn, the Soviet Russian novelist, was arrested. We heard this news on February 12th after listening pleasurably to Verdi's Requiem on the wireless. That had been composed for the funeral of another Alexander, also a novelist, Alessandro Manzoni.

The election took place. I did not vote. I was too busy painting the legs of the kitchen table a delicate green, in preparation for its removal to Pimlico.

On Tuesday, March 6th, Jonathan Goodman rang. The idea was that, for the series of *Celebrated Trials* volumes he is editing, I should do one on Mme Fahmy, who in July 1923, at the height of a record thunderstorm, shot her millionaire Egyptian husband at the Savoy hotel. On Thursday, I went out to the British Museum newspaper library at Colindale and ordered photocopies of the *Daily Telegraph* reports of the trial, the kind of thing no newspaper prints now.

The formula was, as it had been in the *Notable British Trials* volumes, introduction, transcript, appendices. I had not got much for the appendices or even the introduction. As there had been no appeal against the verdict, there was no official transcript to be got. Jon Goodman wouldn't hear of me modifying the formula so as to maintain an element of suspense about the verdict until the five days' hearing was at an end. And so, reluctantly, at the end of another week, I called the Fahmy volume off.

Radio transmission was interrupted at 10.15 p.m. on April 2nd to announce the death of President Pompidou. He was only 62. When I came to think of it, so was I.

As Charles Snow said very shortly after he had been made a life peer, the House of Lords is the best club in London, and (this he did not say) members are paid every time they use it. On Monday the 9th, M. and I were conducted along miles of red carpet to the bar where Charles and Pamela awaited us. Afterwards, we dined at a large, excellent restaurant, not far away, which was later to receive attention from Irish bomb-planters, culturally Roman Catholic. At a neighbouring table sat Longford, who had been speaking in the House of Lords.

It had been at the Snows', when they were in Cromwell Road, that I had first seen Longford. No communication or even greeting passed between the two tables.

Charles, who had once lived near Churton Street, insisted that it was in Belgravia, not Pimlico. He was pessimistic about our political future, though not, I felt, so deeply as myself. He remembered once saying that to dislike the word "culture" is a sign that you are "essentially reactionary". We agreed that I was essentially reactionary. It is in fact the way I define myself politically, that I am a free-lance reactionary.

We chose April 23rd for the move. This was because that week was half-term at the Bousfield. The 23rd was a Tuesday.

OUR FIRST EXPLORATION of the district took us down to the river, by way of Denbigh Street and its continuation, Claverton Street, skirting Dolphin Square to the west. A book called *Murderers' London*[2] explained how Claverton Street had changed but pinpointed where the house had stood in which Mrs Edwin Bartlett, *née* Adélaide-Blanche de la Tremoille, lived briefly, eighty-nine years ago. It is, apparently, difficult to get chloroform into a living stomach, and, after the trial of Adelaide Bartlett for killing her husband by getting a good deal into his, a famous remark in legal history ("Now that she has been found not guilty, she should, in the interests of science, tell us how she did it") is attributed to Sir James Paget, a name in the history of British medicine.

That would have been the most famous murder site in Pimlico and Belgravia. On Saturday afternoon, M. and I looked for another, that of the John Robinson trunk murder of 1927. The house had been demolished, and its foundations lay behind the corrugated iron of a building site. It could not have stood quite so directly opposite Rochester Row police station as more than one book suggests. Also demolished since *Murderers' London* was written and forming part of another building site stood, apparently, a house in Tachbrook Street, just opposite the National Health doctor with whom M. and I proposed to enrol, to whose railings, one December afternoon the year after the Robinson trunk murder, was seen clinging, with blood pouring from a skull broken with a pair of tongs by his frail grandson, a powerfully built, vigorous

1. By Ivan Butler, London, 1973.

septuagenarian, William Holmyard, a bandsman. I had not previously heard of this case, which, it seems, made legal history in that the grandson's plea of self-defence was ably but unsuccessfully presented by the first woman barrister to lead in a murder trial, Venetia Stephenson.

But, indeed, on the acute angle our side of Churton Street formed with Tachbrook Street still stood the house to which Dr Thomas Smethurst retired when, a hundred and fourteen years before, after serving a year's sentence for bigamy, he succeeded in proving the will of the Miss Banks he had bigamously married and, according to a verdict later set aside, murdered shortly thereafter by poisoning, doctors' invariable, as women's usual, means.

29 April

I sit at the typewriter with my back to an interior wall, the left-hand end of my table in the window. All that I then see of ground-floor premises across the road is the top three or four feet of the frontages of the Conservative Club and the Housewarming Centre and the green awning of the men's outfitters, which lies between.

As I have established by going up and down the staircase with a tape measure, our second floor is twenty-five feet above street level. Eye level, when I am standing, is some five and a half feet higher, four feet now that I am sitting at my typewriter. This window faces north-west by west. As the street measures twenty yards across, I am somewhat more than sixty feet south-east of the young woman leaning out of a second-floor window over the Conservative Club. As this window is down and I am four feet beyond it and the late-morning sun shines on her, she cannot see me.

When I stand up, walk round the table and face the window, the green awning and the varnished pine vanish from my view and are replaced, to the left of the Conservative Club, by Harold & Michael's hairdressing establishment, a tea room, a simple barber's and the Constitution public house. If I move or lean a little to the right, I further see the Sunlight laundry. Closer to the window and craning a little, I also see in that direction, to my left, the Greek restaurant and ground-floor premises apparently vacant. To the right of the Housewarming Centre, craning reveals the junk shop and vacant premises past which that side of the street is interrupted by a small square, as this side is by a short, wholly residential street, Charlwood Place, at our corner.

Over the premises designed for and in general still devoted to trade are, on the other side of the street, three storeys intended as living quarters and for the most part evidently so used, though at least one room over the barber's must be a photographic studio, while I imagine that snooker may be played on the first floor of the Conservative Club. Apart from those over the Constitution, each floor has a pair of windows, diminishing in height from first to third. Across the road, even those on the first floor are double-hung, whereas those facing the street on our first floor are casements of the French type. In the earlier part of the morning, any strong sunlight glares reflected through this window from the cream-washed stucco of the premises over the tea room and over Harold & Michael's, whose own paintwork is discordant, that of the tea room plum-coloured, that of Ladies & Gents Hairdressing by Harold & Michael (announced in red, black and green and four styles of lettering by a framed and projecting sign of white glass illuminated at night) divided between lilac and a pink verging on mauve.

Where Harold and Michael themselves live I do not know, but I am confident that, behind each of the six windows over their establishment, as also behind each of those over the simple barber's, is a separate bedsitter. From various indications I judge this not to be the case with the premises over the public house, the tea room or the Conservative Club. I have, for instance, seen Mrs Wrong Hands,[1] the publican's

1. A nickname derived from a comment by the manager of the local Victoria wineshop that "the Constitution has fallen into the wrong hands".

wife, playing with their daughter in a large room behind two windows on that first floor. I have seen the woman at the tea room more than once answer the side door to callers, and it seems probable that the young woman not long since leaning out of a second-floor window over it is the wife of the steward of the Conservative Club. Lack, inadequacy or chaotic diversity of curtaining over windows adjacent to each other I take to be the (not, indeed, infallible) sign of bedsitters. Uniform curtaining at several windows I similarly take to indicate an apartment containing at least so many rooms.

Of the inhabitants of bedsitters across the way, two who live over Harold & Michael's and, indeed, over each other have become the most familiar. Behind the left-hand window on the second floor lives a brisk and cheerful eccentric with a jutting, grizzled beard, a yachting cap and trousers hoisted high. He reminds me of Captain Kettle, a fictional character originally created in the eighteen-nineties but still flourishing in boys' magazines in the nineteen-twenties. The badge on his cap bears two words, one of which M. has made out as WORLD. He is thin, quick in his movements and carries a satchel. Adam says that the man believes himself to be God. In the morning, his smalls may be seen drying on a clothes line behind his window. Thereafter, whenever he is at home, a naked light-bulb of high wattage burns. I cannot see it when I am typing. When I sit in my easy chair, I am aware of it at a level below which it is inconvenient to pull down the white blind.

I do not need to pull it down so low to shut out the view or exclude the gaze of a younger man in a singlet at the window above his. M. has seen him in the street in a respectable grey suit and a hat. To me, he is visible only as a torso in a dingy white singlet, craning this way and that out of his window, occasionally shutting the window and cursorily turning the pages of a stack of magazines. He is an active, as it were aggressive, not a passive or reflective *voyeur*. On the ground floor, Harold (or possibly Michael, at any rate the elder of the two hairdressers) is a bored, compulsive *voyeur*. He stands by the hour behind his glass door, looking out into the street, now and then, reluctantly (one feels), withdrawing to attend to a customer who has made it painfully obvious that he wishes to enter the shop. Then Harold may be replaced for a while by Michael (or Michael by Harold). They have far fewer customers than the simple barber next door but one, and a fair slice of their profits must be taken by keeping the illuminated sign and other lights on all night, not a general practice among the tradesmen in this street.

Where we had been living for the past twenty-three years, M. and I were exceptionally deprived of opportunities to study the life of a street. We indulge our scopophilia at mealtimes in the kitchen, though from today it will be conversationally only at breakfast and in the evening, except at weekends. In the past, it was generally M. who brought me tea in the morning, at any rate during the week. She would have been up since half-past six, cutting my sandwiches. I would begin to feel demoralised only if I were not up to hear the local news at ten minutes to eight. Here, the light wakes me shortly after six and will no doubt wake me earlier and earlier until late June, when it will be shortly after four.

Drawing the curtains and raising the blind in my bedroom, I first see a blackbird sitting on a nest built between a corner of the house round the corner and a bend in a drainpipe. The nest is so little below eye level that, during the bird's absence, I cannot see eggs in the nest. Occasionally, a male blackbird visits the nest from wherever he lives.

Here, I sit facing north-east, with the window on my left. In the kitchen, I sit facing south-west, with the window on my right. I sit closer to the kitchen window. There, I do not see Harold & Michael's or the bedsitters above that establishment but, over my right shoulder, the tea room, then the Constitution, the Sunlight laundry and the Greek restaurant, with the residential premises above these. The kitchen lies beyond the wall at present behind me. From this room at seven o'clock, I may see Singlet shaving, with him a protracted operation, no doubt because he does not like to miss the early life of the street. I certainly see Captain Kettle's smalls on

their line. A little after half-past seven, whether from this
room or the kitchen, a few elderly people may be seen waiting
for the tea room to open, which it does at twenty minutes to
eight. Not long after that, Captain Kettle's smalls have been
taken off the line, and his light-bulb is glaring, though not so
brightly as the stucco if it is sunny. By then, I am drinking
coffee in my easy chair in this room.

At noon or very shortly thereafter, I go into the kitchen, cut
a slice of lemon, measure gin into a wineglass and fill this up
with tonic water from the refrigerator.

A recurrent midday pantomime is that in which a shapely
young woman with close-cut, dark hair wheels a
perambulator from the Denbigh Street corner to the
Constitution, leaves the child in the perambulator and a
toddler she also has with her, goes into the Constitution and
almost immediately returns. In due course, an elderly woman
emerges and makes conversation with the young woman,
who then again goes into the public house, while the elderly
woman moves off with the perambulator and the toddler in
the direction in which these were proceeding before they
halted. I may confidently expect to witness this pantomime
again, with others less predictable, from my place in the
kitchen an hour from now.

With a first gin-and-tonic beside my typewriter, I here and
now witness one which, for as long as it can last, seems likely
to become almost as regular and to be enacted twice daily. A
very old man, small, wearing a long overcoat and a flat cap,
walking with a stick from left to right, has reached the last few
yards before the oak door of St George's Conservative Club.
The door has to be opened and a step negotiated in one
operation. A few yards before these obstacles, the old man
performs a little tap-dance, the object of which may be to
ensure that he approaches door and step on the right foot and
from the most advantageous angle. What I imagine him to
dread most is any lack of dignity at that crucial moment. Now
he has clutched the door post with his free hand and is in.
Oddly, I have never seen him come out.

If either M. or I sees him in the evening, we tell each other of his approach. This is likely to be before we sit down in the kitchen to eat. We are commonly at table when the publican's daughter emerges from the Constitution and plays hopscotch on the pavement. Young Miss Wrong Hands is a graceful child. She does not chalk out the squares but knows her flagstones. It is when his light goes on that we become aware of a young man writing at an uncurtained window on the first floor over the barber's. He writes for long periods, though we have also seen a woman eat with him at the table on which he writes.

The fauna of Churton Street is not sparse, but it would need a television camera at this or the kitchen window to catch, as they pass, from left to right or right to left, the young men with long hair and flared trousers, the working-class girls on their platform shoes, the women with shopping bags, the gentlemanly and the hopelessly disreputable, the remarkably many who limp, the few whose carriage is splendid, so that one would like to know more about them, those whom one can allocate to ethnic groups and those of no interest to anyone but a sociologist, not even to each other, for they are always alone.

3 May

Bernard Wall died yesterday, aged 65, "suddenly, after an emergency operation following a long period of ill health, courageously borne". It must be a year since I visited him. Twice after that, he rang, and we had telephone conversations about the state of the world. As we are no longer in that neighbourhood, M. and I both talked a little to Barbara over the telephone.

4 May

The *Times* obituary states that Bernard "was born of Irish,

Welsh and English stock, though he himself felt that every drop of his blood was green". As I happen to know that Barbara wrote the obituary, I attribute the expression to her. It was always rather in her style, not in his. To the best of my knowledge, his only return journey to Ireland these twenty-five years or more had been for the funeral of his father, a man he disliked. It was a traumatic experience. For days after his return, he was incredibly drunk. If he ever felt that he was incurably Irish, it would be during that period, and it would be with a feeling of horrible fatality, from which in due course he recovered. Even then, I cannot imagine him saying that every drop of his blood was green. His renewed contact with Irish Catholicism had appalled him, and, when he was once more coherent, he told me that he would not be surprised to see Ireland at any moment fall under the papal interdict. The more recent Irish troubles had merely added to his depression about a world which to him meant Europe.

11 May

Alan, one of our son's two principal architect friends, and his father, a joiner, the latter to put up a structure to accommodate press-cutting books and papers in my bedroom, brought Adam this morning. Alan is very strong. Unaided, he picked our son out of his wheeled chair and carried him in turn to the first and second floors, on each floor reinstalling him in his wheeled chair. "Isn't it terrible?" Alan's father breathed to me as they left the big room on the first floor, and, indeed, it was a disturbing experience to see a big, once-active young man, my son, being carried around like that by a young man with whom he had once tramped all over Greece.

13 May

The head of a single chick gaping up from the blackbird's nest.

14 May

All is not well with the blackbirds. The mother has gone away.

15 May

Sparrows are pecking about in the blackbirds' nest.

17 May

The female blackbird reappeared yesterday for a while.
This morning, I saw first the male and then her sitting on the nest, but it is evident now that this has been abandoned, with whatever may remain in it.

20 May

This morning, I paid my subscription and collected a key to Warwick Square garden at an estate agent's in Belgrave Road. I walked round the garden. M. and I walked round it again in the early evening. It is not much of a garden, but what we hope is that Adam, Yvonne and their children will be able to meet us there for a picnic tea. I am also hoping that Adam will sometimes, even without the car, be able to wheel himself to somewhere on the river where he and I can meet.

31 May

Gordon Beadle, in London again to do further research on George Orwell, to dinner. Impelled by her enjoyment of their holiday last year in Ireland, his Jewish wife has become a Catholic. I say that I am sorry to hear it, and we change the subject.

ALL MIGHT HAVE BEEN WELL had it not been for the Launderama below. At first, M. found this a distinct amenity.

It was not until more than a week after the move that I first became aware how strong a chemical odour was rising up the stairs. From the beginning, we had been intermittently conscious of two smells, one presumably that of washing powders and such, the other a dirty, charred smell which might lead us or a visitor to wonder if something was burning. Neither of these smells was botheringly persistent, and, indeed, M. noticed that charred smell also in the street and thought that perhaps it came from somewhere else. The new smell was different.

There was also a new sound, a howl we at first imagined to proceed from a species of drier recently installed. The sound and vibration of the washing machines increased.

The Launderama opened at eight o'clock in the morning. I might become aware that I was breathing tainted air as early as half-past eight, before M. went out to work. By ten o'clock, there would be a nasty taste in my mouth, whether or not I had smelt any distinct smell. In the bathroom at noon, I spat viscous, foul-tasting spittle, rinsed my mouth out with pink mouthwash and perhaps gargled, before mixing the first gin-and-tonic of the day. We adopted a system of leaving all doors and windows open except those of whatever room we were at the moment in.

In the afternoon, if I dozed for longer than usual, I was awakened by a tremendous throbbing and vibration from below at the back. Drawing the curtains apart, raising the blind and the bottom half of the window and leaving the bedroom door open, I came into this room, shut door and window and picked up such papers as had blown off the table and other ledges. It was, unrestfully, in mid-afternoon that the traffic also was loudest, both in Churton Street itself and, a more distant but heavier rumble, along Belgrave Road. By teatime, when M. returned, all was comparatively quiet. As the bedsitter people came in from work, wirelesses might blare through open windows, but the Launderama rarely heated up again before seven o'clock. For it also generated heat.

Had I known how great the nuisances were, the removal would not have taken place.

M. did not mind so much. She was out most of the day, except at weekends. Not that the nuisance was much diminished at the weekend. Saturday was an exceptionally busy day, though rather for washing than for dry-cleaning and only in the morning and afternoon. The Launderama opened also on Sundays and was then busiest afternoon and evening.

On behalf of Adam as landlord, a solicitor's letter went to the launderamist. This letter was eventually replied to by a firm of solicitors, one of whom bore the same name as the launderamist. Any action, said they, would be vigorously opposed. Their client was nevertheless willing to mount his washing machines on rubber and steel and to stop dry-cleaning by eight o'clock in the evening. That evening, the dry-cleaning and its attendant howl stopped at eight o'clock, but thereafter went on until ten or later. There were no signs of workmen coming to mount the washing machines on anything but the floor boards. All mildness, our solicitor took the view that the launderamist's willingness was dependent upon his threat of an action being formally withdrawn.

On the 19th of June, in the afternoon, an hour earlier than he had been told the afternoon hubbub was at its worst, a Westminster health inspector appeared. He examined the premises downstairs and reported that the dry-cleaning cupboards had no top. He had, he said, himself no sense of smell, and the fume-detecting machine he would otherwise have brought was on loan to a colleague for the next week or two. He would bring it next time. We asked him what he proposed to do. There was very little, he said, that he could do. We hoped that he would do that little. Yes, of course.

At midday two days later, Donald came with a consulting engineer, who explored the downstairs premises and went up through the more accessible of our two attics on to the roof. The engineer was to make a report, and this we should no doubt study on our return from Sandwich, where next day we went for a week, staying at the house, Centuries, in Paradise Row. M. had taken the week off school before the strenuous period towards the end of term and of the school year.

The day after our return, Harry Thornton Moore, the D.H. Lawrence authority, rang. He had not been expected in London that year or, by his own account the previous year, perhaps ever again. On Tuesday, July 4th, we had dinner with him at Kettner's in Soho.

It was a hot evening, and we had walked further than was pleasant before we found a taxi home. It was after the Launderama's closing time, but machinery sounded loud from below. In M.'s room, it was as though one stood directly over a ship's engines.

I rang the police. A policeman came round on foot and listened to the noise from underneath. It was bad, he agreed, but what could he do? Break in, I suggested, and stop it. Oh, no, he couldn't do that. The station rang or was rung and said they had contacted the launderamist, who drove round, rang our bell and was admitted by M., I being at the time on the second floor and she quicker at the entryphone.

I stayed where I was and saw only the top of the launderamist's head, heard indeed his piping voice but not the offensive observation M. subsequently reported him making to her, *viz*, that we ought to go and live in Belgrave Square. However, the fan, newly installed that day, one of those on a steel rod, which, one feels, would do equally well as outboard propellers, had been stopped for the night.

A NEW LANDLORD replaced Wrong Hands at the Constitution. Very dear friends were over briefly from Paris. Harry Moore came to dinner, fidgety because due up early in the morning to go on to Paris. A pleasant and intelligent young man from the publisher brought photographs for me to choose from for *Reflections on the Newgate Calendar*. With spare tickets of Lindy's, M. and I went to the Old Vic. Simply going to the theatre was one more reminder, during those dreadful weeks, of an earlier, civilised life. The weather was dull, but through open windows across the way and to either side I listened to other people's wirelesses, to which the sound of road drills just outside was added. On July 20th, M. and I again took refuge in Sandwich, again staying at Centuries.

We visited Deal once or possibly twice, taking a bus to South Street and walking along the sea front northwards past the pier to the coastguard station and the Foresters, an inn we had settled for when staying at the end of Deal four or five years before, the landlord and his wife, Arthur and Pam, being a highly agreeable and efficient couple. Then we, I with dread, returned to London, as our daughter and her children were coming to occupy Centuries for the summer.

The taxi from Charing Cross stopped at the door in Charlwood Place, but M. got out to do no more than pick up post from the floor of the tiny hallway, while I went to the first floor to dump dirty clothes in the bathroom and then to my study on the second, where I picked up one or two things of which the chief was a small, well-wrapped bottle of pink liquid kept behind a row of *Notable British Trials* volumes. The taxi then went on to Campden Hill Square, where M. and I stayed until August 12th, our son-in-law sleeping there for a few nights before going to join his family in Sandwich.

We should have stayed longer in our daughter's house, but by an arrangement of long standing, which could not be cancelled, a university teacher from St Andrews was due to arrive with his family. We therefore returned for ten days to what, with some attempt at jocularity, I called the living death of Churton Street. Then, for ten more days, we took refuge at Bridget's cottage in Buckinghamshire, she having gone off to attend a music camp in the same county, at what I had known before the war as Eric Gill's house, Pigotts, and had indeed visited since, when it was occupied by a daughter of Gill's and her husband, René Hague, and Bernard Wall kept a room there.

On bank holiday Monday, the 26th, the vicar had a party at which I met the poet Ruth Pitter, for the first time since the death of A.R. Orage, almost forty years before, and next day

M. and I went for drinks to her house.[1]

Main-line trains do not run on Sundays between Amersham and Marylebone, so on September 1st we did that part of the journey by what eventually became tube to Baker Street. It was cold that day in the unheated train. We reached Churton Street in the late afternoon or early evening to find that we could not get in. Our keys would not go into the locks, from which trickles of a pale blue substance, presumably paint, had dried on the brown paintwork on the door.

The Launderama was open, and one of the pleasanter girls was on duty, so we asked her if we might leave our luggage there and trudged round to Rochester Row police station. Eventually, before an admiring crowd outside the Constitution, we persuaded a red-haired policeman to attempt to kick the street door open and, when he failed, another to climb up a rain spout to the little balcony outside that landing window and break the glass so that he could release a catch, push up the window, climb in and go downstairs to open the street door from within. Nothing within had been disturbed. As the red-haired policeman explained, drawing no doubt upon past experience, what had happened was that somebody had amused himself by squirting paint into our locks with an aerosol gun. The paint had then hardened inside.

By that time, Donald was there, and we were acquainted with our neighbour in Charlwood Place, whose telephone we had used to summon Donald, luckily back from Sandwich, and who had set before us large dry martinis. He turned out to be a man whose name I knew, Trevor Harvey, orchestral conductor and musicologist. The following evening, he in turn came round for drinks with us. It was the beginning of

1. Ruth Pitter was a friend of George Orwell's (in 1930, her London studio was one of the "drops" where he changed out of decent clothes into rags for empirical research for *Down and Out in Paris and London*). They and RH were contributors to *The New English Weekly*, founded in 1932 by its editor, A.R. Orage, to promulgate his notions on Social Credit.

an acquaintance which would certainly prosper for as long as we remained neighbours.

Out of the past three months I had spent as much time as I reasonably could away from Churton Street, with no other idea than to do just that. I had not intended to go back that Sunday evening. I was unwilling to be found dead there. On the other hand, it would have been unkind to be found dead in the house of someone who meant to go on living in it, Lindy or Bridget. And so my little bottle returned from its travels and again stood behind the row of *Notable British Trials* volumes for the period of a fortnight which I had decided I could further stand in Churton Street.

I was to stand longer than that. Out of simple politeness, I had to show some interest in the outcome of a number of activities conducted on my behalf, though I thought them misdirected and ill-timed.

The public health officer who had no sense of smell reappeared. He walked here and there, holding out a tube of orange-coloured crystals which, he said, would have turned black had the air contained fumes sufficient to cause a smell of the specific chemical, perchloroethylene, currently used in dry-cleaning. The smell at that moment would have seemed overpowering to anybody but him. In any case, he said, perchloroethylene was non-toxic. As I presently learned from an industrialist attached to the French colony in London, although it may be classified as non-toxic in England, perchloroethylene is not so classified in France, where its use is hedged about with every kind of restriction.

Counsel's opinion was sought on the likelihood of a court action leading to the launderamist's forfeiture of his tenancy and licence, which, otherwise, still had three years to run. The prospect was, apparently, rosy only for the launderamist, counsel himself and the expert witnesses who would have to be called. Wisely, as I suppose, Donald allowed the matter to drop.

Meanwhile, some days were better than others, but in general both noise and smell worsened. There was commonly a lull in the later afternoon, increasing pandemonium in the evening and a quiet, odourless night, during which only one's nerves vibrated, unless somebody nearby was having a party.

The life of the street had soon palled, though I did languidly indulge my scopophilia at midday. There were changes. A notable departure was that of Captain Kettle. The young man seen writing had gone. The young manager of the Victoria wineshop was reported ill. He was nice-looking and of an exceptionally pleasing, relaxed personality.

I HAD NEVER walked round the Chelsea Hospital, which, of course, is not a hospital in the usual sense now, but the place of retirement which Charles II, to his eternal credit, endowed for old soldiers. To this day, they seem both to like being where they are and to remain proud of having been soldiers.

It is a wonderful place, with its huge lawns and lovely houses. To occupy one of the latter must be the dream of many a senior Army officer.

If I were a popular writer, I should be nervous of saying that I think that the nicest place in London. For then I should risk causing crowds to mill around where, on a Saturday afternoon, September 14th, 1974, M. and I, with Donald, walked quite alone, very occasionally greeted by a cheerful pensioner.

Being so extremely miserable, I may, it is true, have been more than ordinarily responsive to the occasion. I had also a learned interest in the place, resulting from my recent preoccupation with eighteenth-century trials. One of those houses must have been the childhood home of Elizabeth Chudleigh, later to become the bigamous duchess of Kingston. Her father, Colonel Chudleigh, was lieutenant-governor of the Royal Hospital. Two hundred and fifty years ago, she had played around those lawns with Horace Walpole, who called her Elia Lelia.

Trevor Harvey shared the house round the corner with a clergyman and classics don, Leslie Styler, who, in term, spent part of each week at his college in Oxford. M. and I were

143

entertained by them on the 20th and they by us on the 27th of September. They were not bothered by the Launderama, which was nice for them but a pity all the same.

Regular incidental pleasures were the weekly visits of two of our grandchildren, on their way to and from music lessons not far away.

Apart from Centuries, there was for the moment nowhere to go. M. did not yet want to give up her part-time job at the Bousfield, and her earnings from that were indeed an important part of our income, which had fallen to little more than half the recently published average for the country.

In early December, a further reason for staying on in London arose. Eighteen months after he had gone back to his work at County Hall, our son was still in constant pain below the waist, a thing which happens to a minority of paraplegics and which is poorly understood. Acupuncture had failed. A surgeon at the Maudsley hospital proposed severing the receptor nerves above the break in Adam's spinal column, which had taken place at the twelfth vertebra. It was arranged that this operation should be performed in January.

On the 4th of a mild, wet December, Trevor and Leslie came to dinner, on the 7th Charles and Pamela Snow. On the 11th, M. and I went to the annual Scott-Moncrieff presentation at the French ambassador's residence.

All through those months, I had worked desultorily and with little conviction at a sort of novel. This was almost nakedly autobiographical and documentary in content, placing my son's accident and much of its immediate aftermath in a context of the news of the day and in parallel with the death of a bellringer in the Buckinghamshire village in which M. and I had then stayed for the first time to be near Stoke Mandeville. To compensate for its lack of story and to mask the violence of feeling behind it, the narrative form was highly structured, the phases of the moon during two consecutive lunations being presented on facing pages, of which precisely four were occupied by what was recorded for each day. The book had not been written consecutively. The pages having all been numbered beforehand, I was able to fill them up in what order I chose.

ON DECEMBER 30TH, I filled up the last vacant page of *Two Moons*, as I was calling my novel. A new year began. On January 7th, at the Maudsley, my son had the first of two operations, both of which failed, in that the pain persisted, reaching the brain by what path nobody understood.

On the 20th, my *Reflections on the Newgate Calendar* came out. I was interviewed by William Hardcastle on BBC radio and on London Broadcasting by a young man who wasted no time. Nor, it appeared, did London Broadcasting waste money on its contributors, though it sent minicabs to fetch them and could even be persuaded to send for minicabs to take them home. My reflections received little notice in the public prints, most of that little designed to show what clever fellows the reviewers were. It is true that Charles Snow wrote a long review (that is always the main thing) for the *Financial Times*, though it made the book sound like a mistake on the part of an interesting but misguided writer.

On February 3rd, for what will doubtless turn out to have been the last time, I attended the French Institute party after a lecture which I did not attend by a lecturer whose name I have forgotten.

On Saturday, the girl on duty at the Launderama set a dry-cleaning cupboard on fire, and we had a fire engine at the corner.

The following Saturday, I went to see Adam in Lambeth. That day, P.G. Wodehouse and Sir Julian Huxley died, aged respectively 93 and 87. On Sunday, I shaved off a beard I had started to grow, and on Monday, the 17th, M. and I went down to Sandwich again, she taking a fortnight off school, its second week the half-term holiday.

On almost all of upwards of a hundred early evening visits I have paid to the King's Arms, the first customer in the saloon bar has been Brigadier Hobbs, a man who carries himself well and moves briskly, with a fine head of silvery hair and moustache to match, the floridity of whose complexion is in part due to the round of golf he plays at St George's every morning, whatever the weather. As a rule, he came into the bar through the interior door. If neither Ann herself nor anyone else was behind the bar, he would go behind and serve you, as also himself with whisky and water.

Some evenings during that fortnight and for a while thereafter, not Ann but Barbara would appear behind the bar. Brigadier Hobbs, whom we had not yet ventured to address as Godfrey, though everyone else did and even we referred to him by that name, lived in a cottage next door to the King's Arms along Strand Street. Barbara lived in a cottage next door to that. Both she and Ann were widows. Barbara, indeed, had been twice widowed, first by a journalist and then by a regular Army officer. In her incarnation as a journalist's wife in London, it somehow transpired that she had known Dylan Thomas in Charlotte Street, she and I failing to meet during that period because the year she was most around was 1936, whereas that year I was out of London most of the time, having been much in Charlotte Street the year before and to be fairly often there the year after.

Ann, the proprietress of the King's Arms, is Welsh, her given name Angharad. The fact is sometimes evident in her speech, while in build and colouring one saw that she could belong to the short, dark Welsh.

It was some time before one discovered that she was deaf and not intermittently off-hand, because she was a faultless lip-reader (M., who is deaf in her right ear, has never developed this facility, but gets along without it and sometimes hears things I miss). By marriage, Ann is related to the composer, Sir Arthur Bliss. She is a woman of great energy and capability, high intelligence and tireless generosity. I dote on her.

With one exception, the regular customers in the King's Arms saloon bar are Conservatives, a high proportion of them actively so. Josephine, a retired doctor, is the one tolerated (more than tolerated) Labour voter. The oldest of us all in years, she is small, lean and quick in her movements, darkly bright-eyed, Eton-cropped, pipe-smoking and trouser-wearing, yet withal gently feminine in the general effect of her personality.

WITH A CUT LOAF, soft margarine, and a selection of transparent packets of cold meat, each stamped with a date by which it should be eaten, making sandwiches presented no serious difficulty, while for Monday evening I had the shepherd's pie to heat up, the remains of Sunday's shoulder of lamb having been minced by M. before her departure. On Tuesday morning, I even attempted a cooked breakfast.

On Wednesday morning, a young man from Harrap's rang. He had tried Churton Street, and M. had given him my Sandwich number. He was an Australian boy who had once been brought by Charles Osborne to dine with us in Ladbroke Terrace. He had soon got on in publishing. He wanted me to read and report on a book in French on the work of the Swiss centre of the International Red Cross in German concentration camps towards the end of the Second World War.

As there was little pressure of work at school, M. felt able to cut an occasional Friday. She reappeared on Thursday afternoon. I had three cooked breakfasts and a Sunday lunch, and then she was gone again, not by train but by a long-distance bus about which Barbara had told us.

For a week, I have nothing whatever noted in my diary, except the weather, which did not much incline me to go out until, with almost perfect regularity, come half-past six, I walked round to the King's Arms. Having warmed up my dinner, on Monday a shepherd's or swineherd's or poultry-farmer's and on Tuesday a fish pie, on Wednesday opening a tin and heating the contents, I watched, if it chose to work that evening, a portable Russian television set with a defective tuning mechanism and a screen measuring six inches by five.

After a bright Sunday afternoon, the following week had a little frost and snow. On Wednesday, I saw in the *Radio Times* that Radio 3 was that evening repeating a programme I had written on Eugene Aram.

On Thursday, as he came through the inner door, Brigadier Hobbs sang out:

"Good evening, Rayner!"

To me, he was thereafter Godfrey.

M. was not coming down until Friday that week. On Thursday evening, I got my well-wrapped bottle of pink liquid out of the drawer in which I had put it. I did not like the look of it. The wrapping was stained pink. I hoped that this discolouration might be due to the fact that, at Churton Street, I had kept the bottle out of sight behind a row of *Notable British Trials* volumes, which had red bindings.

I read and reported on the Red Cross book. Much in it reinforced what had not long before leaked nervously into the papers, *viz*, that the figure of six million Jews killed by the Nazis was mythical. Most of us had accepted it without question at the end of the war. Not quite all of us. Godfrey said that he had never accepted it. I believed him.

That week, M. came on Wednesday, to stay for a fortnight over Easter. On Good Friday, March 28th, it snowed in earnest. M. and I spent Sunday morning before our tiny television set, watching the papal ceremonies in windy St Peter's Square, Rome.

I was in Deal that Tuesday, with M. looking again only at the outside of a house in North Street, opposite one in which we had stayed five years before.

The following Thursday is the day I have marked for the suicide, in Brighton, of a young poet, Robin Lee, at the age of just thirty. Twenty years before, he and my son had played together in Ladbroke Square. They had later quarrelled, but M. had remained close friends with his mother, an over-indulgent widow. That Robin might one day commit suicide had always been on the cards, but latterly, after unneeded plastic surgery and a marriage which quickly failed, he had stayed at Sussex University long enough to take a first in English and be kept on with a research fellowship. I do not know how good a poet he was. I had attended his wedding reception and watched his father-in-law, a Canadian cavalry colonel, trying to cut the cake with a sword which had no edge but only a point.

On Saturday, post forwarded by M. included a jury summons.

That was a weekend without M. I got up very early on Sunday morning, the second after Easter, and unwrapped my bottle. Half of the pink liquid had oozed away.

A potted history of that bottle is to be found in the space provided in last year's desk diary for Wednesday, 26th of February, the day of a full moon, continuing on the first of six pages allowed for Notes at the back. It was the day on which we had taken a bus into Deal and walked along the sea front to the Foresters, where we found that the management had changed. I fancy I may have begun it in the morning before we set out.

It must be eleven years since I dissolved some thirty Soneryl tablets in vodka, drained and bottled the pink liquid off the presumedly inert sediment. Later, a further precipitation took place, which, on straining it off, I found to be crystalline, dried, pounded and put in a small, waxed stamp envelope. The purpose of dissolving the pills was to spare myself pill-swallowing, which I have sometimes found difficult (commonly needing to push each pill down my throat with a finger), but also to speed up the reaction with alcohol and to make the use of a stomach pump futile if I were found within, say, four hours. I have always intended to drink the bitter, pink solution with tonic water to make it palatable, first tossing back the pounded crystalline precipitate in water, as the necessarily disagreeable swallowing of a powder.

I am afraid of the quantity of barbiturate being too small. I am afraid of being discovered too soon....

I interrupt the quotation here to say, first, that the initial preparation of my suicide draught had coincided in time with the impending dissolution of Features Department, of which I was a member, at the BBC.

I left three years later, and for five years not all went well, but much did. For a year more, the consequences of my son's accident continued to provide me with the sense of a purpose in my life, though also to leave me poorer. The move to Churton Street had been, in low key, an adventure undertaken in good faith. Within three months, it seemed to be ending in disaster. After the July stay at Centuries, when M. and I stayed for ten days or so at our daughter's house in Campden Hill Square, I had taken the bottle with me and meant to use it or even to walk under a bus before I would go back to Churton Street.

Also while at that house, I had thought of staving off the act for some months by first writing a book on suicide, its history and statistics, its moral justification, some other people's and my impending own. Statistically, it is as common as road deaths, with fairly determined attempts perhaps as common as serious injuries in road accidents, say a hundred thousand a year. Within the past two years, three writers of my acquaintance had succeeded. I had known others both succeed and fail. The one book I knew on suicide by a writer who had attempted it and failed, then tried again and succeeded, was *Récit Secret* by Pierre Drieu la Rochelle.

With failure there always goes the supposition that the attempt was not really serious, but only (this is the *cliché*) a cry for help. It had certainly not been so, even in the first place (he had been misinformed about the dose needed). Another *cliché* is that those who talk about suicide never commit it. Well, of course, there are many who talk about suicide and do not commit it, just as some unsuccessful attempts were cries for help. But those who successfully take their own lives (it is the "take" which is wrong there, a residue of the belief that lives belong to God or the State) are commonly found to have talked a fair amount about suicide previously. A third *cliché* runs that it is cowardly to commit suicide. This can never be quite so. It may be selfish, and there may be moral cowardice in the refusal to face in some other way what seems an intolerable situation, but the actually committing suicide requires some physical courage, even with a quantity of barbiturate sleeping pills to hand. I am sure that, in many cases, as in my own, cowardice of some kind has more often prevented suicide than brought it to the point of final success.

Here, I introduce another quotation from myself. This is typed. It had been done straight on the typewriter a month or six weeks before M. and I went to Sandwich that February and was intended to constitute the beginning of a document addressed to whom it might concern and left by my bedside.

It is some years since suicide ceased to be a criminal offence. I have a perfect right to put an end to my life, and nobody has a right to stop me or in any way to interfere, so long as I do it in decent privacy and by means which do not endanger property or the lives of other people.

If I should unfortunately be discovered before the means I have chosen result in my death, my removal from the place I have chosen to another, a hospital for instance, and the practice there of any form of surgery to prevent my death ensuing would constitute a sequence of criminal offences, from false arrest and illegal restraint to assault occasioning actual bodily harm. Should I against my wishes be restored to a life I do not wish to continue, the persons indulging in these offences may be assured that I shall devote the whole of my remaining energy to bringing them to justice, if necessary by means no less illegal but preferably by test cases before properly constituted courts.

In a statement to be left by the bedside of a man who has resolutely attempted suicide, that last sentence clearly wouldn't do, so I had whipped the sheet unfinished out of my typewriter. And here I had better correct what I said earlier. It can hardly concern anyone where he is found dead. What I entertained a strong distate for was the possibility of being found not yet dead in Churton Street. My objection to being so discovered at Centuries was less emphatic, though I do not wish to add, to whatever distress M. might feel on so discovering me, the inconvenience of finding that she could not get into the house.

What I began on the same theme in my diary for February 26th last year is a bit more judicious.

… As suicide is no longer a criminal offence, neither have the police or doctors any right to convey me to hospital or, there, to perform surgical or any operations upon me to resuscitate me against my will. To move me would be abduction. To operate would constitute criminal assault. I am nevertheless afraid of waking in hospital with a glucose dripper connected to my arm and a tube in my throat, myself at that moment too weak to pull them out and threaten legal proceedings. I may also too much lack will to go on with hunger (and, more important, thirst) strike in the usual way.

It has been very unusual for me to be alone in a house or flat for more than six or seven hours or to count on M. being asleep for as much as that, even supposing that I did not begin to gasp or snore in a manner likely to arouse her. When she returns to London on Sunday afternoon, I have established my intention of remaining in Sandwich alone for the rest of the week. What I then propose to do is swallow my twofold draught at normal drink time in the evening, assuming that, even after a Sunday lunch, my stomach will be fairly empty by then and that I shall not be suffering from indigestion or other predisposition to vomit.

When I read this now, it surprises me that at so late a date I

153

proposed to allow myself five days to die in. I had indeed, at one time, been persuaded that death from narcosis takes at least three days and that what you die of is in fact pneumonia. But [the journalist] Kenneth Allsop had managed it while his wife went up to London for the day, and, more recently, B.S. Johnson had been found dead within a great deal less than twenty-four hours of being seen alive and apparently in good spirits. The point of view I had presently adopted was that the night before M.'s next arrival would be soon enough.

Again, that 26th of February statement was uncompleted. I intended to go on with it next day, but on the evening of that day we had arranged to go for our first gin-and-tonic to Barbara's cottage.

What was left in the bottle would hardly amount to a reliably fatal dose. The leakage had taken place from under the screw stopper, despite the tissue paper I had tightened the grip of this with and the Sellotape round it. Lindy kept a variety of medicaments, Elastoplast and so on, in the top compartment of a tall kitchen cupboard. I there found a roll of narrow surgical tape and a small bottle which contained a few tablets. These I put in an envelope. After rinsing and draining it, I transferred what remained of my pink liquid to the smaller bottle. The little packet of pounded crystalline sediment I detached from the side of the old bottle and reattached to the side of the new one (with Sellotape). The new and smaller bottle I then closely bound from top to bottom with surgical tape and again wrapped the whole thing in greaseproof paper. It might yet come in handy.

That was on April 13th. On the 15th, Tuesday, a cloudy day with some rain in mid-morning, we had the Budget. By the addition of further tax on tobacco and spirits, this raised the price of gin to four pounds a bottle and of twenty cigarettes to half a quid. My average gin for the week would cost me six pounds, my cigarettes seven pounds ten. With a bottle of wine, half a bottle of whisky, a dozen half-pint cans of beer and a dozen split tonics, to say nothing of matches and lemons, the whole of my BBC pension, to which I had contributed over a period of twenty-two years and of which a third was deducted at source as income tax, would go on the few simple things I found quite indispensable.

Almost the whole of the increase was to cover an increase in the wages of miners, whose incomes had already been twice mine. Once M. stopped working at the end of the new term, life for us would be, financially, a matter of seeing for how long we could make a few thousand pounds of savings last. Neither of us would be willing to go on National Assistance.

M. again came on Thursday the following week, and on Friday (April the 25th) we took a bus into Deal to look at two cheaper houses, one in Middle Street and one out towards the Castle. This was Coach Cottage. It was a former coach house, attached to Gilford House at the corner. It had been lovingly converted six years before by a woman who had since become too crippled to use the upstairs premises and was buying a ground-floor flat in a new block on the sea front.

Through a wrought-iron gate we looked in at an elegantly formed bow window, three yards broad and containing sixty panes of glass each nine inches by twelve. On the ground floor, what might still be regarded as two rooms were nevertheless separated only by a well-shaped arch. The kitchen was tiny, but would, M. thought, be convenient. It was well-appointed. A hatch opened from it into the farther room, which contained a purely decorative fireplace said to have come from the Old Exchange. The chimneypiece was of nicely carved stripped pine, and in place of tiles were a surround and hearth of dove-grey, pink-veined marble. The far end of this room was almost wholly occupied by four tall window panels, each containing ten panes of glass of much the same size as those in the bow window. The two centre panels opened into a small conservatory, similarly glazed, and through that one walked into a garden with raised flowerbeds. The most conspicuous feature of this garden was a tree, whose name I did not yet know, covered with small, ball-shaped blossoms of an intense, metallic blue.

It seemed very much a *hortus conclusus*, and the house itself was detached in that it shared no wall with any other.

I noted that the house was, like Centuries, heated by the kind of double, thin, ribbed, white-painted radiators which are now widespread and which I had first seen at the Innes Stewarts' wooden bungalow near Wantage, nine years before. M. took more interest than I in the apparently numerous cupboards and glory holes, principally off the two bedrooms and bathroom upstairs, where the roof sloped. I reckoned that the end wall of the room with the bow window, the room you came into first and off which the rest of the ground-floor premises opened, would be the one to cover wholly with books.

That Saturday midday, Donald telephoned. I gave him as detailed a description as I could manage, including the carpet, about which he asked. It was his day for leaping into action, and that afternoon he got the agent for Coach Cottage at home. By Tuesday, he was able to announce that his offer for Coach Cottage, carpets and all, had been accepted, subject to survey and contract.

2 May

This morning, at a quarter to twelve precisely, just after a sharp shower, a goldfinch, its colours equally bright, the total effect less spectacular. For thirty-nine years, I have never seen a goldfinch without recalling one I saw at the foot of a hedgerow near Langham, when I was out walking with a young girl I was to meet again and see quite frequently within the past five years as Marielle Larsonneur. One of the bird's wings had been torn right off, presumably by a cat. I felt that the right thing would have been to kill it quickly, and I looked round for a large stone. I don't think there was any question of her pleading with me not to, but I found I could not do it and simply moved the creature to a less exposed position under the hedge.

With M. here, this evening I cut a large and impressive

bunch of the taller tulips. These I presented to Ann at the King's Arms, where they are now displayed in the saloon bar.

6 May

Godfrey is a cousin of Carleton Hobbs, an actor with whom I had much to do over a period of twenty years and for whom I always felt the highest of affectionate esteem. Hobbo, as everyone called him, was not only a true professional in the sense in which the word is used in show business. He also contrived to make radio acting seem a profession in the sense in which the law and medicine are professions. In appearance and manner, he could indeed well have been a judge or eminent counsel or a hospital consultant of pre-war vintage. This is in part explained by his early background, of which I had never heard much. Godfrey was at Wellington, Hobbo at Marlborough (where he must have been, though I never heard it said, an older contemporary of Louis MacNeice). Both were the sons of Army generals. Like Godfrey, Hobbo started as a regular soldier, was an artillery captain. His father was a martinet of rigid formality. That his son should resign his commission in order to go on the stage was shattering. On the stage, Hobbo quickly flourished as *jeune premier* in the productions of Sybil Thorndike and Sir Lewis Casson, but lost his hair early and took to radio for that reason.

9 May

I could, I suppose, have got out of this jury service on the ground that I was living too far away, but in just over a year I shall be too old, and I have long wanted to see what the inwardness of it was like.

19 May

The Knightsbridge Crown Court building was formerly an embassy, and next door is still the Colombian embassy. The jury assembly room on the ground floor seats about fifty people comfortably, on padded benches covered with black rexine. Off it lead ladies' and gentlemen's lavatories, dumbly indicated by stylised figures respectively in skirt and trousers. Between the two, stairs go down to a canteen, purely for the use of jurors, in the basement. By half-past nine, about two hundred jurors were assembled. We were shepherded up-stairs to a courtroom which accommodated most of us with seats. Several clerk and usher persons made informative speeches.

Seven sets of nineteen names were then called for seven of the ten courts, the defence being allowed to challenge up to seven jurors without giving a reason, the Crown apparently having agreed never to exercise it in this particular place for logistic reasons. The rest of us went to the jury assembly room, where we were presently joined by just under fifty unwanted jurors from the seven courts. We scattered for lunch (I went to a pub in Sloane Street) and reassembled in the afternoon. Conversational groups formed. The class level was in general lower-middle, with fringes of "working" and smarter big gent, these last distinguished by their briefcases, the workers by the way they got together and talked louder, with frequent laughter. I talked with two young women library assistants, who were very pleasant, one a little indignant at her finding that the class she personified as Lady Vere de Vere seemed able to escape jury service.

At about 4 o'clock, the jury bailiff told us we could go home until ten o'clock the following morning.

20 May

A morning of the same boredom, discomfort and irritation.

I talked mainly with a young, fair Jew, long-haired and wearing the sort of complete suit of unfaded blue denim which before the war would have been a factory worker's overalls. He had brought with him three volumes of paperback science fiction of a kind which before the war or at any rate in the 'twenties was found in boys' weeklies. He was very nice and modest and jumpy.

I ate in the basement canteen. Afterwards, with eleven others, I was empanelled and sworn to try the case of a girl law student charged with theft from a bookshop. Counsel for the prosecution was a dull, spotty-faced, thin young man, for the defence plump, a bit forgetful and unprepared but more intelligent, his complexion clear. None of our first twelve was told to stand down, the only *contretemps* being provided by a middle-aged Jew who wanted to swear on the Old Testament. The judge was tall and big-boned but small-headed, with a very close-fitting wig. His surname was Jewish, his appearance and manner not so. The girl in the dock could have been Jewish, but her name was thoroughly English. She was small, dark, not markedly plain but with close-set eyes and heavy jaw.

We heard the temporary shop-assistant who had found the book for her, a woman store detective and the policeman who had been called. The girl had unquestionably left the shop with the book, unpaid for, in her bag. Her defence was, inevitably, that it had got there by mistake. She had wanted to look at that particular book, mentioned disparagingly in a lecture that morning, but had not meant to take it away, paid for or not. It had got between other books.

In the course of her walk round the shop, the girl had, she said, spoken to two people beside the assistant who found the book for her, one a fellow-student, the other a second shop-assistant whom she knew. The store detective, who claimed to have kept the girl in sight throughout the perambulation, denied that this was so. The store detective was a not unattractive young woman, with poor taste in clothes and hairdressing and a trace of what I took to be a Midlands accent. Defence counsel was sarcastic about her ability to keep the defendant in sight throughout, in view of free-standing shelves between them.

In her own evidence, the girl was put through a whole pantomime of putting down an imaginary bag and shuffling files handed to her to represent books, to show how one book could get between others and into the bag. It was the judge who brought out by his questions how very respectable her antecedents were, that she had taken part with her father in an archaeological dig in the Middle East, that in the earlier part of last term, when she had switched after one term from History to Law and when the alleged theft had taken place, she had not been short of money. She was repeatedly told to speak up. I could not hear the half of what she said, far less just how impeccable her accent was. The fellow-student to whom she claimed to have spoken on her way round the shop was named, and we·were told where he was living.

The judge will sum up in the morning. Then we shall retire and decide whether we think she meant to steal the book. I wonder who advised her to go for trial by jury and whether counsel was with her at the magistrates' court.

21 May

The judge was clearly on her side and seemed to think we should not retire, but a hurried murmuring in the jury box revealed that we did not all favour prompt acquittal. We were shown into the jury room, with a woman usher, a blonde, stationed outside. One of the youngest of us had been made foreman because he had served on a jury before. There were four women among us, one of them coloured. It was quickly established that four of us thought the girl guilty, all of us men. We said why, and the other men and one of the women harangued us, the foreman especially. He was a real gasbag. There was no light in the lavatory off the jury room.

The four of us standing firm, it was clear that we could not reach a unanimous verdict. We were therefore marched back into court for instruction in majority verdicts. We could not leave the jury room for lunch, and so we gave our orders for sandwiches and tea, coffee or milk to the blonde usher. We chatted. Two of the woman were very nice, the coloured one and a countrywoman who, after some years in London, had again moved into the country, though not so far away as Sandwich. It never transpired what any of my co-jurors did for a living, though all had class characteristics of a kind.

If any of them ever bought a book in hard covers, it would be as a Christmas present for a child, or it would be a careers or hobby book. If they read much, it would be books from a public library. They had probably never thought of a book in hard covers as a thing to be bought and paid for. They had almost certainly never thought of books as having authors whose livelihood depended on sales. With the possible exception of one scowling young man, I felt sure that none of them had ever stolen a book from a bookshop. It was likely that some of them had never been in a bookshop.

These were the things I could hardly say. What I did say was that, since the whereabouts of the fellow-student said to have been talked to in the bookshop were known, he ought to have been heard in evidence. There could be little doubt that he would have been approached for the defence. As he had not appeared or sent an *affidavit*, it seemed likely that his evidence would not have supported the case for the defence. As he was not appearing, his existence or his non-existence would not have been made known beforehand to the prosecution, which, now that he had been named, was represented by a counsel who was too dumb or timid to ask for an adjournment while he was *sub poena'd*. We ought, I think now, to have sent a note to say that we could not reach a verdict without hearing the evidence of this person, but I did not think of it at the time.

In the course of the afternoon, we sent in two notes. First, at the instigation of the middle-aged Jew, we asked for clarification of the expression "beyond reasonable doubt". We were marched in and told that we could only bring in a verdict of guilty if we were absolutely certain. This, it seemed to me, was misdirection, but it converted the Jew, who had been convinced beyond all reasonable doubt that the girl was guilty as charged. That left three of us for guilty. We presently sent in a note to say that we had failed to reach a majority verdict and were marched in again. The judge asked the foreman whether he was convinced that we might not yet reach a majority verdict. He said he did not know, so out we went again.

I should have liked to see what the formalities were when a hung jury was discharged, but towards four o'clock I found that I had run out of cigarettes. I therefore said that, although I still thought the girl guilty, I was willing to be marked down for not guilty, so that we could get the hell out of there. The girl was therefore acquitted by a majority of nine and my shortage of cigarettes. A majority of eight really, for the overpersuaded Jew was still convinced of her guilt.

After that jury room, Churton Street seemed pleasant. The Launderama was at its quietest and least odoriferous. I had my books around me. I might, I thought, well have stuck a life there if I had been out during the daytime. Later in the evening, however, as the Launderama warmed up, pop music blared from the Constitution. At one time, we barely ever heard the juke-box, which was stationed inside the door and faced inwards. It must have been moved. M. says that this musical nuisance has now been going on for some weeks. The original Wrong Hands was better than the hands that have got the Constitution now.

The young manager of the Victoria wineshop, who said in the first place that the Constitution had got into the wrong hands, had been mysteriously ill for some time. It turned out to be incurable cancer of the liver. He is dead. He was by far the pleasantest figure among the inhabitants of Churton Street. He wanted to go back to Blackpool, where he came from. At the shop, he and I used to indulge a little mild wars-of-the-roses flyting, which no longer means anything to me. He was genuinely homesick for Blackpool.

I had a £4 book token, my Christmas present from Adam and Yvonne. I took this to Harrods' book department and bought a *Moll Flanders,* an *Amelia* and paperback lives of Dickens and Trollope. I had expected to be going straight from court to Broadcasting House, but spent the afternoon in Churton Street, above throb, howl and perchloroethylene. I waited for a taxi in Belgrave Road and by six o'clock was in a small basement studio, where I recorded my narration for a programe on the eighteenth-century case of Mary Blandy, of which the producer was my former boss, Martin Esslin.

24 May

On our way to catch a bus across the river, M. and I met the widow of the Victoria wineshop manager, rather a beautiful woman. We condoled with genuine feeling. Her manner was faultless.

Lindy and Donald have gone down to Centuries for the weekend, so M. and I must stay here till Tuesday. Donald will meet us in Deal, and we shall go to look at Coach Cottage together. It does not look as though there could now be any slip 'twixt cup and lip. He will buy the house, and we shall live there. M. will stay on at the Bousfield until the end of term, which coincides with her birthday.

3 June

First [the artist] Barbara Hepworth and now James Laver have burnt themselves to death at home, in fires presumably started by cigarettes, though James was an eager cook of Chinese meals. I was much aware of Barbara Hepworth when I visited Herbert Read at the Mall studios in Hampstead [in 1937]. I was there, playing rummy, while she, three doors away, was giving birth to triplets. Ben Nicolson looked in every now and then to report progress and take a hand.

The first time I met James Laver was before that. It was at a party at which the Irish mystic, A.E. (George William Russell), read his poems with bearded sonority. I had eaten little and was given a lot of whisky (or perhaps whiskey). The memory of my behaviour thereafter gives me no pleasure. In 1951, James did a potted translation of Villiers de l'Isle-Adam's play, *Axel*, for which I cast his wife, Veronica Turleigh, as Sara, Paul Scofield playing the eponymous hero. For a much longer version, transmitted in three parts on three successive evenings, James and I collaborated on the translation. I had used Bruckner on records for the short version. For the longer one, I had music specially composed by William Wordsworth for choir and two male soloists, organ and two horns. The bass soloist was called Jack Frost, the tenor Edgar Fleet. The horns were played by Denis Brain and Alan Civil. It was hornblowing of a very high order indeed.

Better still, James and I made a stage version in three acts, omitting the banquet, which the National Theatre turned down on the advice of its literary advisers, at that time committed to the kitchen sink.

26 June

Along the edges of the tables, bookshelf tops and the broad wooden arm of the chair I commonly sit in, there are marks where I have put cigarettes down and let them go on burning. In four months, I had not made a single cigarette burn on anything of Lindy's. Today, I made three, inspired no doubt by the examples of Barbara Hepworth and James Laver.

18 July

It is M.'s birthday, and her last day at the Bousfield. To celebrate, we had dinner in the very pleasant little dining-room at the King's Arms. We were the only diners.

The previous owner will today have moved out of Coach Cottage. Our furniture is coming down next Friday.

27 July

We have moved into Coach Cottage. Today is my sixty-fourth birthday.

In earlier societies, that would have made me a respected figure, one of the elders consulted about all decisions affecting the community. There are too many of us now. We may be demonstrably in full possession of our faculties. We may be in

Who's Who. Unless we are rich and powerfully well connected or so demented that our views may be invoked to support those of the idiot young, we are now at best deserving recipients of the charity of the Welfare State we created and paid for. Should I ever want to go to the cinema in the afternoon, I could get in for a ridiculously small sum, no greater than the price of admission used to be. I shall be able to go on the pier or into the castle at children's rate. My income (apart from the diminishing interest on my savings) will be doubled in weeks when I am prudent enough not to broadcast, review a book or sell anything to a publisher. On present form, I shall be prudent most weeks.

When I was young, I hoped to see a better world before I died. The expectation survived numerous setbacks. I welcomed the onset of the Welfare State, ignorant of what it would become. I have seen the world grow steadily worse and my position in it worsen. I have never been markedly serene. I shall be less so in old age.

Across the road, you are already in Walmer, though Walmer sea front, with the lifeboat house, is a quarter of a mile further south. Two hundred yards along what is also the main Dover road stands the Royal Marines' school of music. From its roof rises a graceful cupola topped by a gilded ball and weathervane. These (at night, they are floodlit) we can see, against a wide expanse of sky, through our bow window. The view is pleasant, and to date we have avoided curtaining the window with net. This exposes us to the gaze of passersby, who look straight through the wrought-iron gate and the bow window to the Henry Moore lithograph on a narrow piece of wall between the kitchen and the place where the boiler stands.

FOR THE WHOLE OF AUGUST, Lindy has been in Sandwich with the children, Donald coming down at the weekend. On Sunday, the 31st, M. drove back with him to London. That night she would spend in Campden Hill Square. Next day, she was going into the Chelsea Hospital for

Women, where a hysterectomy would be performed.

All went well. I did not go to London. M. had plenty of visitors. After a fortnight, she was picked up by her son-in-law and was driven to her sister's in Gloucestershire, whence a week later Donald fetched her and installed her at Campden Hill Square for a week, after which he brought her back here.

I had met Simon Raven, once, briefly, in Edinburgh, thirteen years before. I had read nothing by him except articles and book reviews in *The Spectator*, two of these of books by me. The first I had found a bit irritating. The second had pleased me. I had, of course, also read reviews of books by him, novels from which their reviewers had apparently gathered that the author himself had been expelled from a public school and later cashiered from the Army for misdemeanours of a homosexual kind. Latterly, he had received popular attention for a serial dramatisation on television of Trollope's political novels, calling the whole thing *The Pallisers*.

Informing Alan Ross, at *London Magazine*, of my change of address, I had asked him whether he knew anybody in Deal. Simon Raven lived in Deal, and Alan Ross sent me a note of his address. The immediate consequence was that I dined with Simon Raven at the Royal Hotel the day after my wife went into hospital, the day before her operation. The food was middling, the wine extremely good. After dinner, a taxi took us to a public house, the Admiral Keppel, in Upper Deal, near St Leonard's church and close to where Simon lives in a very small cottage. At the Admiral Keppel, we drank with Simon's younger brother, Myles, who teaches at a preparatory school in the town, and a man called Alfred, who appeared to be an intellectual tradesman. Simon had arranged for a taxi to come at closing time and take me home. He is punctilious in that way.

The weekend was horribly wet. To read, I had a typescript of *The Burning of Evelyn Foster* by Jonathan Goodman. My first television play, three years before, had shown a coroner's jury deciding, against the coroner's direction and the view emphatically expressed by the chief constable, that a case based on this dreadful affair was murder, as there can be no possible doubt it was. Jon Goodman had dug up a great deal about the coroner and chief constable, explained the non-appearance of a rich local woman who should have been the key witness and, to me convincingly, named the murderer as the Ernest Brown who, two years later, was hanged for another blazing-car murder near Huddersfield, my native town, a case in which, when it came up at Leeds assizes in December 1933 (I was twenty and commuting daily between Huddersfield and Leeds), I took no interest and of which I do not remember hearing at the time. An important factor in the peculiar fascination of the Northumberland case to those who know it I take to be the closeness with which the evidence compels one to dwell upon Evelyn Foster's prolonged suffering, a thing one is commonly able to avoid with murder victims.

On the 10th of October, Ruby, who comes in to clean, helped me set up a fancy compost bin, which had arrived two days before. That was a Friday. It was the following Sunday when M. and I first mentioned to each other a man, not young but powerfully built and clearly in excellent physical condition if perhaps a little overweight, whom we had severally noticed walking past in bathing trunks, without towel or anything on his feet. He apparently lived or was staying just across the road. We named him The Streaker.

In the afternoon next day, Michael Hosking, proprietor of a secondhand bookshop, the Golden Hind, which he and his friend used to run as a teashop, along the front, opposite the Royal, brought a one-volume edition of Lucy Hutchinson's *Memoirs of the Life of Colonel Hutchinson*, an alternative to the two-volume edition of 1885, which has some bibliographical interest and which I preferred the look of, so I bought it, having already had it on loan for several weeks.

It must, I fancy, have been on that same afternoon that I first consciously heard of Deal's chief literary celebrity, Elizabeth Carter, though no doubt I had seen hers among the names of other women in Boswell's *Life of Johnson* and been vaguely aware that opposite the bus terminus in South Street there was a Carter House bearing a plaque.

I looked up Boswell. The following Wednesday, I went to the Golden Hind and asked Michael what Carteriana he had. I took away, again on loan, the two volumes of the Rev. Montagu Pennington's life of his aunt, a third edition, 1816, of the work first published nine years before, the year after her death. M. had found out what they had under lock and key at the local public library. The first Pennington volume contained letters from Johnson, Horace Walpole and Richard Savage.

On Thursday morning, M. went to London for a post-operational check. Shortly after she had left the house, I was telephoned by our son-in-law. His purpose was to spare M. moments of panic if she heard on the wireless or read in a midday *Standard* of an IRA explosion in Campden Hill Square. The bomb had been placed under a car outside the Frasers' and had gone off at seven minutes to nine, at which time our youngest grandchild was normally thereabouts on her way to school. That morning, she had been kept in bed, feeling off colour. An eminent cancer specialist, whom our daughter and son-in-law knew and liked, had not been so lucky. It was decided that all Donald could do would be to ring up the Bousfield where M. was calling and leave a message there to say that nobody at the house which concerned us had been more than a little shaken.

MONDAY, OCTOBER 27TH, was marked by two deaths which meant a little more to me than that of Arnold Toynbee on Wednesday. Toynbee had been 86. Georges Carpentier was 81, Rex Stout 88. Carpentier would have been in his middle twenties when he quickly knocked Joe Beckett out in London and won me in Huddersfield sixpence from a big boy across the road (whose name was Frank Jessop and who rode a Nerocar, the moped of those days), thus laying the foundations of my later Francophily, in the pursuit of which I was one day to meet him for the time it takes the proprietor of an expensive bar near the Étoile in Paris to go round greeting each of his customers. Latterly, I had taken to reading Stout's Nero Wolfe crime stories with an interest amounting to positive enthusiasm in the case of one of them, *Some Buried Caesar*, for which I suppose that a quotation from Fitzgerald's *Rubá'iyát of Omar Khayyám* supplied not only the title in all its ambiguity but also the story, audaciously flaunting a clue which very few can have recognised as such until the joke is paid off.

Last roses of summer persisted into December. The 5th was a Friday. That day, Paul Ferris, a journalist and occasional novelist, drove down from London to talk about Dylan Thomas, on whom he was writing a book. He was himself a Swansea man, which gave him an edge over other biographers.

Next evening, the excellent pianist, Valerie Tryon, gave a recital at what is called the Quarterdeck, principally a dance hall but with a good bar and lavishly decorated with flowers. To play on, she had been given a six-foot drawing-room grand, which she treated gently during the first half of the concert but hit harder after the interval, without any strings breaking or going markedly out of tune. A young woman of highly agreeable personality.

The Streaker no longer appeared in nothing but his bathing trunks. He seems to have two cars, one of which could be called red, the other being unmistakably pink. Into this one, on December 12th, he climbed wearing mauve jeans, a rosy sweater and a salmon-pink cowboy hat.

A severe frost on the 15th left a hugely spread pelargonium and half a dozen fine bushes of fuchsia, which had gone on producing flowers and berries at the same time, wilting dreadfully and apparently dead, though now the fuchsias are budding. On the 23rd, M. went to Centuries to open the house for our son, Adam, his wife and their two little girls, who were driving down from London for a few days before the Foords came for the rest of the Christmas holidays. Yvonne brought M. back while the vicar was here.

Next day, a beautiful Christmas Eve, M. and I both went to Centuries for luncheon. It was the first time I had seen my son since May. Christmas Day they spent here. Winter jasmine and a *helleborus niger* or Christmas rose were out.

9 January

Simon Raven to tea and to play me at chess. He beat me without difficulty. I have, of course, the excuse that it is nine or ten years since I last played, but Simon also makes me nervous. I feel that with him I cannot wait as long as I should like to before making a move. Psychologically, he is in command.

13 January

Yesterday, Agatha Christie died. This evening, Simon Raven dined us both at the Royal.

I corresponded once with Agatha Christie. This was over one of her novels in which it seemed to me that she had based her story and the murderess on a real-life French case and, if it were so, wanted to say this in *A Little Pattern of French Crime*,

which I was then writing, so that it must have been in 1969.[1]
The French murderess had been of a distinctly lower social
class than Mrs Christie's.

In opposition to what seems to be the common view, I think
that Agatha Christie wrote better towards the end, at any rate
in the detail of her writing. She became a better stylist. If she
had later revised the dialogue of *The Mousetrap*, it would have
become a better play. Her early novels are also disfigured by a
crude anti-Semitism.

16 January

Simon Raven dined here, coming early, so that we could
play a game of chess before dinner. He again beat me.

1.   Winterbrook House
                                                   Wallingford
                                                     Berkshire

                                             13th January 1969

Dear Mr Heppenstall,

I am afraid I cannot be much help to you in what you want to know,
especially as I am just recovering from influenza and feel definitely
muzzy in the head.

As far as I can recall I read an article a good many years ago, I think
in a medical journal of some kind, dealing with various French cases,
on women who had attended patients and frequently children with
great devotion. The patients usually died and the devoted neighbour
wept bitterly over their demise. As far as I remember the article
stressed the pathological side of these cases. Several of them were
cited and I should imagine that Jeanne Weber was prominent among
them. The medical article was the only thing I remember, but as it was
a long time ago I had really forgotten practically all about it, though
finding it interesting to include the possibility of such a thing in my
last book [*By the Pricking of My Thumbs,* London, 1968]. That is the best
I can do.

I wish you the best of luck with your book on French crime during
la belle époque.

                                             Yours sincerely,

                                             Agatha Christie

Reluctantly, I decided that he was out of my class and that we should have to drop chess.

Like all new dinner guests, he got M.'s steak and kidney pie, together with the joke, almost forty years old, that I had married M. for her pastry. I was able to serve an estate-bottled burgundy which was, into the bargain, a *premier grand cru classé*, than which, as I cockily said and wished I hadn't, they don't grade them any higher, for it had a strong, coarse taste which I fancied to be *un goût de P. D.*, of *producteur directe*, which is to say of grapes from the stock of the vine. We had a second drink misfortune, in that the calvados couldn't be found. Afterwards, it was found in the refrigerator, where it had found its way in mistake for a dry sherry that wasn't used, the two bottles being not dissimilar.

22 January

I hadn't been to see a doctor for almost nine years, since the time, in fact, at which, by an unpleasant business with enemas of barium, I was discovered to have diverticulitis. My aching arm kept me awake last night, and I was also wheezing badly, so this morning I took these ailments round the corner to the doctors with whom M. had already had something to do. A receptionist with spectacles pointed sternly at the cigarette in my hand and made a contemptuous gesture indicating that I must get rid of it outside. There were no NO SMOKING notices in the waiting-room, but neither were there any ashtrays. I was sent up to see a small Indian doctor with a Portuguese name, who seemed both competent and nice and who prescribed me antibiotics for my chest and analgesics and another drug, the name of which I could not read, for my arm.

19 February

Picked up by Simon Raven and driven, first, to Ripple, a short way inland, for a pub lunch at the Plough, to which the

Pam and Arthur, formerly of the Foresters, near the old coastguard station, have moved, then on a tour of churches, taking in Westcliffe, Ash, Wingham and Barfreston, of which only Ash and Barfreston were open. Simon is knowledgeable about church architecture and monuments, so the excursion was both enjoyable and instructive.

16 March

I had just discovered the signs of an unobserved late-morning incursion by a cat when M. brought out Robert Hewison, just arrived from London, who is writing a book on the literary life of the war years[1] and with whose father, R.J.P. Hewison, I had much to do in the 'fifties, in London, in Paris and one Saturday evening in Weybridge. When Raymond Mortimer was literary editor of the *New Statesman*, the competitions had often been for translations of French poems. The winners had invariably been Frances Cornford, L.E. (Sir Lawrence) Jones, Naomi Lewis and R.J.P. Hewison, who was a senior civil servant. In 1951, Raymond arranged, for Third Programme, four brief selections from the work of French symbolist poets and recommended these four for the translations, while I went to Paris to record Yonnel, Roger Blin and Madeleine Renaud reading the originals. I continued to use them, with other translators, thereafter. I lost touch with Rob Hewison (who translated under the name "John Petrie") when he went to Ceylon, where he had an accident which crippled him, after which his wife left him, to my mind no great loss. Young Hewison was very nice and devoted to his father, but I fear that his book will be another of those Leftish books.

27 March

Saturday. Martin Esslin drove over from Winchelsea, where he has a weekend cottage, to record my narration for

1. *Under Siege*, London, 1977.

a radio programme on Jonathan Wild and Jack Sheppard.

10 April

Easter. A pair of gorgeous butterflies on the aubretia.

11 April

The foghorn blowing early, but on land no mist to speak of. The same pair of butterflies, no doubt. Tortoiseshells, I fancy.

12 April

Lindy and children mid-morning from a swimming lesson in Dover. I don't care for Tippett, but the bass in *A Child of Our Time* this evening sounds wonderful. Clifford Grant. The name is quite unknown to me.

14 April

A Canadian academic to lunch. To be asked questions about John Middleton Murry is a change from being asked questions about Dylan Thomas or George Orwell. M., of course, can join in about all three.

19 April

The crime pages from *France-Soir* and *Le Monde* are now here, to be trimmed and filed. This periodical task interests me less and less. A curious ocular effect this late afternoon. I looked quickly sideways and found, returning to a normal focus, that the sight of my two eyes was no longer co-ordinated. This was rather alarming, but after an hour or more of resting my eyes, I had normal vision again.

21 April

A profile of me in the *East Kent Mercury* may have produced local effects. The only one manifested to date was the appearance at the door this morning of a woman whose husband, a retired schoolmaster, has written six novels which nobody will publish. He is shy. So, as I tell her, am I, but I am perfectly amiable and ask her in. Read the typescripts, however, when I discover her to be approaching that point, is a thing I will not do. She understands. It is a question of professionalism. I ought, of course, to have said that I would not read them for nothing and to have proposed a normal reading fee. I am sorry for the man. At one time, apparently, he had the six typescripts at six different publishers, and all were returned by post on the same morning. I have never suffered anything quite so traumatic in that context as that.

The house next door has a SOLD notice up. It is next door at the back, but not at the front. That back and our side garden run parallel, Gilford House, at the corner, having no back garden. The neighbouring back garden has been a waste since we came here, containing plants which I have often been tempted to climb over and dig up. I should probably have done that if we were not so overlooked by the guest house across Hope Road and the backs of the houses in Victoria Road and even some upper windows across Gilford Road and above the RAF cadets' drill hall at the corner where part of Hope Road turns left (they practise drumming on Monday evenings, and afterwards the boys chase the girls round the upper rooms).

22 April

Listened to *Jack Sheppard and Jonathan Wild*. Excellent performance by a young man called Christopher Bidmead. Afterwards, Trevor Harvey rang to say he and Leslie had listened and been enthralled. It will be Leslie's birthday on Saturday, May 8th, and they want to come down to Deal for a day out and to see us.

30 April

Richard Hughes died, aged 76. I must be one of the few to

have heard and remembered his radio play about people lost in a coal mine, over fifty years ago, when I was thirteen and lived in Guisborough. Just after the war, I dined with him at his club and he with us in Rosslyn Hill. He was a cousin of poor Marged Welch, whose death, by an accident which could have been suicide, was so great a disappointment to Dylan Thomas.[1] I did not meet him again until he was suddenly to be found staying with Jill, a friend of one of his daughters, in the flat below at Ladbroke Terrace. We fed him for Jill when she was away. I found him no longer interested in pirates.

I have struggled all week with Captain Kidd, a dreary man, a pirate without *panache* for five months in late middle age. Thereafter, just a biz gent trying to hang on to his ill-gotten gains and avoid the gallows.

Dinner at the Royal this evening, with Simon, a youngish American writer, Robert Coover, who lives on some inexhaustible award at Kingsdown, and his Spanish wife, who chatters with a wholly unwarranted confidence in her English.

3 May

The persons of three generations in the next garden this evening were presumably our future neighbours. They looked what I suppose would be called respectable working-

1. RH: "[In the late 1940s,] I often met a disturbed young woman named Marged Welch, whose family was very rich indeed. In the spring of 1950, when I was in Wales to study the home ground of Giraldus Cambrensis and the cathedral of St David's about which his long struggle centred, I stayed with Marged's mother outside Llanelly, which she largely owned. Marged had more than once said to me that she wanted to do something for Dylan Thomas and was, I suppose, the rich woman from whom one of the books about him says that in his last years he entertained expectations, though I have not seen her anywhere named. She died in the course of the kind of incident about which coroners' juries always find it difficult to return a confident verdict.... I am unable to suggest what effect the disappointment of those expectations had on Dylan, who in the summer of 1951 still had two and a half years to live."

class and were rather numerous, but perhaps they will not all be living there.

4 May

M. and I walked along the sea front as far as the Pelican, of which we had heard that it is improved. It must be thirty years since I saw Gordon Crier,[1] pointed out to me in the basement of Colombo's restaurant in Great Portland Street. I had just arrived at the BBC, and he left shortly thereafter. He was in a group sitting down at the Pelican. I introduced myself, and we were incorporated. Presently, his wife, Peggy, came in. She was recognisably the young woman I had seen with him, thirty years ago, in Colombo's basement. They were clearly regulars and introduced us to one or two others, the most engaging being a large man in a red jumper. He was called Stanley Miller.

Our presumed new neighbours around again on our return. Without hearing any words they said, I seemed to detect a north-country intonation in the voices of the older man with spectacles and the woman with a sort of brown, woolly teacosy on her head.

6 May

The second tour of churches with Simon Raven, who first lunched with us. This time, we got into Wingham, where a woman was cleaning. A splendid monument in black and white marble, with four outsize *putti*, of which two stand with shields and two kneel, one with a skull, the other a helmet. Thought to be the work of Grinling Gibbons, though Pevsner opts rather for Gibbons's teacher, Quellin. While we were contemplating this, M. was stung on the neck by a wasp. Very painful, very red, though not much swelling. Treated, on our return home, with vinegar, wasps' stings being said to be alkaline, unlike those of bees, which are acid and require

---

1. Producer, writer and presenter of radio programmes.

bicarbonate of soda.

8 May

Trevor Harvey and the Rev. L.P. Styler, Trevor very stately, Leslie rather thin, both wearing saucy *cravates*. We didn't know just how old Leslie was, but M. had a birthday cake made with eight candles, to be on the safe side in the matter of decades. None had to be removed, as Leslie is 68. At the end of lunch, I was instructed to draw the curtains, and M. appeared, candles lighted. Leslie, almost in tears, extinguished all eight with one well-directed blow. Afterwards, we walked along the sea front to the lifeboat, where we all photographed each other. "Ah," said Leslie as we retraced our steps, "this is peace and beauty!" It was, indeed, a lovely afternoon, and the occasion was wholly delightful.

14 May

The Criers again at the Pelican. Stanley Miller talking about an eighteenth-century play, *The Fair Quaker of Deal*, which the librarian here, a Miss Hooker, is having photocopied for him. It sounds rather good. Deal must indeed have been full of whores when the Navy and East Indiamen used to lie up in the Downs. As many as eight hundred sail at a time lay there, with a constant traffic of ships' boats and the hovellers' galleys and luggers to and from the shore.

31 May

The new neighbours have moved in. My bedroom window, facing north, overlooks their chaos. I am usually awake by five o'clock and up by six. Drawing back my curtains this Sunday morning, I saw that a milkman had left, at their kitchen door, a crate designed for eight pint bottles containing seven, a carton of cream or yoghourt beside it.

9 June

Sybil Thorndike has died, aged 93. I recorded her once, doing a speech of Queen Elizabeth's, when she would only have been in her seventies. Sir Lewis Casson came with her to the studio, the Grafton, which, of all the BBC studios I ever used, had the fewest amenities. For a cup of tea, one had to go to a Lyons' teashop in Tottenham Court Road.

10 June

This evening, M. and I went to the Quarterdeck for a recital by Peter Katin. It was all Chopin and did not include the Barcarolle. We left at the interval. Peter Katin wore a dreadful suit of the colour known as aubergine.

14 June

On behalf of the history society, M. did an afternoon's duty at the maritime museum. She had only two customers. I fetched her, and we looked, in my case for the first time, inside St George's church. From 1712 to 1727, a duty of two shillings was imposed on every ton of coal brought into Deal, to pay for the building of and improvements to St George's. Elizabeth Carter's father was the second perpetual curate, the first having proved unsatisfactory. By 1727, Elizabeth herself was a child of ten, and that year she lost her mother. The memorial tablet behind the altar reads:

> Sacred to the memory of Mrs. Elizabeth Carter, a native and inhabitant of this town, where her benevolence and virtues will be long remembered.
> She was eldest daughter of the Rev. Nicolas Carter, D.D., for upwards of fifty years Perpetual Curate of this Chapel, by Margaret, sole daughter and heiress of Richard Swayne, of Bere, in the county of Dorset, Esq.
> In deep learning, genius and extensive knowledge, she

was equalled by few; in piety, and the practice of every Christian duty, excelled by none.

She was born December 16, 1717, and died in London, February 19, 1806, and was interred there in the burial ground of Grosvenor Chapel.

That mural monument of marble, as he calls it, was put up by her nephew, the Rev. Montagu Pennington, then himself perpetual curate of St George's, a man towards whom, for no very good reason, I am always inclined to adopt a mocking attitude, as I never am towards Elizabeth Carter.

18 June

Last evening, Dorothy Blain brought her British stamps for me to look at. Dorothy, nurse and paid companion to Madeline Mortimore, the previous owner of Coach Cottage, has become M.'s shopping and morning-coffee friend in chief. A Cumbrian, she married in West Africa, where her husband still lives and works, seeing her every two years on leave in England. She has a house in Kingsdown, but rarely sees it. Her mother died recently, leaving her house to her son and its contents to Dorothy. Among the contents, which otherwise did not amount to much, were the remains of a stamp collection, of which Dorothy's mother had sold off the part she thought most valuable. This must, I fancy, have included the Cape triangles, of which only a few remained (as I saw this evening) loose among depleted pages. But among the British stamps were pages and pages and pages of penny blacks and twopenny blues and penny reds, these last arranged in almost any order except the right one, but copious enough to make up whole plates.

Nothing is more tedious than to look at page after ill-arranged page of penny blacks, twopenny blues and penny reds, unless, of course, you are going to be in a position to regard them as yours and to rearrange them. I had been meant to keep the stamps for twenty-four hours, but I packed them

up there and then for Dorothy to take away with her, first
pointing out one or two oddities, as that for example a block
of four George V postal union congress £1 stamps of 1929
had been curiously misplaced.

Next week, Dorothy is taking her stamps up to London to
be looked at by a man at Phillips, the auctioneers. I suggested
that that block of stamps should be put in its proper place. I
looked up that stamp in a 1970 catalogue and saw that
individually the stamps were then already priced at £75
unused. The block, I said, could hardly be valued at less than
four or five hundred pounds now.

Next evening, at Madeline's, I looked at the foreign and
colonial stamps. About some of them I felt sad. I would have
liked my pick, for instance, of the earlier French ones. I did not
feel that, scattered haphazard through numerous albums,
Dorothy would get a proper price for them. If anyone was to
get them as a bargain, it might as well be me.

21 June

This evening, M. and I walked along the front to the
Pelican, where Gordon Crier holds court. Stanley Miller had
at last brought along his photostated copy of *The Fair Quaker
of Deal*. As Gordon could not give it his attention for a week
or more, I was allowed to take it away.

It is by Charles Shadwell. From references in the prologue,
it appears that he was a younger son of Thomas Shadwell,
Dryden's MacFlecknoe, and from other references that the
play, a farce, was first produced in the reign of Queen Anne
with Booth in the cast. I have found it not at all contemptible.

1 July

Two Jehovah's witnesses at the door. When the last pair
appeared, I had not looked up a book I have to make sure that
1975 was the year when the world should have ended and the
faithful begun their perpetual life on a new earth. Those

182

today simply denied it. They were a trendy-looking young couple.

Dorothy got £700 for her foreign and colonial stamps. A reserve price of £4,000 has been put on the British stamps.

6 August

On what must have been July 1st or the evening before, Myles Raven, Simon's younger brother, had a stroke which put him into hospital, where he lay in a coma until Saturday, the 3rd, when he died in the evening. He had been a sweet man, and Simon had clearly been very attached to him. We imagined that Simon might no longer feel attached to Deal, but would go and live elsewhere, which would be a grave loss to us.

The news of Myles's death did not in fact reach us, on a postcard from Simon, until the morning of Wednesday, the 7th. On that day, M. went to the Social Security office and brought back a form N 127 A, on which I could apply not to pay National Insurance from the previous April, that is to say from the beginning of the financial year in which I was to be 65. On Thursday morning, I filled this form in. The whole system of the Welfare State seemed to me nothing but a gigantic confidence trick, bent, at the moment, on depriving me of any old-age pension until I was 70, because I was self-employed, making no money but compelled to pay for self-employment stamps, since I had no other status. Even if I were to draw an old-age pension for a year or two, I should never recover what I had already paid into National Insurance. I raged loudly.

M. took the form in and did her shopping. When she came home, I said I felt wobbly. However, I ate my sandwiches and went upstairs for my usual afternoon rest. I slept a bit. In the course of the evening, my right eyelid and the right-hand corner of my mouth drooped, a pain crept down my left arm, and two brief diary entries I tried to make were quite illegible. My speech was blurred. My sense of balance was disturbed, so that when I went to bed, I had the greatest difficulty in getting out of my trousers and into my pyjamas. It was as though I were drunk.

I fancied I must have had a slight stroke. M. had made a friend of the receptionist who had been so severe with me on my one visit to the doctors, and by the resource of this Sheila a doctor from round the corner was here before ten o'clock on Friday morning, a youngish man with a beard but with his top lip shaved. This was Dr Dyer. He seemed very pleasant. He also concluded that I had had a stroke. He prescribed Valium and said that he would look in again on Monday.

I tried the Valium once, found it made me sleepy and stopped it. I could not read. My attention wandered. On the other hand, I could not sleep at night, so that it would have been sensible, had I thought of it, to take Valium as sleeping pills. I cannot now recall whether, when Dr Dyer called again on the 12th, I told him that I had stopped taking Valium or not. What he must have noticed himself was that my speech remained blurred. I cannot remember whether he performed any tests which may have shown a marked incapacity in my right hand, but I could hardly use a pen at all. I could not swat flies. I cut myself shaving.

What is more immediately relevant is that I could hardly type. That is the reason why this diary contains no proper entries after July 2nd and why everything that I want to note for a month from July 8th has to be noted retrospectively. In my desk diary, I continued to make legible scribbles with great care, but I also have to tax my memory, which was unimpaired. My typing will no doubt improve with regular practice. My handwriting is better than it was, but it is still far from good. My mouth still droops at the right corner, but my speech is not bad except when I am tired or when I talk for too long. I still cut myself, shaving. I can sometimes swat flies, though already there are fewer flies to swat.

27 August

August is almost over. My chest X-ray showed nothing.

There has been some rain at last, though not enough to put an end to the drought.

I do not seem to have made much improvement during the past week or so, but am now less inclined to cut plants, white alyssum, rocket, sweet peas and everlasting flowers, the dill and borage and pinks being already in pill bottles. The sensitive plants in the conservatory are still in bloom. There are, indeed, eight flowers today, which is more than have previously been out at one time. They last a day or so and are then reduced to small, brown, soft things which do not contain seeds. Sutton's seed catalogue says that the pink flowers are insignificant. I do not find them insignificant.

11 September

I have a book on Baudelaire to review for *The Sunday Times*. Raymond Mortimer cannot have wanted it. I suppose that Raymond must view Baudelaire as an enemy of pleasure. I am not sure whether Baudelaire was one of the poets from whom he arranged a selection twenty-five years ago. That was the occasion of the first of my many trips to Paris to record French actors reading verse. I remember the tremendous *comédien*, Yonnel, who read with a tremolo, and Roger Blin, who could not conquer his stutter at the microphone. Jean-Paul would line up, count down, give Blin his cue ... and nothing would happen. I rather fancy that we already had Madeleine Renaud that time.

The book[1] is by Alex de Jonge, currently a fellow and tutor of New College, Oxford, aged thirty-eight. I looked Enid Starkie up in an outdated *Who's Who* and see that her *Baudelaire* first came out in 1933, though from de Jonge's bibliography I also see that it was reprinted as late as 1971. The bibliography lists Sartre but does not list Michel Butor's *Histoire Extraordinaire*, a book-length analysis of a dream of Baudelaire's, which was the last thing I have read on the poet and perhaps the only kind of thing there is still room for.

1. *Baudelaire: Prince of Clouds*, London, 1976.

12 September

Donald brought soil for the roses. This happened as a result of the discovery that Lindy had a copy of Enid Starkie's *Baudelaire* with her in Sandwich.

It is as I thought. There is nothing in de Jonge which was not in Starkie. This does not mean that he plagiarises. I am sure that he felt he had something new to say. He lacks the command of language which would have enabled him to say it, and it wasn't new anyway. I suppose that he became infatuated with his title, which is a quote from *L'Albatros*. He manages to show what a bloody awful life Baudelaire led, but of the machinery by which he transcended it knows nothing. Here, Starkie had the advantage of a Catholic upbringing.

15 September

By this morning's post, the contract for *Two Moons*.[1] This evening, on the wireless, the recording of an American performance of Berlioz's *Romeo and Juliet*. I am not sure that I had ever previously heard this in full. The voice of the mezzo, though she was good, was a bit metallic, but then, as Adam first pointed out to me, the voices of young girls are metallic. Those infinitely refined, pure voices are the voices of mature women. Romeo is never heard, the tenor being only a gibing Mercutio near the beginning and the baritone Friar Lawrence, who has a long aria. He was good. The orchestra was good, as one expects American orchestras to be, the choir adequate. Berlioz must surely have intended an opera, writing the interludes and less important passages first. The best things are those one commonly hears. Friar Lawrence's aria is tremendous, but belongs to an operatic tradition alien to Berlioz. I am addicted to Berlioz, perhaps the more so for a certain vulgarity which is every now and then apparent in him, in his cymbal-clashing for instance, though in his time that was highly excusable.

1.   From Allison & Busby.

17 September

Raymond Radiguet died in 1923 at the age of twenty. At the age of nineteen, he had published a best-seller, *Le Diable au Corps*. When he died, of typhoid through gorging on Mediterranean oysters, he had more or less finished a second novel, *Le Bal du Comte d'Orgel*. Both novels have been translated three times into English, and *Le Bal du Comte d'Orgel* was filmed by Marc Allegret, with adaptation and dialogue by Françoise Sagan. The son of a well-known cartoonist, Radiguet had been on the literary scene from the age of fifteen, at which age he met Jean Cocteau and presently went to live with him, though by no means essentially homosexual.

I knew some of these facts. I have gathered others from a new book by Margaret Crosland.[1] I once tried to read *Le Diable au Corps*. I could not get into it or on with it, but that may have been due to a purely temporary state of mind. I also glanced at *Le Bal du Comte d'Orgel*. I saw the film. At my one meeting with Cocteau, he recorded a long poem by himself on Radiguet asleep. I know Margaret Crosland, though it is some years since I saw her.

I rather fancy that we first met at an exhibition of paintings by Cocteau, which convinced me what a very bad painter he was and in fact somewhat set me against Cocteau altogether, which I had not previously been. Margaret Crosland has, of course, both written about and translated Cocteau. This might be gathered from her book on Raymond Radiguet. There had, inevitably, to be a lot about Cocteau in it, but there is more than there need have been, and it is not all relevant to Radiguet.

The fact is that, although he had a great many friends who were writers, some of them very well known, either they did not write about him or Margaret Crosland has failed to turn up what they wrote. For her account of his short life is almost

1. *Raymond Radiguet: A Biographical Study with Selections from his Work*, London, 1976.

wholly based on Cocteau material and that provided by a maddening woman called Nina Hamnett, whom I used to see in the Charlotte Street pubs and who had written a book, *Laughing Torso*,[1] which apparently speaks much of a woman of whom I think I have heard, Beatrice Hastings, who fell in love with the young genius. Still, I do feel that I now know more about Raymond Radiguet than I did and even that I know something about his two unread novels.

I was also led to meditate on literary precocity. My son's development made it clear to me that an intelligent boy is mature in mind at the age of twelve. Thereafter, he will be assailed by the madness of sex, which is likely to plunge him into a state of confusion from which he will not emerge for at least fifty years. It looks to me as though in the two novels I have not read there was no sex except, in *Le Diable au Corps*, the interference of an older woman, whom the young Radiguet very properly kills off. Outraged by his experience of sex and homosex, he, after further writing a novel about an imaginary world, *La Princesse de Clèves* put into modern terms, ate oysters until they killed him.

Also by Margaret Crosland, I have a second book in proof, *Women of Iron and Velvet and the Books They Wrote in France*.[2] It begins with George Sand, goes back beyond her to Margaret of Navarre, Christine de Pisan, Madame de La Fayette and so on, says a little in a more general way about the nineteenth century and is then devoted almost wholly to modern writers from Colette onwards. Of the later among these I have not read the half.

I once met Dominique Aury, generally thought to have been the "Pauline Réage" of the indecent *Histoire d'O*, oddly enough at the house in the Rue Jacob of Natalie Clifford Barney, but I have read only articles by her. Hélène Cixous was once kind enough to describe me in print as the founder of the *nouveau roman*, and I might well have supposed that she has also written books.

1. London, 1932.
2. London, 1976.

Margaret has, apparently, read them all, indeed in a fair number of cases makes it plain that she has, by analysing plots. She has read Nathalie Sarraute beyond the point at which, with *Les Fruits d'Or*, I stopped. It is apropos Nathalie Sarraute that, apart from a few polite kowtows in the direction of progressive ideas, Margaret most distinctly voices a point of view. Of "the charming, dignified Russian woman" she says that she feels "compelled to be honest about one aspect of Sarraute's work as it affects me personally: I admire it intensely but cannot enjoy it.... Perhaps my response to Sarraute is related to my allergic reactions against Ivy Compton-Burnett...." Well, I feel a little the same myself, though it is Ivy Compton-Burnett whom I can enjoy or disenjoy and leave alone, while, in the case of the charming, dignified and paranoid Russian woman, I find both the tropisms notion and the endless rows of dots a blight. Margaret has not found out what tropisms are. She could apply to a biologist or a natural historian or consult the *Encyclopaedia Britannica*.

Simone de Beauvoir I find an utter bore, though I fail to see on what grounds Mary McCarthy (who is) considers her "odious". I remember in 1948 christening her in my own mind, wittily I thought, *la grande Sartreuse*.

No feminist can ever have so abjectly betrayed what men consider the feminine condition by tagging along the way she has always done behind Jean-Paul Sartre. She was, however, kind to a far better writer, the late Violette Leduc, who thought herself conspicuously ugly, whereas she just looked typically French.

Simone Weil, whom I have read comprehensively, Margaret Crosland clearly hasn't read at all. While she gets the facts of that infinitely pathetic life right, she cannot even whip up for her bibliography more than two titles in English and none in French. On my shelves alone, there are eleven titles in English, all posthumous. A woman of velvet and iron, Simone Weil died in England during Churchill's war through refusing to eat more than the official rations in occupied

France. She was a more scrupulous philosopher than any man or woman in our time. A title not on my shelves, because unpublished, is that of Sir Richard Rees's translation of a very *Venice Preserv'd* she had almost completed.

In a recent issue of *London Magazine*, a book by Monique Wittig, *The Lesbian Body*,[1] was interestingly reviewed by a man called Graham Martin. More than one of these women writers is or was lesbian. I do not think Margaret Crosland is, but there is a kind of lesbian effect brought about by a woman writing about women. Male critics writing about male writers do not write about them *as men*. This kind of book may even, in its small way, encourage lesbianism, just as Women's Lib. does. Not that I am at all opposed to lesbianism, any more to male homosexuality. I only wish that both would become rife among the "working" class and coloured immigrants. Then they would not breed so.

As to women, by all means let them play with each other's titties and bottoms and those convenient holes between their legs. They presumably contrive to induce orgasms in each other. For, of course, only women have orgasms. Men don't, they merely ejaculate. Their pleasure is a reflection of the woman's. There is a certain science in the achievement of this, but the essential thing is simply that, having induced an orgasm in the woman, a man should refrain from ejaculating until it is almost finished.

More lesbianism would mean that women were less frequently in mixed company, so that we should be spared their childlike voices, while perhaps women announcers could be confined to lesbian radio. Women, it is true, are needed for singing up beyond any counter-tenor's range, an advantage especially now that choirboys are so hard to find.

19 September

Ann Bliss's grandson, Toby, was christened this evening. I had never been to a Church of England baptism or stayed for a

1. Translated by David Le Vay; London, 1975.

C. of E. communion before. The communicants had to walk quite a long way to the high altar. Their manner on return was odd. They all looked as though they had been doing something they shouldn't.

What were alleged to be champagne cocktails, having a slice of orange in them, were subsequently filled up with tepid champagne. There were good *canapés,* but not enough to serve as a supper. With so many voices bouncing off a low ceiling, I could hardly hear what anyone said and concluded that I must be getting deaf. I went and sat down. In the car afterwards, we agreed that Ann is quite wonderful, more especially in that she so enjoys her own parties. Afterwards, Godfrey said, she goes out like a light.

It is clear that I am suffering from urethritis. I must see Dr Dyer tomorrow or the next day.

20 September

I have a photograph of Dylan Thomas, with Augustus John and Caitlin, taken outside the Red Lion inn, Newlyn, in July 1937. A woman at Hodder & Stoughton rang up about it this morning, the idea being to use it in Paul Ferris's life of Dylan. I spent the whole morning finding and trimming two pieces of cardboard to fit an envelope of suitable size, pasting a sheet of flimsy typing paper to one of the pieces of cardboard, writing on the back of the photograph, addressing the envelope and writing on it: PHOTOGRAPHS WITH CARE. It is astonishing the time it takes to do these little favours. However, if Hodder & Stoughton use the photograph, I shall receive a fee of eight pounds. If I did this every morning and again every afternoon for a five-day week, my salary would be eighty pounds, which is now average industrial earnings. I did not take a coffee break. And, of course, they may not use the photograph.

All that while, my son was being driven north to Sheffield, in his own car but by his friend Johann. They did not reach the Royal Infirmary there until about two o'clock. Adam will be six weeks in that hospital. They are to explore the area of his spinal injury and clear things up there, this not having been done at the time and the suspicion being that that is the source of the pain which Adam has been having ever since. It is only Sheffield which has entertained this suspicion. At the Maudsley, all they could think of was severing the receptor nerve above the twelfth vertebra, an operation which, for some reason, resulted in my son becoming terribly fat. This, however, does not seem to worry him.

27 September

Picked rather more than fifty quinces. The rest will be very difficult, if not impossible, to get at. Almost all are split, a consequence no doubt of the drought. Helped M., minimally, with the cutting up, which I found hard work. She didn't find it easy, but M. is a real sticker. We are to make jam, not jelly. Jam is more trouble than jelly, but apparently worth it. The quantity will be larger.

After lunch, I started a bonfire. There came a ring at the door. It was the young husband from next door. He wondered if I could arrange to have my bonfires a little later in the day because the smoke blew over on to the washing. Well, of course, I could hardly be said to have bonfires in the plural. The last had been about six weeks before. I could not, had I been so inclined, have stopped that bonfire, which would presently burn itself out. There was just as likely to be washing out next door later in the day. Quite often it was left out all night.

All this I pointed out to the young man, who has enormous arms which are partly powerful and partly chubby. In profile, he is quite good-looking. From the front, it was a rather smudgy face, of clear and boyish complexion. In profile, I had noted what I took to be complete humourlessness, the young man's general expression being resentful. I further told him that we were a little tired of the washing next door, particularly of the strings of knickers and underpants that were so often stretched across our kitchen window.

I am never at my sweetest in the early afternoon, when I feel that I should be resting upstairs. Warming to my subject, I informed the young man that we found him and his family unpleasant neighbours, and I told him to piss off.

Only a few minutes later, the doorbell rang again. It was a policeman, rather young, thin, dark, immaculate, quiet-mannered. He enquired whether I had a bonfire. I said yes and invited him in. He took his cap off, but would not sit down.

The course of that conversation I cannot quite clearly recapture. It ended in perfect happiness and even with jokes, and before that the young policeman had told us about the trouble his own wife had with a neighbour who lit bonfires every day when she hung up her washing.

2 October

The evening was taken up with a La Scala studio production of *The Barber of Seville,* also going out on television. It would have been nice also to see it, but on radio alone it was magnificent. Hermann Prey, a German, was Figaro, Teresa Berganza Rosina, a tenor I had not heard of, Luigi Alva, Count Almaviva. I was especially taken with this last. This was tenor coloratura singing such as I have never heard before. I suppose I must have heard the *Barber* in full before, but I had never realised that the thing is in coloratura, the effect of which was particularly magical in the ensembles.

It rained heavily in the night and was still at it when we got up this morning. No sooner had it cleared than a ring at the door revealed Mrs Johnson with a box of vegetables and fruit. As she explained, the vicar had meant to send me (me, not us) a share of what was distributed after the harvest festival, but had forgotten. Last week a woman had gone to the vicar with a load of garden produce which she had meant to be for the harvest festival, but had failed to take in until afterwards. This, as Mrs Johnson said, had been the answer to the vicar's prayer. A coincidence, she said, and then hastily added that, but, of course, they didn't believe in coincidences.

M. goes to the public library at least once a week and brings, in general, thrillers, perhaps half a dozen. Usually, I find that I have read one or more of these before. There may, occasionally, be an unread Ed McBain or Rex Stout or Erle Stanley Gardner, but in general they are sad stuff.

I can hardly ever read a straight novel. Often enough, I cannot read a thriller, not even caring who done it or repelled by the sex, while at other times I skip to the last chapter, thinking that, while the author writes intolerably, he may have a good story, that who done it and why may be of some interest. Inevitably, after a few days, I begin to complain that I have nothing to read.

Unless they are very recent, the books are grubby. At first I would only read the clean ones, but such fastidiousness is a thing of the past.

9 October

A week in the life of a senior citizen. On Tuesday, I saw young Dr Dyer again. He suspects prostate trouble. I am to go into Deal hospital for a cystoscopy.

I had a cystoscopy eleven years ago. After a dab of some local anaesthetic, a steel tube with a flashlight bulb at the end was pushed up my penis. As I climbed the ninety-two stairs at Ladbroke Terrace, blood was flooding my trousers, and for a week I pissed fish-hooks. However, I am told that they have flexible tubes now, and I shall have a general anaesthetic.

On Wednesday evening, the Vienna philharmonic was playing Mozart's last three symphonies on the radio. I am particularly fond of the E flat, or rather I am particularly fond of the minuet and of the first subject of the first movement in the E flat. The recording was one made during the last Edinburgh festival, and the man who introduced the programme was good. It had never occurred to me how unusual it is for a first movement to be in three-four time, and it had never struck me that every movement of the G minor is in the minor. This was a welcome change from the kind of rubbish with which musical programmes are commonly introduced.

Dorothy's daughter-in-law had said that bonfires are not supposed to be started until six o'clock in the evening, a matter about which the policeman had been vague. On Thursday evening, with branches sawn off the quince tree, I began a bonfire as six struck from the cupola of the Marines' school of music. It was the best bonfire I have had to date, with flames leaping upward from the funnel at the top of the incinerator.

I had another bonfire on the stroke of six yesterday. Afterwards, M. and I walked along the sea front and down King Street to the town hall, where the history society was having its annual wine-and-cheese party. We had made up our minds to eat as many sausage rolls and sandwiches as possible, so as to obviate any need for supper afterwards. Most of the others clearly had the same idea, even Sir Rex and Lady Niven. Sir Rex, who is 78 but very brisk, told M. that he is still writing and that his books sell a hundred thousand copies, which I find hard to believe. They are all about Nigeria.[1]

13 October

M. went into the church to take a bagful of matchsticks, which at her last Sunday evening visit the vicar had asked for to help somebody who was making something (a ship, a church) with matchsticks. We use a very large number of matches, as I smoke about sixty cigarettes a day. The vicar was at the altar, beginning his weekly service of healing, and a woman helper took the matches from M., but then the vicar left the altar and walked to the back of the church to ask my Christian name, so that he could include me in the list of

1. In which country Sir Rex Niven was a colonial administrator from 1921 until 1954.

people to be prayed for. I consider this to be under false pretences, as I feel pretty well at the moment and am only threatened. M. asked him also to pray for our son.

She came back with another rose from Lipton's. This was Pascali, a white hybrid tea. M. had forgotten that she had previously got a white, the Iceberg, and that what I wanted particularly was a Whisky Mac, which is yellow. We had, however, agreed that there is room in the rosebed for three or even four more roses, and I was glad enough to have Pascali, though it is not a fragrant rose.

Adam rang from Sheffield, reversing charges. He is again at Lodge Moor, on the edge of moorland. He said he wondered why I had ever left the moors. He felt marvellous, he said. His feeling is, we all feel sure, largely due to the two anti-depressants they have been giving him, but it seems that he will be going home at the weekend (prematurely, we fear), and he wanted to stop my sister and her husband from driving from Preston to see him, as they proposed to do (Adam likes my sister, who is indeed a very nice, genuine woman, Adam being appreciative of genuineness in women). Johann will fetch him.

Unexpectedly enjoyable programme on the radio. First, Bartok's music for strings, percussion and celesta (it ought to specify piano too, for the piano is more important than the celesta, and, if the piano can be considered percussion, so can the celesta), which I am not sure of having heard before. Then Walton's 'cello concerto, with Zara Nelsova. Perhaps I had never heard this before either, or perhaps it was that Nelsova gave it a particularly splendid performance, with the conductor, Yuri Ahronovitch, helping. Now there is Stravinsky's *Firebird* in the version with reduced instrumentation. It has often been said that Stravinsky could not write tunes, but the princesses' round dance is wonderfully melodious. Ahronovitch is, indeed, taking it very slowly to bring this out, but why should he not? It is not being danced to.

25 October

Last Tuesday, Clive Allison rang to say that proofs of *Two Moons* were in the post and asking me not merely to correct them but to make a mock-up of the book in its eventual form, left-hand and right-hand pages having been set separately. The rest of the week I spent doing this, hitting various snags.

It rained most of the week, but Saturday and yesterday were beautiful days, with night rain between. On Saturday evening, M. and I went to a Schubert concert at the Quarterdeck. After the interval, four string players joined the pianist to perform the "Trout" quintet. This, I suppose, is everyone's favourite chamber music. It is certainly mine. The pianist played competently but too loud, so that at times the strings were heard as mere buzzing in the background. It is difficult for solo strings to compete with a piano, which is a violently percussive instrument.

While we were at the concert, Clive Allison had been trying to reach me by telephone. He rang again late, and we arranged that he should come down next day to Sunday lunch, collecting the proofs and discussing any awkwardness, bringing also a set of proofs which someone else had read. He asked if he might further bring his girlfriend.

She was a nice, unassuming girl who works in the firm. The one thing I felt I knew about Allison & Busby, *viz*, that they published Piers Paul Read, turns out not to be the case. He is published by some other Allison or Alison. I was struck by Clive Allison's appearance of extreme youth, which a beard does nothing to disguise. He no doubt was struck by my appearance (which, in my case, is also the reality) of extreme decrepitude. I liked him. On the other hand, the only mutual acquaintances whom we discovered were people I heartily dislike. They must somehow have failed to inform him that I am a Fascist beast, not to be encouraged at any price. For, to judge by the contents of his catalogue, a copy of which was produced and left with me by the young woman, Valerie, the firm's policy is Leftish. Indeed, it appears that he used to write regularly in the *New Statesman*.[1] So, of course, did I, but that was long ago, when the literary contributors were allowed what politics they pleased. In any case, I was a socialist then.

1 November

Pitter patter, bloody raindrops.

Trying to read *Can You Forgive Her?* I have never yet read a novel by Trollope, indeed only tried once with *Barchester Towers*. My two most reprehensible failures to get into a novel were, I suppose, with *War and Peace* and *Middlemarch*.

8 November

Friday being fine, M. and I went after lunch to the chrysanthemum show at the Quarterdeck and then walked on the pier. My reason for wanting to walk along the pier was to see the town from the end of it and to make mental notes of what I could see. This was connected with an idea I had for a novel, which was to begin with a man walking in the morning from the end of the pier towards the town and to end with him in the evening returning to the end of the pier, with what intention I had not yet decided. What in fact one sees is the coast from the high point beyond Kingsdown, behind which lies St Margaret's Bay (this on one's left), to where, past the coastguard station, the land curves away to the remains of Sandown castle. One cannot see much of what lies between Hope Point and the lifeboat station, where inland are golf links and Walmer castle, but the rest of the sea front is built up. It looks quite attractive.

Passing through the exit turnstile, we had the Quarterdeck immediately in front of us, the Clarendon a little to our right. We turned left. The owner of a boat whose petrol engine had been hauling it up the shingle as we passed on our way to the chrysanthemum show had now set out a little stall and was selling herrings at 8p. each. We bought four.

1.   RH was mistaken about this.

M. marinaded them for dinner, and a very nice change they made.

At five o'clock this morning, there was a thunderstorm, remarkably noisy and with rain of extraordinary weight, but only feeble lightning. The phenomenon had the feeling of being purely local, and the south-east weather bulletin spoke of the day starting sunny inland. Not that weather forecasts are often to be paid much attention to. They are wrong at least fifty per cent of the time, which is as often as they would be wrong if they were based on no information at all. Yet the forecasters go on confidently stating that this or that will happen. They might be modestly useful if they said that, according to their information, this and that ought to happen, but that of course there is no guarantee that it will.

It rained all afternoon and was heavy again at half-past six, though with no thunder until the rain was a little abated, and then only one clap, not very close. M. had just returned from the library, where she found what I take to have been the latest Maigret. Having abandoned *Can You Forgive Her?* a little under half-way through (looking, of course, at the end in order to find out broadly what happens in the course of the second half of the book), I had taken up *The Duke's Children* (which should tell me what has happened in the course of the other political novels). I shall put it aside until I have read *Maigret and the Black Sheep*, which I am likely to finish before I go to bed. I do not read in bed here. I have never read in bed since we left Ladbroke Terrace.

16 November

In the small hours, I had to get up and, going into the bathroom, I found my sense of balance curiously adrift. All morning, I swayed when I walked and had to put my feet down carefully. After lunch, with the usual amount of alcohol in me, I was stumbling. It was the same after I had lain on my bed and slept briefly. M. went to see Sheila, receptionist to the doctors round the corner. Young Dr Dyer came at a quarter past four. He got me to walk and turn. He also got me touching his finger and my nose, at first with my eyes open and then with them shut. His diagnosis was that my arteries were furred up. I had thought it was perhaps a very slight further stroke, with no symptoms apart from the disturbance of my balance. It could, he said, be that the furring up of my arteries had been responsible for my stroke in the first place. He prescribed some pills, with no evident confidence that they would do any good.

17 November

I find, this morning, that I am again making far more mistakes on the typewriter than I was, and, when I had to sign a cheque for M. just now, my signature was again shaky.

When I went up to bed last night, I noticed that M. had once more taken to leaving her bedroom door open. This morning, she asked me whether I should like Lindy to come down and see me. I said no.

18 November

The morello cherry I had ordered arrived just as M. was on the way out to do her shopping. The hole I dug two months ago was far too wide and not deep enough. Less aware of a defective sense of balance than of general weakness, I dug down through very stony soil, every now and then feeling peculiar and having to go and sit down, the plant meanwhile standing, stake and all, in the water butt. M., returning, fetched me a drink. By the time she had cut our sandwiches and laid the table, I had the thing in position. After lunch, M. did much of the filling in of the hole, I most of the stamping down of the soil, for, after all, as she said, my feet were bigger.

I suppose that this bush will bear fruit next year. I ought to be there to see. It looks very nice, standing four feet tall in the angle between north and east walls, between the compost bin and the end of the shed.

Berlioz and Ravel on the wireless, with Boulez conducting, from the New theatre, Oxford. By Berlioz, the usual three scenes from *Romeo and Juliet*, by Ravel *Daphnis and Chloë* in its entirety, which is not often heard. M. responding like anything to the Berlioz, especially the Love Scene. I find it all a bit of a treat.

25 November

On Sunday, Fr. D'Arcy died, aged 87, on Monday André Malraux, 75. It is forty-one years since I stayed at Campion Hall, under instruction to Fr. D'Arcy, eventually dodging the font. He came to dinner with us twice in Ladbroke Terrace, and that I suppose is already about twenty years ago. I never met Malraux, but everything I read by or about him annoyed me.

We had not been so much aware of the Streaker this summer. The week before last, on a cold day, M. saw him walking home from the beach in nothing but a pair of bathing trunks, his feet bare. He is, I fancy, a man in his late forties or early fifties, powerfully built but with a little too much flesh. I noted last autumn that he had had his roof painted pink. Yesterday, a man with a spray gun was up a ladder against the gable of his house, painting it a pale but appalling green. The front of his house is still, for the moment, inflamed-looking brick, with white windows and white above the windows and above the little porch, the door being black picked out with white. It is an ugly house, and no amount of painting it will disguise the fact. It is, I am sure, the Streaker himself rather than Mrs Streaker who so loves colour. The curtains on his upper floor, at a window in the green gable and two bay windows at the front of the house, are plain violet, but at a smaller window between the two bays are blue patterned with black. Of the two bay windows on the ground floor, one is curtained plain orange and one yellow with a large pattern of black and orange circles.

Last evening, Boulez did all *Daphnis and Chloë* in the choral version. I liked this less well. Voices singing "Ah!" were a thing that caught on between the two world wars, the effect in general being one of mystery and the ineffable. This was before Hollywood went in for heavenly choirs.

Arrived this morning seeds from Dobie's. After lunch, I spread all my packets and bottles of seed out on the table, partly to give M. an idea of what I meant when I said that I had too many seeds and that it was crazy. Three jars formerly containing olives now contain, respectively, dill seed, red gladiolus seed and red gladiolus spawn or cormlets. The rest of the seed I have collected myself is contained in seven pill bottles and seven small stamp envelopes. From Dobie's and Unwin's, I have twenty-two packets of seeds, of which thirteen are of herbs and four, outsize, of radishes. In addition, there are four leftover packets from Sutton's, one intact, three of herbs. It is an impressive display. Two packets on order have yet to arrive, and Sutton's catalogue is still awaited. The seeds I collected myself would easily sow all the vacant ground. I further have rather more than thirty gladiolus corms. I don't even know where I shall put those, apart from the three white, the three pink and the one yellow one. The rest are either red or of unknown colour, not having flowered this year. As to the few hundred cormlets and the jarful of seeds, the only thing I can think of is to arrange with Donald and Bushell, the gardener, that I shall have a patch of ground at Centuries and there start a gladiolus farm.

7 December

With a *paté* at lunch, we ate the alfalfa which had been growing a mere four days in a jar, kept moist and capped with muslin and a rubber band, over the pilot light on the gas stove. It was crisp and delicious, tasting of young green peas.

8 December

This afternoon, M. went with me by taxi to the hospital to

see Mr Standeven, consultant surgeon. I was first to be called. The nurse in attendance took me to a cubicle and asked me what my trouble was. When I said that it was waterworks, she told me to take the bottom half of my clothes off. I did just that, removing my trousers and underpants, putting my shoes back on and then sitting down to wait. When she returned, she made it clear that I should have done more than blindly obey the instructions I had been given, that I should also have taken my jacket off and put on a kind of bathing wrap that was in the cubicle. These things I did and was then, carrying my jacket, taken in to Mr Standeven. Instructed to hang my jacket on a hook behind the door, I was shown to a chair facing him across a table.

"Mr Heppenstall is rather deaf," said the nurse.

"Oh, not really," said I.

My exchanges with Mr Standeven proceeded in normal voices. Towards the end, I had to take the bathing wrap off and lie on my left side on a bed, bottom towards the edge of the bed, and hoist up my knees to, the nurse said, my chin. I could not quite get them to my chin, but she said this did not matter. Then Mr Standeven dipped his fingers in something of the nature of Vaseline, shoved them up my arse and felt around. He washed his hands, while I put the bathing wrap on again and sat where I had sat before.

The nurse had to get some form which had to be filled in. While this was waited for, I asked Mr Standeven how his name was pronounced. It was pronounced as though it had been two words, "Stand Even". It was a Yorkshire name, and there was only one family of Standevens, who came from near Sowerby Bridge. That, as I pointed out, was quite near the village of Heptonstall, from which my name came. He was interested. He was a small man, not at all distinctive in appearance, in late middle age, very nice. I having mentioned it in case it was relevant, he told me that my impotence was due to the condition of my arteries.

Once the form was brought and filled in and the nurse had got me out of that room and into the cubicle, she began speaking to me as though I were very deaf indeed, telling me what I next had to do, which was to reappear at the hospital between nine and ten o'clock in the morning one day soon, as it might be tomorrow, in order to have blood and urine specimens taken. These would then be sent to a hospital, the Buckland, in Dover. An X-ray there would then be arranged, and an ambulance would fetch me. I must have looked as though I were not taking this in, for, presently, the young woman left me in the cubicle and went to sit down beside M., to whom she repeated the instructions, leaving with her the two forms which had to be handed in when blood and urine specimens were taken.

She was a very nice, conscientious nurse, not particularly pretty but not plain either, clearly a married woman. No doubt she was worried about time. There were a good many people waiting, and the next customer had been in his cubicle for half an hour. M. had recognised him as one of a homosexual pair, of mature years, who had been in the Ship when we were last there.

10 December

Yesterday morning, the same taximan took us to the hospital again to give blood and urine specimens. This morning, Martin Esslin came, driving over from Winchelsea, to record my narration for *The Trials of Captain Kidd*, which I did badly. He stayed, of course, to a lunch of braised steak, followed by cheese and a home-made chocolate *mousse*. It was very good, and he enjoyed it. *Vaut le voyage*, he said.

Martin is leaving the BBC at the end of the year. He will thereafter spend six months in the United States, teaching drama at Stanford university, and six months in England, writing. I do not much expect to see him again, though he spoke of keeping in touch.

15 December

I had long been in the habit of drinking two gin-and-tonics

and a martini before dinner, no large quantity of beer or wine with the food, with latterly diminishing frequency a cup of white coffee afterwards and then two carefully measured whiskies and water. For some time past, this quantity of liquid had ensured me a bad night. I woke at about one o'clock and then again at half-past three, in each case to pee into a chamber pot kept beside my bed. Too often, the heaving my legs out of bed would seem to activate my bowels, and I would have to go next door. That was unpleasant on cold nights. Moreover, I rarely got to sleep again after the half-past-three do. I lay in a half-doze, full of anxiety.

Last evening, I had four whiskies and water after dinner. This had to do with the emotional effect that a performance of Handel's *Messiah* always has on me, though the performance was rather a bad one from Birmingham. I awoke at a quarter to four, wanting to make water but unable to do so. This I found truly alarming. In the course of the morning, the curious blockage ceased.

17 December

This afternoon, I lay for an hour on a table bed beneath a massive and rather beautiful X-ray apparatus, while a tall, stony-faced girl with a lot of blue on her eyelids told me to breathe in, breathe out, hold my breath and breathe away, while at one point a wild-eyed Indian doctor very slowly injected fifty cubic centilitres of dye into a vein in my right arm, this being known, according to Adam, who has repeatedly had all these things, as an intravenous pylogram. I was then strapped up with an apparatus into which air was pumped, with the intention that two inflated pads should block the ducts from my kidneys to my bladder, a series of further pictures then being made.

M., of course, went with me, but at no point at which she could help was my intelligence overtaxed, though I did contrive to lose my way between the lavatory, to which I had been directed to empty my bladder before a last photograph was taken, and the room in which my particular table bed stood.

The day had begun wet. As we drove to and from Dover, there was a heavy mist. Late in the evening, it began raining heavily again. The red rose bloomed splendidly. On the wireless, we listened to Vivaldi's *Seasons*, a wonderful work. It is only during the past fifteen years or so that one has become much aware of Vivaldi, the first revelation being how much Bach owed to him, sometimes whole movements, in his instrumental music.

20 December

The rose wilted yesterday afternoon. The *Mail* today shows on the front page a terrible photograph of Vladimir Bukovsky, the Soviet dissident recently freed, and on page two a photograph of Mrs David Markham at the cottage in Coleman's Hatch, Sussex, where Bukovsky is to go. She was Olive Dehn, a writer of children's books and sister of Paul Dehn, and David, whose real name is Peter Harrison, is the hero of the hour, whose campaign on Bukovsky's behalf secured his release. He is an actor, at one time much seen on BBC television. The fact that his brother, Stephen Harrison, was a producer there advantaged him, but he was a satisfactory actor and a man of great charm. I used him twice on radio.

I first met them all before the war as friends of Eric Cocks, who died towards the end of the war with disastrous effect on my finances.[1] During the war, I, then stationed outside

---

1. Eric Cocks is portrayed, as "Richard St Hilda", in RH's autobiographical novels, *The Greater Infortune* and *The Lesser Infortune*.
   M.: "We met him before the war through the writer Oswell Blakeston. He was homosexual. We were both fond of him. When our ceiling fell down in Boundary Road, Hampstead, Rayner and I went to live in Eric's flat in St John's Wood. I went with Lindy to his sister's in Wiltshire when the air raids started on London. He had left Rayner some money in his will but, owing to events in a relative's life,

Manchester, was put up for a weekend at an inn in the Cheshire village where the senior Dehns lived, Olive being at that moment with them, Peter having just been released from prison as a conscientious objector. Old Dehn had been a merchant in Hamburg. He was chairman of his local Conservative Association and addicted to the stories of Guy de Maupassant. His great boast was that he had once killed a nigger in Jamaica.

A hero now, Peter/David was regarded as a crank while his campaign on Bukovsky's behalf went on. He is a bit of a crank. A disciple of Bertrand Russell, he also followed Wilhelm Reich. He and Olive used to revitalise themselves by sitting in an orgone box. For this practice, it may be said, they were a good advertisement. They had great vitality. This is evident in Olive's photograph, taken delightfully with another Russian refugee, Dr Martin Voikhanskaya-Fainberg, who, smiling radiantly (Olive seems helpless with laughter), looks as though she, too, had been sitting in an orgone box.

24 December

M. had a headache and felt dizzy. Yesterday, she went to see Dyer. By mistake, my notes were sent up instead of hers, which turned out to be a good thing. M. had a virus infection, a kind of 'flu (which antibiotics seem to have dealt with promptly). With my notes was a letter from Standeven, saying that there was some obstruction, but it was benign, and that he did not want to operate because of my stroke. It is Christmas Eve. The doctors are closing for Christmas. M. has made a date for me next Thursday, by which time the results of blood and urine tests and X-rays will have reached Dyer.

---

changed the will. Towards the end of the war, he came home on leave, ended up in hospital and died of a perforated ulcer. Rayner always felt rather bitter about the changed will. I suppose, on looking back, that when he came out of the army, having a bit of money would have made a difference to our lives, instead of just having í27 gratuity and a demob suit.''

30 December

There have been comings and goings in both directions. We have a great vase of daffodils in the bow window, brought by Donald on Wednesday, when there was a thick white frost. This morning, I saw Dyer. He still has no report on my blood and urine, let alone on my X-ray examination. I had thought that something could be done with drugs to shrink the prostate, in view of the fact that Standeven does not wish to operate. It is apparently not so or so only in the case of cancer.

1977

3 January

A major stamp operation is in progress. I had not intended this. At the end of a year, I normally deal with the larger French stamps and with such English stamps as have accumulated. I had missed doing it last year, so that there were more larger French stamps and more English stamps to deal with. However, I got this out of the way, needing to make only five new sheets, headed 1975-6.

I then had but the miscellaneous stamps which had accumulated in a Japanese box of modest size in which I dispose them evenly and keep them flat with two packets of twenty cigarettes. These also were more numerous than I had thought, and, while I am still putting back into the box stamps of countries of which there are very few, I have found that there are enough stamps of twenty countries to require new sheets.

The reason for so many Ghanaian stamps is the presence in Ghana of Dorothy's husband. The reason for so many Spanish ones is Isla Cameron's correspondence with Robert Graves on Majorca. I am making no attempt to arrange the Ghanaian stamps in order of date or in any other order, for none seems to have governed their issue, though there are, indeed, Christmas stamps, and others commemorate world population year, international women's year, Ghana going metric or the first anniversary of the revolution of January 13th, 1973 (unless it was 1972[1]). That must be when they kicked Nkrumah out. I wonder what became of him.[2]

1. It *was*.
2. Dr Kwame Nkrumah, overthrown in February 1966, died in exile in Romania in April 1972.

Because of the neighbours and my various disorders, I have somewhat lost interest in the garden. I no longer feel that I can attempt to make a real garden of it. I shall simply concern myself with growing bits of this and that here and there. I wish I felt that I could afford to spend any length of time at a hotel in Pewsey and really do something at Easter about the ground at Adam's church.[1] If he, alternatively, could install beds there, M. and I could perhaps go down and, isolated as the place is, also make it habitable for him in the summer.

17 January

I pay some attention to the crimes reported in the newspapers. I noted that on Christmas Eve in Paris the Prince de Broglie was shot by a policeman's son, hired by another policeman on behalf, it presently appeared, of two businessmen who owed the prince a very large sum of money. It seems a very good motive, but I have never come across it before either in a detective story or in a real-life case. Of course, you will still owe the money to your victim's estate if there is documentary evidence of the loan, and to secure and destroy that was presumably the occasion of many of the péripéties which have attended the case since.

26 January

Isla is very good at forwarding letters.[2] This one was dated Monday, the 24th. It is from a Mrs E. Gotch, assistant to Victor Bonham-Carter, secretary, The Royal Literary Fund, at an address in Ludgate Hill. It reads:

1. Adam had bought a disused church near Pewsey, Wiltshire, and was having it converted to his own design. RH and M. did spend some time at Pewsey in September 1979.
2. Isla Cameron was now living in the flat in Churton Street.

Dear Mr Heppenstall,

A friend of yours has suggested that you might care to apply to this Fund for some financial help, and for this reason I enclose an application form, together with some notes on its completion. We also need some examples of your most representative works and two letters of support from people who know you and your circumstances well.

As forms are so impersonal I wonder if you would agree that I pay you a visit to discuss problems at firsthand. I could also collect one or two of your books to save you the trouble of posting them.

I need hardly say that any application to the Fund is treated with the strictest confidence.

If you wish to apply perhaps you could telephone me one afternoon *after 2.30 p.m.* and we could fix a time for me to call. (I shall not be in tomorrow, Tuesday.)

Yours sincerely,

(Mrs) E. Gotch.

I had not heard of *Victor* Bonham-Carter, but am prejudiced against anyone with that surname.

Now, the fact of the matter is that some years ago, I did think of applying to the Royal Literary Fund, which advertises in *The Author*. That I should do so was further suggested to me by Peter Owen. It occurs to me that he could be the "friend". It could, on the other hand, be Margaret Crosland, who moves in Peter's orbit, who was officious on my behalf once before and who, alas, will suddenly discover that I think poorly of two recent books of hers, what was an interestingly unfavourable review in *London Magazine* having been so cut as to leave it merely unfavourable.

I shall reply politely to Mrs Gotch, saying that I am not at the moment in such distress that I could properly apply to the

Royal Literary Fund for financial aid, but that it might yet come to that and that I am glad to know that the Fund exists and would perhaps be willing to help me. The application form, incidentally, is so inquisitorial that I do not think I *could* fill it up, even if I wanted to. It is far more inquisitorial than an Income Tax form.

30 January

Two winter aconites out on the rockery. Out also, in frosty sunshine, on the street, the Streaker in an exiguous pair of bathing trunks, striped black and white, and nothing else. His body has taken on no winter pallor, so perhaps he uses a sunlamp. M. thinks Ruby said he was a grandfather.

9 February

Dr Dyer has wavy hair, and his beard waves. He shaves his top lip. This adds to a slight oddity of appearance conferred on him by his, by its, certainly illusory youthfulness. If he were clean-shaven, he would be handsome. His bedside manner consists in a sudden switching of all his interest on you, all lights on like a pin-table into which a penny has been newly inserted. If he is not smiling, he is ready to smile. As he must often be feeling tired or harassed, there must be a certain falsity in this, and at times one feels that he wonders who you are and what you have come to see him about. But he has soon connected. He is there. He is with you. Everyone speaks highly of him.

M. saw him on Monday (her chest) and had asked to have my notes sent up, so that we already knew the contents of Mr Standeven's further letter to him about me. It contained much what Standeven had said to me, plus the information that my blood and urine were normal, which I had forgotten to ask about. I had also omitted to ask why I continued to feel a stinging sensation when I passed water, and to this question the letter contained no answer.

4 March

On Tuesday, the 1st of the month, M. went off to London, to stay for two nights at Lindy's but mainly to see Adam, who has been depressed.

I see her very occasional absences as opportunities for committing suicide. As we sleep in separate rooms, I have wondered whether it could be done at night when she was here, but, although M. is deaf in one ear, she does hear me coughing and getting up in the night, and I fancy that going into a coma after taking barbiturates may be accompanied by heavy and unusual breathing and even moaning. If you have a strong enough dose, a day will be enough. Kenneth Allsop did away with himself successfully when his wife had gone up to London from Bridport for the day, while, according to Diana, Michael Bakewell's assistant, she had seen Bryan Johnson, apparently in good spirits, one evening, only to find him dead next morning. Indeed, I read somewhere that, although, when you take barbiturates, you may, falling into a coma, linger for some days and die of pneumonia, it is also possible for a sufficient dose to kill you in four and a half hours. But my dose is weak. I ought, I felt therefore, to do a bit of lingering.

It would probably be a long time before M. was again away for three days. On Wednesday morning, I took the small bottle containing my depleted pink draught from its place behind some of the bigger French books on my shelves and stripped off the surgical tape with which I had bound it, in part to protect it and in part to make it airtight. On its buoy out at sea, the foghorn was blowing. A blackbird sang atop a chimney on the Streaker's house. Though not strongly, the sun came out at nine o'clock.

I was still in my dressing gown at eleven o'clock. My intention was to start drinking gin-and-tonic at twelve o'clock, as usual, or a little earlier, and, after drinking three or four all at once (I had chosen that time of day because my stomach is then pretty empty of food and my digestion at its best, and so there was little chance that I would be sick), I would then take my draught and the powdered precipitate, the draught with tonic in it to make it palatable, upstairs, swallow the powder, drain the draught, rinse the glass (so that what I had done would not at first be apparent to M. when she returned) and put myself to bed. I was on my third gin-and-tonic and trembling with excess of adrenalin when I decided that I would not make the attempt just then. I did not like the opportunism whereby the timing of so important a step should depend on the accident of my wife's absence. The moment ought to be more adequately chosen. I could see how my digestion was that evening. Even tomorrow might not be too late, for M. would not be back until late afternoon.

That Wednesday afternoon, I sank forty gladiolus corms in the raised centre bed between the foliage of the hyacinths, and between the hyacinth foliage and the gladiolus holes, not for the moment filled in, sowed thyme seed. Yesterday morning, I sowed sorrel, summer and winter savory and lovage. This Friday morning, with M. around, I sowed tarragon, burnet, rue, balm and pot marjoram. I also pruned roses. The forsythia at the front is full out, and there are blue squills out.

19 March

Last evening, Lindy, Donald and the children came down to Sandwich and today were with us to lunch. In the afternoon, Donald took the girls to a children's concert. Andrew played me at chess. We played on a little board he had brought with him. I did not know that he had even learnt the rules. He was surprisingly good at the game. He had, he said, got a book. After a while, he suggested that we call a draw and proffered me his hand.

26 March

It is very cold. Today is the hundred and fiftieth anniversary of Beethoven's death, about which at one time more fuss would have been made. However, Radio 3 has had a reproduction, on Viennese recordings, of Beethoven's last concert, consisting of the *Consecration of the House* overture, the Kyrie, Credo and Agnus Dei from the *Missa Solemnis* and the ninth symphony. The chorus in this last was the Vienna State Opera chorus, and I do not think I have ever heard the sopranos' top notes less strained at. Each item was introduced at irrelevant and maddening length by Martin Cooper, who also made the surprising statement that Beethoven's reputation was based on his last string quartets.

4 April

Peter Grimes on the wireless, direct from Covent Garden. Thirty years ago, its undoubted originality meant more, because, just after the war, one was in a frame of mind to expect significant development in opera, as elsewhere. There has been no more. I still like the way the first sea interlude persists through the first scene proper and, indeed, with that widely spread arpeggio, continues to dominate the opera. I am now quickly irritated by Britten's (undoubtedly original) vocal line and his (no less undoubtedly original) ensemble writing. Opera is not about originality, unless the originality is either very discreet or on the scale of Wagner's.

5 April

This evening, Godfrey fetched us to the King's Arms in Sandwich, where we had one drink and went on to St Clement's church for a performance of Bach's St John passion. The soloists were rather poor, especially the two women, but the choir was good, the young conductor very much in control. At about nine o'clock, all the lights went out, not only in the church but, as it was to turn out, in Sandwich. It was a long time before candles were found. Godfrey, M. and I felt our way round three sides of the church and out into the churchyard and to the George & Dragon, where also the lights were out, the customers loudly and nervously witty. Then we went to try and get Godfrey's car out. It is a wide Ford Executive, and the operation was difficult. Ann had gone into the George & Dragon just as we left and, by walking, arrived at the King's Arms at the same time as ourselves. The lights came on during a very nice supper for ten people. Godfrey drove us back here. It had been a very nice evening.

6 April

A dull morning, with not much wind in the south-west. I have never been so aware of the weather as here. The general direction of the wind is apparent to us from the gilded weathervane on top of the cupola over the Marines' school of music. M. also sees the one over the ball tower, on her way into town if she goes by the sea front. The two do not always agree. Perhaps they never agree, and it is not a matter of the wind being different where there are more houses, but of one or the other weathervane being set wrong, the ball tower one I should think, though, as there are more fishing boats along there, you would think the fishermen might spot it and complain. I must get M. to look every morning and see whether the variation is constant and always in the same direction.

Desultorily in recent weeks, I have done almost a hundred pages of what I intermittently hope may turn out to be a book. It is about Elizabeth Carter, but also about Mary Blandy[1] and the bigamous duchess of Kingston, who were almost exactly contemporary with her, but had no other connection. After lunch today, M. and I kept an appointment to view Carter House. The owner is a Mrs Barrett, a tall, handsome woman of what could be a great age, but presumably isn't, since her husband was a desert rat in the last war. With her to stay was a daughter, who is a highly placed officer in the probation service in Winchester. We met the daughter after being

1. Executed in 1752 for the murder, by poison, of her father, a wealthy lawyer of Henley-on-Thames.

shown two portraits of Elizabeth Carter in the hall, both of her when young, one dressed as Minerva, with helmet and breastplate, owl, acorn and the rest.

We sat in a nice room with a big coal fire. Mrs Barrett brought out a box of bits and pieces, most of them of no great interest, and talked mainly about how she and her husband had acquired the house, in 1947, from a Pennington, a descendant of Elizabeth Carter's brother-in-law and, like him, a parson. One thing which came out of the box and at once engaged my interest was a framed broadsheet telling, in the first person, very circumstantially and well, the story of one Ambrose Gwinnett.[1] The print was too small for me to read. The daughter, about whom I had till then wished that she were not there, read it to us with great zest.

It had been spitting with rain as M. and I walked to Carter House. After our return, it came on heavy. This evening, the St John passion on the wireless. Dear me, Bach's arias are awkward for their singers. If I were a singer, as I so nearly was, I think I should refuse to sing Bach, whereas, if I were a trumpeter, I should want to play little else.

One thing one doesn't know is how good performances were in Bach's time. I feel sure that he was often faced with situations when, for instance, like last night, there was no flautist, the harpsichord was inaudible, and one wretched tenor had to double evangelist with the tenor arias and so sang in too much of a head voice all through so as to save his voice. Luckily, things are not always perfect even on the wireless. Robert Tear just then got a frog in his throat while dispatching a particularly affecting bit of recitative. He is now already in better voice again. I would like to be able to say that I enjoyed last evening's performance better than I am so far enjoying this. It would not be true. Oh, dear, Tear is squawking again. What an unfortunate evening he is having.

1. Retold by RH in an essay, "The Half-Hanging of Ambrose Gwinnett", which appears in the anthology, *The Pleasures of Murder*, edited by Jonathan Goodman; Allison & Busby, 1983.

What Godfrey, M. and I missed last night was the wonderful final chorus, which is perhaps the best bit of the whole work. I believe that, after we had gone, they made some attempt to set this up by candlelight.

19 April

Sunday was a lovely day, but turned dull in the late afternoon. Yesterday and today were grey and cold. Coming into Deal to shop and meet for coffee-drinking, Dorothy brought M. my Deacon Brodie review from the *Sunday Times*. They only, *mirabile dictu*, cut one sentence, without greatly affecting the sense of what I said.

It is almost a week since Adam brought down the *Observer* containing a first instalment from Paul Ferris's biography of Dylan Thomas. Only today have I sent a letter to *The Observer* to correct Ferris's statement that in early 1936 I kept a diary. It was, I suppose, a reasonable deduction that only so could I, in *Four Absentees*, have given a precise date to the occasion when, while proceeding in the direction of Charlotte Street to find a pub, Thomas coughed, spat, regarded the spittle and said, "Blood, boy! That's the stuff!" In fact, I was able to date this occasion through the combination of a good memory with the date on a letter from Dylan. I don't like it to be thought that I was keeping a diary in those days or at any rate one in which I noted the sayings of the potentially great, for to me Dylan Thomas was already that.

23 April

This morning, M. saw a white flag with a red cross flying over St George's church. It is, of course, St George's day. Three years ago, we moved into Churton Street. It is rather more than two years since I moved out. The question is whether we are better off now than we were then. I certainly could not have gone on living at Churton Street, with the noise and the smells. We have noise here, but no smells. Take it by and large, Deal is a dreary hole. There were occasional parties in London. But they are not possibilities between which one could still choose, and my health has deteriorated. M.'s, too, I suppose, though not so conspicuously. No doubt we shall die here, or one of us will and the other go to live for a while in Campden Hill Square. For purely selfish reasons, I hope that I shall be the one to die first. I can't think how I should manage with a dying woman.

21 May

A paperback and a hard-cover copy of *Two Moons* this morning. Nicely done, though the drawing on the jacket is puzzling. I thought of ringing Clive Allison, whom I have an excellent reason for ringing, since he writes of meaning to live in Deal and says that he has been negotiating for a tiny cottage. I decide to wait until tomorrow, when there may be reviews in the Sunday papers.

22 May

There are, in *The Observer* and *The Sunday Times*, and both are incredibly vicious. They are by Lorna Sage and Ronald Harwood, whoever they may be. Both devote their space to the way the book is laid out and hardly mention its content. Indeed, Harwood says nothing whatever about the content, but simply makes clever remarks about the form. To him, I am, though a distinguished man of letters, in this novel merely eccentric. To Sage, I am mad.

29 May

Nothing again in *The Sunday Telegraph*. There was a bit in *The Guardian* on Thursday, by Christopher Wordsworth, whom I suppose to be a respectable kind of bloke. M. saw it at the public library and tried to get it down in shorthand, but then could not read her shorthand back. It was short, but contained the word "riveting". There are in fact possible quotes in the *Observer* and *Sunday Times* pieces, too. "Insidiously interesting" (*Observer*). "One was bound to admire the prose and the author's acute powers of observation" (*Sunday Times*). The reviewers are indignant. It is possible to read most novels skippingly, but of *Two Moons* every word must be read, not in the easiest order. A fiction reviewer expects to give so much time each week to reading. With *Two Moons*, he would have to double the time. This he resents. He refuses to do it. I wrote to John Whitley at *The Sunday Times* to say that, as Mr Harwood had found himself unable to read the book (he said that), he should not have reviewed it and that he, John Whitley, should not have let the non-review appear in print. I suggest that he now gets a second review.

With the pork for Sunday lunch today, we are eating homegrown spinach. For several weeks now, homegrown radishes have been speared and put in the martinis instead of olives.

2 June

The weather has turned colder, though it is the same north-east wind which keeps blowing.

On Tuesday, the duke of Kent was down to view the *Hampshire Rose* lifeboat and dedicate the auxiliary inshore boat. He wore a light suit and no overcoat.

As his party were ready to move off, he remarked to a bystander: "It's very healthy down here."

Two better reviews today, in *The Times* and the *Financial Times*, especially good in the latter. Martin Seymour-Smith is a man about whom I have long had mixed feelings and who clearly had mixed feeling about me. These now seem to have become wholly positive and sensitively, modestly so. I am much pleased.

1 July

There has been much commotion all year about the prospect of the Marines leaving Deal and going to Portsmouth. We have all signed petitions. Now it appears that they are not to go for three years and that we are in fact to have five hundred more Marines, the 41st commando, recently disbanded in Malta and to be reformed. This will delight wholesale tradesmen and anyone who can supply married quarters. The rest of us will be glad to keep our musicians.

This morning, four hundred of the existing Marines, with some reservists, marched through Deal, led by the staff band, exercising their right as freemen of Deal to march with drums beating and bayonets fixed. The march celebrated the Queen's silver jubilee, which has not otherwise caused a great to-do here.

A small crowd had gathered at our corner. I invariably become tearful on these occasions and hoped that I should not attract the attention of other spectators either by visible moisture or, what would be worse, by a sudden, audible gulp. I need not have worried. The well-shone pairs of club feet marched, five abreast, round the corner, and the young, pink, solemn and, I suppose, stupid faces (but all faces, especially young ones, look stupid when they are held expressionlessly rigid) all passed, without me betraying myself.

15 July

Death of William Gerhardi, aged 82. A brilliant novelist fifty years ago, a fearful ass since.

It rained heavily in the night, and this morning my vine was down. But we live in a bower of roses. Every morning or almost every morning, a few new ones are brought in, a few old ones thrown out. The colour pattern changes. So does the scent pattern.

1 August

Some neighbours had a frightful shouting match, very clearly audible to us throughout the house and garden, especially in the kitchen, though we could not make out what was being said. The man, in a raucous, working-class voice, went on yelling for half an hour with such hate-filled fury that I felt sure the row must end in physical violence and possibly murder. I hoped it would.

3 August

A beef stew, heavily seasoned with coriander seeds. A great success. M. had the excellent idea that next time we would put the coriander seeds in the pepper mill. The orchestra in the promenade concert was the BBC Welsh symphony orchestra, which I commonly speak of as the worst of the regional orchestras, though in fact the Scottish is just as bad. The great thing was the Mendelssohn violin concerto, in which the soloist, of whom I had not heard, was Iona Brown.

"And," the announcer said, "if I may be forgiven for saying so, since it has nothing to do with the music, Miss Brown looks a picture." A pretty little thing, one imagined, probably dark in colouring, dressed in *chiffon*. But, of course, she might equally have been a big, splendid girl with flaming hair.

That was certainly the picture her performance suggested. It was tremendously strong, with occasional odd displays of impulsiveness. The last movement she took at a terrific lick, and the orchestra went along with her. In the applause at the end, there was less shouting than one expects from prom audiences, but the clapping was massive. If this was Iona Brown's prom *début*, she is made.

The horrible Archbishop Makarios is dead, at only 63. We have a blue rose. Of course, it isn't blue, it is lilac, but as roses go it is blue.

14 August

The promenade concert on Monday evening was preceded by a half-hour talk with gramophone records on Solomon, who I was again persuaded was the best of all the pianists of our time. I first heard him on a Sunday evening in a theatre in Rhyl, where I was at a school camp, in 1929. What I particularly remember is a Chopin nocturne in a great many flats, D flat or even D flat minor, to which I became addicted.

Yesterday, Henry Williamson died, aged only 81. I had thought him more. He was an enchanting, though rather a foolish, man, perhaps the more enchanting for being so foolish in so friendly a way, without any malice.

30 August

The end of another month, and summer is certainly ended. It has been a poor summer, not wet but almost uniformly grey and cold. I have managed to collect a fair herb harvest, but had a disaster with my coriander seeds. I thought I had dried them well, but they went mildewy in the jar. I decided that I would wash off the mildew and dry the seeds again. I ran them under hot water, and this washed off a brown liquid which contained all the flavour, so that, when I had dried the seeds again, they were tasteless. I had become very fond of a beef stew heavily flavoured with coriander. I even liked the smell, though I have seen this described as fetid.

There is the usual end-of-season fair in Victoria Park, which is past the end of Gilford Road, therefore inland and to the west of here. At intervals during the week, I have seen the big, luxurious caravans driving past in strings of two or three. The wind is in the west, and we hear the dreadful music, which is not at all what fairground music used to be, but pop records enormously amplified. Despite this, M. and I might have walked up but for the coldness and windiness of the grey evening. As Friday is, though not to the same extent as Saturday, an evening of motor-bikes and lechery, there may be some custom at the fair now that it is dark. In the morning, I shall find beer bottles and cans and curious food packages thrown over the wall on the Gilford Road side of our garden, more of them perhaps since I cut the big lilac down a foot and a half.

8 December

The main Britten work at St Clement's in Sandwich on Tuesday was his *St Nicolas*. This time, the lights went before the performance began. However, a system of emergency lighting had been installed, and the lights came on in due course, though at first the organ would not play and had to be replaced by a piano. *St Nicolas* began to liven up when Peter Pears came in at tremendous volume, to be joined presently by the organ. The selection called "Nicolas and the Pickled Boys" (I have not, alas, discovered what pickled boys are) was both pleasurable and impressive.

Yesterday, Sir Rex Niven looked in for drinks in the evening. He is 79, but used to do all the shopping even while his wife was still alive. He is also in far better intellectual form than I am, thirteen years younger. We did not get him much on Nigeria, but he was first-rate on a subject which is divisive in Deal at the moment and which has got into the national Sundays, both the *People* and the *Mirror*. This is the vicar's attempt to get two people out of the other half of his divided vicarage, where they pay £5 a week, not to him but to the church commissioners, and install rent-free two young people with whom he wished to live in community.

I had only two views on this matter. First, I did not like Peter Bowers, in the parish magazine, indicating that it was by divine guidance that he wished to make the change. On the other hand, I was annoyed by ----, who never goes to church and is an old Lefty, expressing indignation, which led me to support Bowers, M.'s churchgoing last Sunday having been quite specifically an expression of solidarity with him.

Four snowdrops have poked their tips through the soil under the ceanothus tree.

16 December

I have several times had rather a bad pain across the chest, sometimes thought it might be indigestion, at other times wondered whether it was due to excessive smoking and whether this had affected my lungs. Late yesterday morning, it was quite bad. A cold sweat broke out on my forehead, and a pain crept down my left arm into the hand, which made me wonder if it could possibly be angina. There was little of the pain left this morning, but M., without my agreement, went round to the doctors' and spoke to Sheila, the head receptionist, who took it upon herself to say that one of the doctors would presently visit me.

First came round, in fact, a nurse, Sister Ellender, who is permanently employed at those doctors', a thin, married, fairly pretty and terribly nice and friendly soul. She made me go upstairs and lie on my bed and carried out an electro-cardiogram, which took quite a long time. Then, Dr Dyer being away, appeared Dr Cameron, darker-bearded, his hair receding a little, older than Dyer. He studied the electro-cardiogram tape, then informed me that I had had a small coronary thrombosis.

He wanted me to give up smoking. He also wanted me not to walk up or down stairs. I shall obey him in neither respect. I shall go up and down stairs twice a day, to rest in the afternoon and to sleep (or so I hope) at night, though I will not go up or down unnecessarily. I am sure that he would rather I walked slowly upstairs than that I exerted myself to bring my bed down. As to smoking, I will try to cut it down a bit and not to inhale.

On the wireless this evening, a performance of Berlioz's *L'Enfance du Christ*, a work of which I have been particularly fond since hearing it at St Bartholomew the Great, a wonderful church, conducted by Colin Davis, some ten years ago. I immediately bought a recording, under Charles Münch, and borrowed Adam's record-player purely in order to be able to play it. Of the singers in the Colin Davis performance, I remember only that Peter Pears was singing the narrator, as he was this evening, but this evening wobbling as he did very little at St Clement's in Sandwich ten days ago.

The singers this evening should have been all right. There were Janet Baker, who has many merits, though she ought not to sing in French, which she does very peculiarly, and Donald McIntyre, who is a very adequate Wotan in this year's *Ring*, which we are getting all day on Sundays. It would have been better if the work had been sung in English. Then Sir Charles Groves might have understood the libretto, might have understood that what followed the opening narration was a march and that the first singers were conducting a brisk exchange as they passed each other in the street at night and that the singing of the sorcerers should have been quick, building up to the massacre of the innocents. Sir Groves's only idea seemed to be that this was all sacred music and ought therefore to be taken slowly. Even in parts two and three, all his tempi were too slow, or, if they began right, soon *ritenuto*'d, with never a corresponding *accelerando*. This was even the case with the flute and harp dancing. The effect throughout was dirgelike and lifeless. I suppose that I ought not to have expected it to be otherwise, but, even after the dreadful first part, I thought it would be all right for the shepherds' chorus and that even Sir Groves might understand that Joseph was growing desperate as he knocked at door after door or that the singer would take matters into his own hands. I almost gave myself another coronary or stroke by inwardly urging them to get a move on. M. in fact warned me.

18 December

Another thing that is likely to give me a further coronary thrombosis is the juddering of Gwyneth Jones's voice as Brünnhilde. This morning, for the first thirty-five minutes, she was better than she had been in *Siegfried* last Sunday, and I wondered if the conductor, Pierre Boulez, had dared, between the two operas, to tell her about it, for it must be as difficult as telling somebody that they suffer from B.O. It is not that Gwyneth Jones's breathing apparatus is irrevocably broken down and that she can do nothing but wobble on long, loud notes. This morning, she did not begin to wobble until she was bidding farewell to Siegfried. And then it was not on her highest notes, but on those in the middle of her range. The whole thing suddenly became insufferable. As a matter of fact, in the hall of the Gibichungs, Gutrube was almost as bad, but she has less to sing, and her thinner voice had not the same volume as Gwyneth Jones's, so that one was able to listen to Gunther, Hagen and Siegfried with a fair contentment, all three having reasonably steady voices. Not that their music is of the finest.

Then back to Brünnhilde on the mountain, at her wobbliest. Waltraute was better. Another English singer, Yvonne Minton. A mezzo and less taxed, of course. In came Siegfried, pretending to be Gunther, and what Gwyneth Jones mainly had to do, after wobbling for a while, was scream when he took the ring from her. This, naturally, she did very well.

Thereafter, I missed the whole of act two and the interesting part of act three, including Siegfried's funeral march, which I particularly wanted to hear. I came back only in time for more of Gwyneth Jones's screeching and wobbling, which then went on to the end of the performance. After it all, the audience sounded in an ugly mood. In general, the booing and so on has been taken as a sign of dissatisfaction with the sets and stage effects in this modernistic production, but I do not believe it. This was Gwyneth Jones's *Ring* and will be remembered as such.

2 February

I have just had a second look at some ivory from the Congo which Dorothy gave M. because Adam has started carving ivory.

Dorothy's connection with Africa goes back forty years, though she has been back in England at least twenty-five. She first went to Nigeria as a teaching nurse and there married George, by whom she had two sons. When the boys were settled at a school here, George went back to Ghana, which must then still have been known as the Gold Coast. Last year, he lost his job in Ghana and has been home in Kingsdown ever since, but all the time applying for new jobs in Ghana. He is seventy-two or seventy-three years old, a small and insignificant-looking man . He is now planning to return to Ghana. None of our numerous black men or those in the West Indies and the United States seem to fancy the place or anywhere in Africa. There is, that is to say, no black equivalent of a Zionist movement. To say no more about it, this is strange.

22 February

Hallam Tennyson here on Monday, recording me on Dylan Thomas. That day, maddening letter from Inland Revenue, charging me £23.25 on my old-age pension for 1976-77, pretending that it was impossible to deduct this for that year.

My tax for this year on the said pension will be up by about £350. That is £600 to be paid. The lower bank rate means that there will be less interest on my deposit account. My current account had kept fairly steady, but I had ignored the fact that what was keeping it steady was my old-age pension. By the end of this year, I shall be having to keep it steady by taking money from my deposit account, which will further lower the interest on that, an important part of my income. The skids are under us financially, quite apart from rising prices.

M. went out shopping this morning and again, for eggs, which she had forgotten, after tea. I cannot help. I can no longer walk as far as the shops.

I have nothing to read, and, as usual now, there is no music worth listening to on the wireless this evening. Over recent weeks, we have had a surfeit of Schoenberg, Berg and Webern (we were getting quite a lot of them before) and of somebody call Berio and of another humbug, Lutoslawski, with, oddly, constant Beethoven piano concertos and, of course, Shostakovich. Most of it played by the BBC Welsh and Scottish orchestras, the Liverpool Philharmonic, the Birmingham this, the Bournemouth that and so on, all of which it seems the BBC had to support on pain of a general strike by the musicians' union.

25 February

Margaret Belassis lives in one of the small, pretty houses in Victoria Road. She is a writer, her greatest success having been a novel called *Attic and Area,* a Victorian pastiche.[1] She is a robust woman, with strong legs, who must have been pretty at one time. I suppose that she will be sixty, though it may be less. She is a fearful chatterbox, but we rather like her.

I am very reluctant to lend books, even to people who I feel certain will return them. She managed, nevertheless, to talk out of me one of the later volumes in the Jackson *Newgate*

1. Published under the pseudonym of "Francesca Marton", London, 1948.

Calendar. She turned up the following, which is of local interest and will be going into the next issue of the magazine she edits for the Deal Society. On a date towards the end of 1793,

> ...A man of shabby appearance called at the New Inn, Deal, and dined there, and after having gone out returned and supped there. He appeared particularly anxious to remain in the house unseen, which, together with his appearing to be disguised in a wig that did not fit him, led the waiter to suspect that he had done some act which had induced him to disguise his person, and to wish to sail from thence by some outward-bound vessel. The waiter the next morning sent to the Mayor in order to relate his suspicions, and on the way thither observed some bills pasted up describing the person of Lyons....

This was James Lyons, a forger awaiting trial, who had escaped from Newgate.

> ...and offering £200 reward for apprehending him, he was accordingly secured, and Carpmeal [a Bow Street runner], from whose custody he escaped, and who was at Dover in search of him, was sent for, and identified his person; but the Mayor refusing to send him to London without a warrant from one of the Bow Street magistrates, Carpmeal came to town and obtained a warrant to bring him, with which he returned to Deal.

There are interesting details connected with this case. What Lyons was charged with forging were "receipts for scrip in three per Cent Ann. for 1783, to the amount of £16,000, with intent to defraud the Bank of England". This, it is true, may be as clear as daylight to anyone less financially illiterate than myself. He had sent his sister in man's clothes to the Stock Exchange to give these receipts to a stockbroker who would sell them and meet her with the money next day. He had told his sister that the reason for sending her in man's clothes was that the scrip was to be sold for Lady Bridget Tollemache and that, if he brought it to market himself, it would be understood for whom he was selling it, and he should be prevented from getting so great a price for it as he otherwise might. This was, of course, only a tale for the sister, who seems to have been an unreliable woman, but it does suggest that he was known on the Stock Exchange and also that he was credibly connected with Lady Bridget, of whom I fear I know nothing. The sister had failed to keep her appointment next day with the stockbroker, and so, of the first £10,000 sold, Lyons had received nothing. Forgery being perceived in the receipts for the remaining £6,000 and officers from Bow Street appearing at a correct address she had given the stockbrokers for herself under the man's name she was assuming, the sister had blabbed.

The trial was interesting. It took place on January 17th, 1794, presumably at the Old Bailey. Lyons pleaded guilty on all twelve counts in the indictment, though forgery was at the time a capital offence. The judge advised him "in a very pathetic manner" to alter his plea, and the indictment was read again. Lyons still pleaded guilty, which, of course, meant that, by English law, he would be automatically convicted, sentenced and hanged. Counsel for the prosecution now joined in and urged him to alter his plea, without effect. The judge asked him why he persisted in pleading guilty. He said that it was due to the poignancy of his feelings on reflecting that his sister was the principal evidence against him. Whereupon his counsel (who in those days were not allowed to address the court in defence of their client) directed him to demur to the indictment, as the determination of the case would then devolve upon the judges. He demurred.

In a few days after, his demurrer came on to be argued at the Old Bailey, but the decision of it was postponed to a future day.

It was postponed in fact for over a year.

May, 1795, Mr. Justice Grose informed the prisoner that it was the opinion of the Judges that the crime which he was guilty of was not that stated in the indictment, and upon these grounds it appeared not sufficient nor a good one. The Judges were therefore agreed that judgment should be given against the Crown.

Lucky Mr Lyons, it seems we must say, unless we suppose that he wanted to be hanged. The determination not to convict him was quite extraordinary, since there is no suggestion that he was a gentleman or in any way a privileged person, and, anyway, gentlemen were hanged for forgery. The only explanation I can think of is that Lady Bridget Tollemache was fond of him and very influential. Knapp & Baldwin miss the case out of their *Newgate Calendar,* presumably because it so contradicts what they say about the bloodiness of English law.

3 March

The late morning turning out sunny, M. hurried back from her shopping and urged me to make today the occasion for doing what I have for some time been saying that I wanted to do on the first propitious day, *viz*, make a note-taking excursion to and along the pier. Not expecting her back before noon, I was in fact thinking of doing this without her. My anxiety that the weather should be just right was due to a felling that to walk to the pier would so tax me that, the moment I was on it, I should need to sit down, but the interest of pacing the distance to the pier and of noting, every hundred paces, what boats I had come to or what lay across the road was such that, walking with a stick, I continued pacing to the end of the pier, where I counted the steps down to the lower level and examined, as far as was possible, the outside of the building which housed a bar, a tea room and the public conveniences.

Here, I did indeed sit down, in the bar, which we found

open and where we drank gin-and-tonics, but felt that this was part of my research, that I needed to know what sort of a bar it was and could hardly look around without drinking something. The fact was that I had received a disappointment, expecting to see fisherman on the lower level and to walk down there, but finding that repairs were still in progress after the January gales and that the lower level was closed to the public. Anyway, after one drink, we set off back, counting shelters, lamp-posts, litter-bins, fishermen and their rods and, on the promenade, boats and petrol engines, houses in Deal Castle Road and so on, arriving back here not too tired and with pages of notes, which I have now started trying to incorporate into a narrative, goodness only knows to what purpose. I was bucked up, and M., whose bronchitis had come back, seems better.

11 April

I am reading, for the first time, a book by Gore Vidal, *Myron*, apparently a sequel to the more famous *Myra Breckinridge*. It has not so far made me laugh, which is remarkable in view of its uninterrupted jokiness. I do sometimes laugh at homosexual jokes. I am also very much in favour of homosexuality. If everybody were homosexual, the world's greatest problem, that of overpopulation, would be solved. Any breeding that was still felt to be necessary could be done by artificial insemination.

20 April

Music one takes the trouble to get up and go out for is generally more satisfying, if it is at all good. This evening, Ann and Godfrey called and drove us to the Marines' church for Lieut.-Col. Paul Neville's farewell concert, a performance of Verdi's *Requiem*. We had been led to expect only a modest attendance, but the long church was full to capacity and may have held as many as a thousand people. I have very little impression of the exterior of the church, but inside it is splendid in, I fancy, a between-wars manner, austere, a bit Lutyenesque.

The acoustics are good, which is as well, because we were sitting in the back row. After the interval, the woman on my left, who at the beginning of the concert had sung "God Save the Queen" with great conviction and a pronounced wobble, started joining in the choruses. At last, in exasperation I said, "For Christ's sake, woman!" and put an end to this nuisance.

23 April

At a quarter past two, Olga Rickard[1] came round and wondered if we would care to go for a drive to the other side of Canterbury and look at the cherry in bloom. Well, the cherry was not yet in bloom, but Stanley drove us far into west Kent, and we looked at two churches, those of Eastling and Doddington. The day was sunny, though with some mist. Stanley Rickard is a good, fast driver. He was more interested in Doddington, but Eastling pleased me more, by reason of its Elizabethan family monument (husband and wife kneeling, with their sons and daughters kneeling behind them, sons behind father, daughters behind mother, a little as at Wingham, though with fewer daughters) and its yew trees, one of enormous antiquity. We got back a little too late for M. to go to church, as she had intended.

Tomorrow, the *Waverley* is supposed to paddle across the Thames estuary to Clacton and back. Given better weather, I might have been tempted by this, had it not been for the prospect of the disco blaring in the bar and on deck. The young are lucky in their love of noise. It fits them for the life of today, which they would not be able to face without it.

28 June

Today is grey, and a western wind is blowing with small rain. M. is off on a coach outing with the history society to

1. A near-neighbour.

Great Dexter, a fifteenth-century manor house at Northiam in Sussex, beyond Rye, where they will stop to eat their sandwiches. They are not expected back until half past seven, so that I have ample time for a suicide attempt. In case I was able to screw myself up to this, I carefully ate only a piece of toast for breakfast.

M. left the house at a quarter to eleven. I got my suicide dose out, put it on the table by my typewriter and from eleven to twelve contemplated it. At noon, I mixed myself a gin-and-tonic and put the dose back, behind the books in the crime room where I now keep it. The pink liquid occupies about two-thirds of a sizeable pill bottle. Attached to one side of this by Sellotape is a small stamp packet containing the pounded crystal precipitated earlier by a larger quantity of pink liquid. The visual effect is pleasing.

The weather here brightened a little at about four o'clock in the afternoon, but was then overcast again. Though it was spitting in Rye at lunchtime, the bright period in Sussex was longer. M. greatly enjoyed her outing. She has brought back six coloured photographic postcards of Great Dexter. These are for Adam.

30 June

I have been reading *Nelson, the Essential Hero*, by Ernle Bradford,[1] and bits of *Sir William Hamilton, Envoy Extraordinary*, by Brian Fothergill,[2] both from the public library and both remarkably clean. My purpose was to learn as much as I could about the Hamiltons' visit to Deal in 1801, when Nelson was in the Downs. This was after the battle of Copenhagen, and he had been put in command of a large flotilla of frigates and other small ships to protect our south-east coast, from Beachy Head to Orford Ness, against any incursion by Napoleon, whose grand army was then encamped at Boulogne. I had

1. London, 1977.
2. London, 1969.

hoped there might be some mention of Elizabeth Carter, then presumably here after a bad attack of erysipelas in London the previous winter.

The Hamiltons stayed a fortnight at the Royal hotel or Three Kings, as it then was. There were excursions to Ramsgate, Walmer and Dover castle, and Sir William fished, and Emma "could take the benefit of sea bathing". On the way to Walmer and Dover, the carriage would pass Elizabeth Carter's house, and somebody would no doubt point out to her which was Nelson's frigate, the *Medusa*, while, as the Three Kings was barely a quarter of a mile away, she may have seen the small, one-eyed, one-armed man come ashore there from a pinnace. His infatuation was already a public scandal. Lady Hamilton had already borne him a daughter. Mrs Carter would hardly have approved, but indeed was not a gossiping sort of woman and may not have known.

10 July

This evening, we were dined at the Royal, with its new carpet in the dining-room, by Simon Raven, whom we had not seen for almost two years, though we know that he was in Deal last summer.

20 July

M. to London to see Adam. The usual routine here, with the usual lack of effect. In the afternoon, I greatly regretted this, but by then had food in my stomach and too short a time before M.'s return.

There are no further entries until April 1980. RH gives reasons for the lacuna in the entry for June 10th, 1980.

1980

4 April

Two days ago, I at last received from Benjamin Glazebrook at Constable's publishers, a letter, fifteen weeks overdue, in which he expressed the firm's reactions to the type-script, which I had sent them last December, of *Tales from the Newgate Calendar,* a book they had commissioned. They found too much that was personal and even autobiographical in this.

After a day's resistance to the idea of making changes, which under contract I am not obliged to do, I have started making them on a carbon copy I have of the typescript and shall presently type these out, with page and line references, on sheets which I shall send them, letting them copy or insert them in the existing typescript, which I was determined not to have back here, with the trouble and expense of sending it off again.

This typing will be unwelcome. Before doing it, there is at least one passage I must copy out from a borrowed copy of Christopher Sykes's life of Evelyn Waugh. I don't think I shall write to Sykes. It would be difficult not to sound too polite.

8 April

Christopher Sykes's biography of Evelyn Waugh came out in 1975. I have only just read it, having been loaned a copy of it by Alan Brien's friend, Mike Hill. It contained the following passage:

It was the custom then [apparently in 1945] for the Home Service (now Radio 4) to introduce the Sovereign's Christmas broadcast by an hour's "world round-up" programme. It had been decided to approach Evelyn in the hope that he would take on the task of introducing the programme. It was felt at Broadcasting House that the Corporation should send as their ambassador a literary man. An appointment was made at the Hyde Park Hotel. With singular maladroitness the emissary chosen was a disappointed novelist, a deeply class-conscious man whose self-esteem bordered on mania, and who regarded Evelyn's work as decidedly inferior to his own. Being a man who looked on good manners as servility unworthy of genius, he did not attempt to win Evelyn's agreement by any exercise of charm, wisely perhaps as he had little to exercise. He preferred an attempt at impressing the other.

Evelyn was angered by the incident which he long remembered. He said to me once, "Why does your Corporation send people like Kurkweiler to me and expect to get anything out of me?" In fact the BBC emissary bore a sturdy English name, but Evelyn always insisted that this man (who later displayed some sympathy with Nazism) was a German Jewish refugee whose real name was Kurkweiler. The proposition came to nothing.

That Kurkweiler was myself readers will recognise if they remember my account of my one meeting with Evelyn Waugh. That Waugh must have given Sykes my real name and that Sykes therefore knew it was me follows from his statement that "in fact the BBC emissary bore a sturdy English name" (as perhaps only a fellow-Yorkshireman would know for certain, for the name "Heppenstall" is often supposed to be foreign, while "Sykes" is only less common than "Walker" in Huddersfield). Whether Sykes's memory or Waugh's original account to him is at fault I do not know, but the meeting took place not at the Hyde Park hotel, but at White's club.

My immediate boss, Laurence Gilliam, was the only man who with certainty knew of the meeting at the time. It was Laurence who, maladroitly or not, had deputed me to arrange the meeting. This was because it was I who had suggested Waugh as an alternative to T.S. Eliot, known or supposed to be unavailable. The great inducement was the amount of foreign currency to be put at the disposition of whoever introduced the round-up from whichever European capital he chose (having visited others during the period before Christmas). Despite certain misgivings about Waugh's social posture, I greatly admired his writing.

I could only be regarded as a "disappointed" novelist in that I had been lugged into the ranks of the army for four and a half years so soon after the appearance of my first novel, which had been a succès both de scandale and d'estime. At the time of my call-up, I had just begun work on a second novel, which I did indeed finish while in the army, during an exceptionally pleasant interval in that seemingly interminable servitude. This had gone pretty well, despite being put out in a limited edition at a high price by publishers who feared repercussions from certain passages. I had not yet begun a third novel, having come out of the army with a gratuity totalling twenty-seven pounds and needing a job at once. I had signed on the first dotted line to appear under my nose and, if the date of my meeting with Evelyn Waugh was indeed in the autumn of 1945, I had been at the BBC for no more than a few months, still finding my way in that complicated world, never having produced a programme, not even a member of staff but under probationary programme contract for some months more.

It is true that I should have voted Labour had I received voting papers for that year's general election, but I have never been "class-conscious" in the sense in which the paragraph immediately preceding the two of Christopher Sykes's which I have quoted makes it plain that he understands by the expression, as well as what he means by a "disappointed" novelist.

> Though the Corporation had several distinguished writers and poets working for it, a larger proportion of those responsible for the literary part of its output were men of talent who had not fulfilled earlier promise. They were naturally envious of one whose gifts, in their own estimation, were in no way above theirs, but who, nevertheless, had hit the jackpot. Most of such people were extremely class-conscious and thus repelled by his extreme conservatism, and his openly expressed contempt for the age of the common man. They represented that host of readers who had resented Evelyn's unsympathetic portrayal of Hooper in *Brideshead Revisited*. When Evelyn offered the BBC *Helena*, the novel by him that they most despised, these people instinctively obstructed its chance of success.

I myself have never expressed or even felt any resentment against the portrayal of Hooper, having met too many Hoopers in my time. I don't remember ever expressing an opinion of *Helena*, though I did think it Evelyn Waugh's least successful novel, as Sykes himself evidently considers it earlier in his book, and as it evidently was commercially, whence Waugh's anxiety to increase his earnings on it by having it broadcast. The only thing I can remember saying to Waugh which he might have considered an attempt to impress him was my telling him that I had once stayed at Campion Hall. If he had doubted my word on this, he could easily have found out that it was so by asking Fr. D'Arcy. As to class-consciousness in general, I should have thought that Sykes was to make himself appear prone to it by his contribution to Nancy Mitford's dreadful U and non-U game. As to my supposed later sympathy with Nazism, I cannot even guess what that may have resulted from, something I said jokingly, no doubt.

What follows my first quotation is peculiar:

> This had happened six years before, but the memory lingered on, and "Kurkweiler", accepted by his employers at his own enormous valuation, was of weight in Third Programme counsels. The opinion was circulated, propagated, encouraged, and almost turned into a decision that *Helena* was not worth any considerable expense and need not involve first-rate actors. I wanted something very much more ambitious, and in the end obtained it. Evelyn had made the offer in January 1951 and from March the battle of *Helena* occupied most of the year till I recorded the production, before the December broadcast, in October.

I don't understand how there can possibly have been a battle of *Helena* in 1951, while Harman Grisewood still controlled Third Progamme, unless he objected to Sykes's intention of dramatising only the novel's second part. For what I believe was his very first production, he also seems to have insisted on a programme budget which would enable him to employ two such expensive actors as John Gielgud and Flora Robson. I, certainly, had nothing to do with such difficulties as he may have experienced over this wasteful employment by a novice producer on a programme I did not even listen to.

In the difficulties he more probably experienced in placing a talk by Waugh on P.G. Wodehouse in 1961, even Sykes does not pretend that I played any active part, but only says: "The 'Kurkweiler' affair was not forgotten." As a matter of fact, I thought this talk a thoroughly good idea and believe that it did much to dispel the cloud which had hung far too long over Wodehouse. I had myself just published, in *The Times Literary Supplement*, a middle-page article in praise of P.G. Wodehouse.

Sykes's onslaught has filled me with shocked surprise. The whole time we were colleagues, he had appeared friendly to me. So he had on the one occasion when we had met since. At any moment, he could have asked me for my account of my one meeting with Evelyn Waugh, whom even he shows to have been a frequent mythomaniac. If he had nursed an intense dislike of me for years, he had been guilty of sustained hypocrisy, to say the least. Perhaps his enmity dated only from 1969, when he read my account of him in *Portrait of the Artist as a Professional Man*. It may be that Christopher Sykes is too sensitive about his wobbling jowls and that to see these mentioned may have touched off a streak of paranoia.

15 May

No fewer than twenty-five pages of revision to *Tales from the Newgate Calendar* were posted off to Glazebrook on April 9th, many of these on foolscap paper and much of it single-spaced. This represented a mighty effort on my part.

On April 11th, I have a handwritten diary note which reads simply, "Saying things". It stops there, as though I were unable to find the word "wrong" which I later adopted or any other form of words to describe the disability of speech I had begun to exhibit. I was becoming tongue-tied. I used the wrong words. I put my words in the wrong order. I also failed to find the words I wanted and would lapse into silence in mid-sentence. At the same time, I had formed a disinclination to read, together with a failure to concentrate for long on what I was reading, and a growing confusion as I read, so that I would keep having to go back to the beginnings of paragraphs.

This was particularly awkward in that Julian Symons, who recently came to live in Walmer and with whom and his wife we had enjoyed three social occasions, had just sent me a copy of his new book, a novel based on the case of Adelaide Bartlett.[1] I did my best to read this book with care, but found in the end that I had missed the half of it, and to this day I have not thanked Julian for it, in part because I was afraid that on the telephone I should become confused, while, after so much exemplary typing, I had suddenly again become unable to type so much as a short note, let alone write one by hand.

At first, I thought that I was just tired. Saturday, April 12th, was the date of a splendid dinner in Ramsgate, to which we were taken by Michael Hosking and Clive Allison, who shared its cost. At this, I was all right, though next day I noted that I was "saying things wrong" and did so again on April 18th and 19th. I began to wonder if I had had a further and even slighter stroke, which had come on bit by bit and not all at once, brought on by annoyance with Christopher Sykes and by heavy, urgent typing.

I had no further symptoms, except that on certain days I was a bit wobbly and very weak. I did not visit Dr Dyer and at the moment I seem recovered, at any rate as far as typing is concerned.

10 June

The nuisance from neighbours in part accounts for my failure to keep up this journal for over a year, this and the depression over the pains of my jaw (I have never been back to Bone or gone to any other dentist, and I have given up seeing Dyer) and my chest, which remain much as they were. I nevertheless, last year and earlier this year, wrote and revised *The Pier* and also put together a small group of potted biographies provisionally entitled *Three Lives and a Bit*, the lives being those of Colonel John Hutchinson,[2] John

1. *Sweet Adelaide: A Victorian Puzzle Solved*, London, 1980.
2. The subject of the book bought by RH on October 13th, 1975 (page 167). Hutchinson was, to all intents and purposes, a supporter of

Gabriel Stedman[1] and Elizabeth Carter, the bit Victor Hugo's table-turning in Jersey.[2] I can hardly walk, though I get round the garden and sometimes perform great feats there.

The garden is or has just been at its best, with splendid lupins and irises and the ceanothus covered with blue pom-poms, the pinks coming into bloom, and the first roses, of course. I say its best. It has had a previous best, with daffodils and other narcissi, squills, hyacinths and crocuses, most spectacularly the mauve botanical crocuses, but also the white Dutch kind, which had greatly multiplied. Sparrows picked all the yellow Dutch crocuses to bits.

We have at last given way, and for three months we have been addicted to television. This evening, we mean to watch (and I mean watch, though also, of course, to listen to) half an hour's music by Cantilena, a Scottish chamber orchestra.

16 June

On television, Caravaggio's *Supper at Emmaus*, first of a long series of programmes on "One Hundred Great Paintings". As the man said, Christ has an extremely gross face. M. wonders whether he could have been posed by a woman. I have wondered whether sudden adoption of the habit of watching television could have had something to do with my tongue-tying and saying things wrong the month before last, perhaps even with my typing incapacity. It was a quite new or at any rate renewed habit. The change seems to have passed off. I type much as I did. I speak with some fluency. My words may come haltingly, but they come in the right order.

Cromwell, though a certificate presented in his favour after the Restoration asserted that he secretly served the royalist cause during the Protectorate.

1. Author of (shortened title) *Narrative of a Five Years' Expedition against the Revolted Negroes of Surinam, in Guiana, on the Wild Coast of South America, from the year 1772 to 1777.*
2. See January 22nd, 1969.

24 June

I have given up stamp-collecting. That is to say, I shall stick no more stamps in any of my nineteen albums unless I improbably acquire one which fills a gap. I shall still soak any foreign or new English stamps off envelopes and put the more interesting into the little wooden Japanese box, the remainder into a big twicer box which once held chocolates.

Any children who call here may have their pick of the twicers. I wanted to divide up my albums among my five grandchildren, but their interests, in so far as they have distinct interests, differ impossibly and are either too changeable or too rigid. They like looking at my stamps when they are here, and they like collecting their own stamps, and there it stops. It may change.

The day has been wet. The fact that I have finished collecting stamps does not, alas, mean that I have finished with stamps. Here I am, after midnight, still engaged in getting rid of pseudo-stamps or, rather, separating them to put in envelopes in the big box mainly devoted to accessories. Pseudo-stamps are what are commonly known to stamp-collectors as stickers, but further include the stamps of such places as Tangier, Lundy, the Republic of Malaku Selatan and the state of New York, commercial and tax stamps (these mainly Italian or Spanish), stamps cut off postcards, stamps wholly covered with Arabic or Chinese characters and, in general, anything which I cannot find in a catalogue. This will go on all tomorrow morning, when I have to be up early to unbolt the garden gate for the dustmen.

7 July

C.P. Snow died last Tuesday, the 1st, the coldest July day on record. I wrote a letter to Pamela on Thursday. It was not a very good letter, I fear. Charles was seventy the October after we came here and invited us to his seventieth birthday party. He was three months younger than M. In a way, he meant a great deal to me, yet we have never written to each other during a period of over five years, mainly, I think, because of my depression during most of that time.

Charles was a very heavy drinker at times, but never, I would say, in danger of becoming what is known as an alcoholic. Pamela is, to my mind, or was when I last saw her, an alcoholic. She had also not long before had a stroke, which had left her with different symptoms from mine.

Vernon Scannell is coming to Deal this week to read his poems at the public library on Friday evening. His new wife is "preposterously young". Her parents are Deal people. He hopes "we can meet for a jar". At fifty-eight, he thus nips out to pubs, whether with young wife or not, and there drinks beer, to which he refers as "a jar". This is terrible. I remember him as quite a good poet, though not a good reader of verse. Not that I care for poetry readings at best.

19 July

V. Scannell first came round at teatime on Thursday with his tall, quite pretty young wife, whom he first met as a barmaid in Canterbury, where he was poet in residence for a year.

At the poetry reading on Friday, we met the Dover librarian, Ricketts, and, in my case for the first time, the local librarian, Mary Ward. She and Ricketts went round with us afterwards to the bar at the Royal, where Ricketts bought the first and third rounds and Vernon the middle one, with me attempting to butt in, and where Mary Ward had only one rum and Coca-Cola. The Scannells brought us home and had two further whiskies.

I have always thought of Vernon as rather a heavy drinker, though mainly a beer drinker. Angela keeps up with him, except that, when it is beer, as it was at the Royal, she has half-pints to his pints. She also keeps level with him in smoking cigarettes, which he rolls by hand. She is a very nice girl.

Vernon read only six to eight poems, talking about them

and inviting questions afterwards. The reading meant very little to me. He evidently made jokes and had jokey last lines to some of the poems, for there were intermittent ripples of laughter, in which I was unable to join, for he dropped his voice at the punch lines, and my hearing is a bit hard. I was sitting at the back, between M. and Angela. I told Angela that I had missed all the jokes. She said that she could tell me them if I wanted to hear them.

It was the young men in the audience who asked all but two of the inaudible questions. I wished they would stop. Eventually, Ricketts stood up and passed a vote of thanks. This was very boring, but he turned out afterwards to be a very pleasant fellow. Vernon also had to sign books afterwards. He offered to take us home before the signing began, but we declined the offer. Mary Ward is a businesslike young woman, with nice hair and rather special eyes.

20 July

This evening, on independent television, *Murder at the Savoy*, the trial of Mme Fahmy, played by an actress who gave her evidence in English (Mme Fahmy had an interpreter) and was thus able to put on a performance. Fahmy Bey's secretary, who was Egyptian, was played by an unmistakable European, who did not look or sound particularly homosexual, and Marshall Hall by Robert Stephens, who was unmistakably himself, though he took pills and limped every now and then.

24 July

Lindy and her two daughters are down here. Andrew is in Brittany, Donald not yet down. This evening, the regatta procession, held up by sewage repairs at the corner. I paid almost no attention. It was just so much noise. Recorded pop brought up the rear. Dogshit on the pavement. When the withdrawal began, I trusted that so many feet would remove it, but no. It was still there, noticed and avoided by everyone.

Somebody will perhaps tread on it in the dark.

25 July

Somebody did, but not sufficiently.

26 July

Phyllis Lawson or Sedlacek, *i.e.*, Sedlacek, *née* Lawson,[1] wants to play chess with me and told me yesterday that she had been playing since we last met with Jiri, who beat her, this doubtless by way of reassuring me, who had told her that I was so out of practice that I barely remembered the moves or the position of pieces on the board. It is doubtless this which has led me to reflect how like a game of chess the present world situation is.

A game of chess ends when one player's king, already in check, cannot move out of check and the player cannot move another piece so as to cover the check. This is then checkmate. Russians are very good at chess, though eight years ago an American beat the Russian champion.

I do not suppose that either the Americans or the Russians wish to destroy each other's countries or even their capital cities, but only that they wish to establish positions from which one or the other could unmistakably achieve this, according to the rules of the game. The nearest thing to a checkmate the Russians achieved was when, but for President Kennedy's timely intervention, they would have established in Cuba missiles capable of reaching New York.

27 July

My sixty-ninth birthday and the fifth anniversary of our moving into this house. Luncheon at the King's Arms in Sandwich, with Lindy and the two girls, M. and Donald,

---

1.   A painter, married to a Czech, Jiri Sedlacek.

notably including some of the best beef I have ever tasted. Ann Bliss has had two car smashes in rapid succession and is still a bit shaky. Godfrey was in the bar, very purple.

For our birthday presents, M. had a jade brooch and I what I understand to be called a treen. This is a tapering cylinder of boxwood, four inches tall, the top of which takes off to reveal a small, green tumbler. It will come in handy next time I enter the pump room of a spa.

2 August

The musicians' strike is over. The proms will start on Thursday, and this evening on ITV, beginning at 9.45 and going on till 12.20, we had Stravinsky's *The Rake's Progress* from Glyndebourne with a very irritating *décor* by David Hockney, but well sung. I found some of the action obscure. I had only heard the work in a concert performance before. There is not very much of the later Stravinsky I care for.

7 August

I have been reading a book on William Godwin. I had not realised that, in his *Essay on Population*, Malthus had mentioned and criticised Godwin's *Political Justice* or that Godwin was later to publish a feeble refutation of Malthus. I had not in fact thought much about Malthus at all, though I had thought much about overpopulation.

Godwin I see as the late eighteenth century's chief optimist and therefore (with Bentham), politically, progressive, Malthus as its chief pessimist and therefore, politically, reactionary. Malthus thought that populations tended to double every generation. In this he was wrong. The tendency is rather for them to double every century. Since Malthus was wrong about the rate of population increase, his views are ignored. But populations do increase, and the population of this country is now dangerously large, as well as intolerable.

9 August

Concern over the size of our population, not unmixed with colour prejudice, may be thought to have begun with an act of the Privy Council for August 11th, 1596.

> Her Majesty understanding that there are of late divers blackamoors brought into this realm, of which kind there are already too many, considering how God hath blessed this land with great increase of people of our own nation, ... those kinds of people should be sent forth of the land.

But it was not until the eighteenth century that Jonathan Swift published *A Modest Proposal for preventing the Children from being a Burthen to their Parents, or the Country, and for making them Beneficial to the Publick*. The proposal was to pay beggars to fatten up their babies to one year old and then to serve them as food at the tables of the more prosperous. As Swift was a satirical writer, it has always been regarded as satirical, though of what it would be difficult to say. At the end of the century came Malthus.

This evening, we saw on tv a programme we had heard on radio on Thursday, the belated first night of the proms. It consisted of Mahler's fourth symphony, a recent favourite of M.'s, in which the soprano solo of the last movement was beautifully sung by Jessye Norman, an enormously fat Negress or mulatto with a face of splendid dignity, rather aquiline in profile.

14 August

My insect bites, now fairly comfortable, have been replaced by a burn on my left arm. This was received while refuelling a bonfire last evening. By pouring water on the lid handle, I had managed to remove the lid and push further garden rubbish in. While replacing the lid, I caught my bare arm on the rim of the incinerator, which was hot. Afterwards, I rubbed the burnt place with water, thinking it merely dirty, and this took off a lot of top skin. I then rubbed on Savlon ointment. The pain was inconsiderable until this evening, and in the afternoon I had made love with great enjoyment to M., who was delightful. Now the pain is extreme, and M., after bathing the place with liquid Savlon, has put on a Melolin pad with Micropore sticky tape, of which one end is on a patch of inflamed skin. Loosening the tape, of which there was very little left, I am afraid that the pad will come off during the night, and I cannot sleep on my left side, which I prefer to do much of the time because of my aching right arm, aching the more after much sawing and snipping during the past two days, and the continuing pain in my jaw. I had been intending to go to bed with M. again.

20 August

The Woolleys are returning to London tomorrow. Next week, David starts rehearsing *The Ring*. We had them in for a drink at midday, and Lindy looked in for half an hour. Lindy's interest in David was due to his professional oboe-playing, she being a recent amateur. The Woolleys have been coming to Deal these fourteen years. David has already spent ten years editing Swift's prose for a two-volume, thin-paper Oxford edition, intended to replace one published in more volumes by the Bodley Head. I cannot imagine how anybody spends ten to twenty years editing anything. I do not know why an Australian oboe-player was contracted by the Oxford university press to edit Swift's prose. David Woolley's qualifications must be more impressive than I have yet heard. He is a very gentle-mannered man, frail-seeming, with steely depths. He remembers my name from *Penguin New Writing* during the war, almost forty years ago, he cannot remember as the author of what, but doubtless of a story called "The Wild Man of the Woods".

The French fishermen's blockade remains in the news. The Polish dockers' strike is far graver and less idiotic, though it will certainly be crushed, no doubt with Russian help.

22 August

While we were having lunch, a man called Paul Binding rang up from the *New Statesman* to ask if I would review Evelyn Waugh's letters. It is at least ten years since I was asked to review anything for the *Statesman*. I have believed that it was on political grounds. I wonder why I have suddenly been asked again and why it should be Evelyn Waugh.

According to Phyllis, Deal is full of vice. According to Dr Reynolds, it is famous abroad for its homosexuality. Phyllis also had a story about a man who came to clean for her and who left a cinema projector in the house. She later discovered that he went round showing blue films at various houses and fancied that he may have been showing them at hers. The man came round to her house in the small hours, drunk, and was told to fuck off by a son of Edward Ardizzone, who lives next door. She has had the lock changed and a chain put on the door.

- - - - is very disturbed. She is behind with pictures for an exhibition. She wonders whether to leave her husband, but also asked me to make her a reading list, so that she could keep up with his fat girl friend, who is apparently highbrow. We advised her against reading for such a purpose.

4 September

L'Enfance du Christ this evening from Westminster cathedral, with Rozhdestvensky conducting. It overran ten minutes, though not with the dirgelike sameness of Sir Groves's *tempi* last time I heard this favourite work. The singing I found little more than adequate. How many years ago was my favourite performance? It was, I fancy, the year before the death of Victor Gollancz, who was there with his daughter, Livia, a handsome woman who had once played French horn in the Hallé orchestra.

5 September

The morning post brought me pleasure, especially a

friendly letter from Clive Allison, enclosing a cheque and two marvellous reviews of *The Blaze of Noon*, one from *The Times* and one, by Martin Seymour-Smith, from the *Financial Times*, together with the news that he and Val will be down here next weekend, inviting us to either lunch or supper, whichever we prefer, they having friends staying.

9 September

Copies of *The Blaze of Noon* arrived on Saturday. It looks very nice, with a reproduction of Bonnard's *Nude in Yellow* on the jacket. I posted off a letter to Clive, saying that we opted for Sunday luncheon, but could equally manage supper on Saturday evening if they preferred it, and explaining in broad terms, without names, the origin of the rumour about him and Val splitting up. I am not quite satisfied with this explanation, since it leaves it possible to be believed that it was I who put the interpretations on the facts reported to me.

M. came home at lunchtime with sad news about Peter Bowers, the vicar, and his "commune". Diana Bowers is still in the house, but "unwanted". Peter Bowers's "sincerity" is never in doubt. The inverted commas there mean something different from in the two previous uses. I believe that he is sincere, but quite hopelessly misguided, one wonders from just what lack of previous experience.

11 September

The new bishop of Dover has intervened in the affairs of Peter Bowers and said that people other than his family must leave the vicarage.

A letter from Nancy Bush, Michael Head's sister, married to the composer Alan Bush, tells me that Pamela Snow is very ill. This she presumably knows from seeking permission to reprint a letter of Pamela's in a Memoir she is writing about Michael.[1] The letter, from the *Listener*, was about the *petite*

1. *Michael Head: Composer, Singer, Pianist*, Thetford, Norfolk, 1982.

phrase in Proust, which Pamela and I, after listening to records, had decided to be a phrase from Saint-Saëns's first violin sonata.[1] This was used by Michael in his versions of the Vinteuil sonata and septet for Pamela's Proust reconstructions.

14 September

We went to Clive and Val's for supper last evening. A girl staying there called Bryan Healing, who works at *Encounter*. Clive came here late this morning. Val and Bryan joined him at midday for drinks. He has seen Sillitoe, who was apparently speaking kindly of me, and Alan Burns, who has now got himself fixed up at an American university and separated from Carol, who did not want to go to America.

I gave Bryan a little packet of lovage seeds. In return, she is to send me seeds of bronze fennel. We forgot to ask her to remember us to Margot Wormsley (or is it Walmsley?[2]), Anthony Thwaite and Mel J. Lasky at *Encounter*, where they all three still are. I have not seen this magazine for at least six years.

15 September

Barbara Wall rang this evening while I was in the middle of my greatest bonfire yet. Our last communication was almost five years ago, not long after Bernard's death, when she was about to move to her mother's house in Sussex and she wanted to know about removal men we had used. I gave her the very sound advice to use a firm in the neighbourhood she was moving to rather than that she was moving from, in her case

1. From a letter from Pamela Hansford Johnson to RH, July 12th, 1976: "I shall never forget those gorgeous Prousting days (I think I was never happier) and the inspiration you breathed into my dead scripts. I shall never forget the day we skimmed through two Saint-Saëns sonatas to find the Right Piece, and lo, there it was!"
2. The latter.

Ladbroke Road, London. She had rung this evening because she had seen somewhere a review of the reprinted *Blaze of Noon* and was taken with nostalgia, as I was when I heard her. She grows vegetables and had a novel published during the year by Gollancz, called, I fancy, *Widows and Widowers*[1] and, I suppose, under her maiden name, Barbara Lucas.

She has, she says, become very Left, almost a Bennite, her neighbourhood being hopelessly Tory. That I had become very Right did not surprise her, since I read the *Sunday Telegraph*. I pointed out to her that it was the cheapest of the Sundays, indeed of the weeklies, and therefore proved nothing. We first met forty-five years ago, when Bernard was editing a Catholic monthly called *Colosseum*, entirely pro-Franco in Spain, where Left and Right meant something. I remember an article by her called "The Cadets of the Alcazar". It was a celebration of the heroism of those under Republican attack. But we had no dispute. I attributed my Rightishness to the Leftishness of the Deal intelligentsia. I had been very fond of Barbara in those remote days, when I myself was under instruction to Fr. D'Arcy with a view to reception into the Roman Catholic church, which did not take place, largely because of the Spanish civil war.

20 September

Last night, a horrifying and protracted thunderstorm broke out just as, on tv, the film based on Edward Abbey's *Brave Cowboy* (which I had read when it was new) was ending in heavy rain on the road where Jack Burns was dying and his horse had to be put down, both having been injured by a big lorry. This seemed like a special case of pathetic fallacy.

24 September

Graham Greene's second volume of autobiography[1] (really

1. London, 1979.
2. *Ways of Escape*, London, 1980.

a miscellany arranged in chronological order, including the introductions to a Collected Edition of his novels) contains a glowing tribute to Herbert Read, most quietly glowing of men, whom he met at about the same time as myself, in 1935.

I wonder how successful the Collected Edition will be at today's prices. For the past forty years or more, we have all grabbed eagerly at Graham Greene's latest novels, but I wonder how many of us read them a second or third time. Each had an unexpected point of view, easily remembered. Evelyn Waugh stands up better. He was the better writer of English narrative prose.

28 September

The vicar, Peter Bowers, has gone. I use Weedol in an attempt to kill the acanthus which keeps putting up shoots between my wallflower plants. This is a paraquat compound from ICI. I have wondered whether to drink it, but the symptoms sound unpleasant and lingering, though death is apparently certain.

30 September

M. has been washing one of our heavy back curtains, rinsing the nicotine out. I helped her to wring it and hang it on the line, bringing it down from the bathroom. I also finished cutting a plum-tree trunk with my small pruning saw, which becomes steadily blunter.

2 October

A telephone call from Julian Symons, inviting us to lunch on Sunday. He said he had been pleased to see me in the *New Statesman*. I said I could not think how I had come in favour there again, he (wittily, I thought) that they had no doubt discovered my secret Left-wing leanings. At any rate, I am glad not, as I feared, to have upset him or not permanently.

6 October

Finding a quince on the soil, I decided that the time had come for picking quinces, though they did not look quite ripe. M. and I went out, at some time after five o'clock, with stepladder, secateurs, colander and walking-stick. We had picked twenty or thirty of those easiest (though not easy) to get at when a small man with spectacles offered to help. He said that he was younger than I was (he was not very young), I that he was not so tall. He was used to it, he said. I asked him how this came about. He said, "We've got an orchard." He went up the stepladder and stood on the very top, which I have never dared to do, except very occasionally, with M. holding my legs or my trousers, more to give me a feeling of security than to make me secure. Altogether, we collected sixty quinces, including three small, split ones. It would have been sixty-one, but that one rolled out into the middle of the road while I was holding down branches. Just as I was ready to go out and get it, a car ran over it and squashed it flat. I thanked the man and asked his name and where he lived. He is Mr Berkshire of Middle Deal Road.

The quinces are now set out on a table in the conservatory. Their smell is ambrosial.

12 October

The first boiling of quince jam is jarred and labelled. The second boiling, which contained a few green Japanese quinces (the fruit of the spiky bush usually called japonica) was started last night to the accompaniment of thunder and lightning, wind and rain (the wind from the north-east), which continued until half-past six this morning. The milkman had faithfully delivered milk.

A letter from the editor of *New Society* informs me that I shall presently receive a formal invitation to the unveiling at noon on Tuesday, November 18th, of a GLC blue plaque on 50 Lawford Road, Kentish Town, where in 1935 I shared a flat with George Orwell. I was surprised that Orwell should be made the object of blue plaques and should have thought this one better applied to a house in Islington where he lived longer. Among those present will be Bernard Crick, author of the official biography.[1] Sonia Brownell, who married Orwell on his death bed (a *mariage blanc*) and who has since received the royalties and controlled the copyright and who later for a while became Sonia Pitt-Rivers (another *mariage blanc*) may also, I suppose, condescend to put in an appearance.

There is no midday news on Sundays (or on Saturdays), but there was a "Crime Writers" at a quarter-past one, so we had to have lunch in here, the appearance of Ross Macdonald being announced, to say nothing of a further appearance of Julian Symons (to whose very great credit be it here recorded that he did not wish to watch the programme last Sunday, when we were at lunch with the Symonses, he being on, although he had not been announced in *Radio Times*). Ross Macdonald has a sensitive, sad face. He does not look as if he were capable of performing the feats of his private eye, Lew Archer, but one understands why he writes as he does. One could have done without the interventions of Gavin Lyall, a writer whose name I know, but of whose novels I do not think I have read any, at any rate have not remembered any. But the fact is that I have not found Julian's own crime novels memorable, though he was good in this programme, talking about Dashiell Hammett and Raymond Chandler.

All BBC tv series programmes have to have a signature tune, accompanied by a sequence of images either photographed or drawn, a source of expense and annoyance. The tunes, some of them at any rate, recur to one's mind in the most irritating fashion, so that one remains discontented until one has traced them to their source. They "haunt" one, that is to say. That a tune is "haunting" is no guarantee of its merit or of its nostalgic quality. I am continually haunted by the dreariest tunes. The worst of all sets of preliminaries was those which preceded a book programme, "All About

1. *George Orwell: A Life*, London, 1980.

Books". This was interminable, badly drawn and showed pigs trotting across the screen, while voices sang some form of pop music to the accompaniment of a band. The programmes themselves were not at all bad, better than those chaired by Robert Robinson, who himself does most of the talking.

As to those long lists of "credits" which conclude so many programmes, it is one's own fault if one is irritated by those, though often the programme continues behind them. My own favourite is the Dubbing Mixer. Dubbing used to be grease prepared for the treatment of leather, often prescribed by Army Council Instructions and ignored in regiments, which preferred polished boots. One might easily imagine somebody mixing that, especially if it was black in colour. I also, when working in sound, became familiar with a dubbing as meaning a copy of part of a recording. I still cannot imagine what a Dubbing Mixer on television does. What a Vision Mixer does is more easily imagined, and Graphic Design would be simple had there been any drawings in the programme.

3 November

Clive and Val Allison down at the weekend, with two friends. We had dinner with them on Saturday. They came for drinks here with us on Sunday. He has taken *The Pier* to read.

He mentioned a letter from Christopher Sykes in answer to a reference to him in my review of Evelyn Waugh's letters. It goes:

> Allow me slightly to correct Mr Heppenstall's mistaken correction of my biography of Evelyn Waugh . . . . He claims that in the biography he is maligned "under a false name". This gives a false impression. I avoided using Mr Heppenstall's name, but I revealed the name of Kurkweiler by which Evelyn came to refer to Mr Heppenstall.

I am replying:

> You must forgive your literary editor and myself for the
> fact that I have only just seen Christopher Sykes's letter,
> with its references to me, in your issue of October 10th. I
> cannot see that a name is any the less false for having also
> been used by the late Evelyn Waugh.
>
> I am reluctant to say anything complimentary about
> Sykes, but it does seem decent of him to provide a clear
> identification of Kurkweiler with me. This is bound to ease
> the task of any barrister I may employ to bring him to book
> for his libels.

I have no solicitors and no intention of taking Christopher
Sykes to law. The idea is to keep him on tenterhooks.

16 November

The galley proofs of *Tales from the Newgate Calendar* arrived
yesterday from Constable. The main trouble for me has been
to do with dates and with noblemen's titles.

Nobody *says* "sixteen November". People say either "the
sixteenth of November" or "November sixteenth" or even
"November the sixteenth". Nowadays, however, English
printers print (and, for all I know, writers write and type, or
their typists type) "16 November". I should have let this stand
if the compositor here had been consistent, but in a large
number of cases he printed, as I had typed, "the 16th of
November" or "November 16th". I shall have to go back to
the typescript and see which of the two forms I had used in
each particular case, lest it should seem that in some cases I
have made an alteration, for which I could be charged.
(Another thing is that nowadays English printers always put
commas after closing inverted commas, which I find
disgraceful and which American printers still do not do.)

As to the titles of noblemen, I used small letters for "earl"
and "duke" and so on, as at least the fourteenth edition of the

Encyclopaedia Britannica does throughout. A copy-editor chose to substitute capitals, but has again not done it consistently throughout. Glazebrook said that I could have it my way if I liked, and somebody has been through the typescript altering some capitals back to small letters, notably in the case of Earl Rivers, where I had put a capital, as I did with Earl Ferrers and various Lords. I have felt quite uncertain what to do.

28 November

Andrew was here for two nights early in the week. He has done marvellously well in the common entrance examination, coming top of all those who took it and for Westminster. A fortnight later, he was still in a state of reaction and very tired. The dull skies and inaction suited him. He is a beautiful boy and very nice. On Tuesday at midday, we had one of my best bonfires to date.

I now have two copies of Bernard Crick's life of Orwell, one from *Encounter*, which Bryan Healing sent together with the bronze fennel seeds she had promised when she was here with Clive and Val. All but the *Lit. Supp.* have reviewed the book this week at considerable length. All but Nigel Dennis, in the *Sunday Telegraph*, commend the book highly. I shall not be able to.

After almost a fortnight of mild weather, it has turned cold again, with quite heavy snow. I do not remember snow in November, even in Huddersfield.

30 January

There was some frost this morning, but January has been a remarkably mild month. This is the more remarkable in view of the cold start the winter got off to. The month got off to a letter from Glazebrook to which I have not yet replied, nor to a later, briefer one he wrote, though this one required a brief answer. I want to wait until I have the page proofs.

The foghorn is booming. There is not much mist on land, though there was earlier in the evening.

3 February

Copy of *Encounter* containing my review of Crick's *Orwell* and nothing else of much interest. The woman whom Orwell married on his death bed, known as Sonia Orwell, though she became Mrs Pitt-Rivers after being Mrs Blair and who started life as Sonia Brownell, died in time for me to have added something about her, and the review was short of the three thousand words asked for. I am not much of a *de mortuis nil nisi bonum* man. I am more conscious of the fact that, once a person is dead, he or she can no longer be libelled. I did dislike Sonia, I think with good reason. Jane Degras's word for her was "black-hearted". It was the right one.

As a young person at *Horizon*, she was greatly admired for her looks, but it quickly became known that she had a morbid fear of sex. Despite this fact, she did very well out of her two marriages, marrying first Orwell when she knew he was dying and subsequently Michael Pitt-Rivers when he was released from prison after a notorious homosexual offence. Two *mariages blancs* with great financial consequences. In the case of Orwell, she made no attempt to be a mother to his adopted son. As controller of the Orwell copyright, she was a *veuve abusive*, denying Abrahams and Stansky all quotation and agreeing to a radio programme on Orwell (to be produced by Christopher Sykes) only if I were excluded. This was, I suppose, because my own radio programme had contained only one, slighting reference to herself. She must have imagined that I had cut out other references, but I had not. Of those I recorded, only Avril had referred to her brother's second marriage, which, she said, had taken place to her surprise. I should like to know what sort of will Sonia made, if any. Doubtless Richard would do best if she died intestate. Not that I cared much for him the last time I saw him.

The snowdrops are out. Also a few rather small violets and primroses. And now I see that yellow crocuses are almost out. The sparrows will peck these.

On the wireless, from Covent Garden, *Un Ballo in Maschera*, with the tenor Luciano Pavarotti, said to be even better than Domingo. I have not found him so, but then I do not think I have heard Domingo in anything so devoid of human and melodic interest, the chief memorable aria (*Eri tu*) being one for baritone, here modestly sung by another Italian. I am sure that *Un Ballo in Maschera* is splendid on the stage, where I have not seen it (M. has). Merely in sound, it is routine middle-period Verdi.

We switched it off two-thirds of the way through in order to watch the tenth of Robert Kee's *Ireland* programmes on television. These started well, but the last few have been full of old men reminiscing (some of the old men ought clearly to have been hanged) and far more nationalistic in tone, so that

Kee seemed about to become an apologist for the IRA. I have various memories of Kee, one of him pouring wine into my lap while I moved my glass, containing whisky, to the side, one of him bringing a child to a party of ours and this being rather a nuisance. I was very taken with the Jewish wife he then had.

4 February

It is too cold to sow my pansy seeds, but I have opened the packet. At £1.20, it contains about forty seeds. These have to be distributed over a flat box and four six-inch pots. The seeds are small, and I shall probably have to pick them up with tweezers.

15 February

Last evening, Mahler's *Symphony of One Thousand* on tv from Vienna. The second half was enjoyable, but how absurd Goethe's *Faust* seems when it is flashed on the screen in bits. He brings everything in, from Jesus to Abraham feeding his flocks, all to prove that Faust (whom we last saw sinking through a trap door to Hell) should have been redeemed through the love of women, while thousands of others were no doubt rightly damned.

This evening, a programme of boundless fascination showed film going back to the early years of this century. Such early film could be shown on television ten hours a day, and I should sit glued. Nothing of the kind exists for past ages, when nevertheless human beings, both famous and obscure, were co-existing on earth. How, for instance, one would like to see, however dimly, Horace Walpole entering a ballroom.

20 February

I seem to have started work on putting my periodical critical writings together into a possible book (or, indeed, books), with many revisions. When I have thought of doing this before, I have, oddly, been tied to the notion of putting them, mainly, in the order in which I wrote them, doubtless with the idea that my views were temporary and should be shown thus. Now I have started putting the pieces together in a chronological order of a literary history. This has already paid off in one way. I had vaguely supposed that the horrible *Malleus Maleficarum* must precede the highly civilised Charles d'Orleans. Not so. It comes almost thirty years after Charles's death, admittedly in a less civilised part of Europe, the Alsace-Lorraine from which Joan of Arc also came, not then or for two hundred years more part of France.

14 March

After a dry and frigid February, which seems to have killed the fuchsias, already putting out shoots, March came in mild and wet. Glazebrook has stopped writing to me, but sends little messages by his secretary. The book will come out with my name on it, hardly recognisable as my work. Apropos the *Blaze of Noon* reprint, Julian Symons has published a general article on me, part complimentary, part not, in the *London Review of Books*, missing out *The Woodshed* and *The Shearers* and, with *Two Moons*, grumbling, like reviewers at the time, at the way it is set out and not saying what it is about. On Thursday, Kathleen brought me a clump of day lilies.

4 April[1]

This morning, Julian rang to invite us to lunch tomorrow. It was impossible. Lindy and all her family will be here, with a boy called Stefan. I find Julian's article patronising, but am determined not to quarrel.

---

1. The last typed journal entry.

11 April

Right hand semi-paralysed. Couldn't attempt to shave.

13 April

Very weak. M. blew her top.[1]

19 April

To Lindy's for lunch and to meet Lindy's old school-friend, Maureen, and her husband Paul.

26 April

Julian and Kathleen to lunch. Got a bit tight.

6 May

Francis Booth[2] came down from London.

7 May

Hadn't slept. Rain in the evening.

8 May

Hadn't slept. Rubbish collection a day late. Am very uncomfortable.

---

1. M.: "Over nothing very much. I rarely lost my temper. But Rayner couldn't bear it if I lost my temper with *him*. Sat huddled in his chair, 'you've spoilt my day,' etc."
2. An admirer of RH's work, particularly *The Woodshed*; he was writing a thesis on the modern novel.

16 May

1.00 a.m. Thunderstorm

Shortly before noon on May 17th, when, as was his custom on Sunday mornings, he was at his typewriter, Rayner Heppenstall suffered a stroke which paralysed him down one side and made him mute. He was taken to the hospital in Deal, but his condition worsened, and he died in the early hours of Saturday, May 23rd.

CONSOLATION IN JULY

Father, be praised for a white jasmine
Thrown over a balcony of falking iron.
The odour faint, florets quickly discoloured,
It roots in builder's rubble and the vile,
   sour clay of London,
A soil for which none living feels affection,
Rubbing it amorously between the fingers.
A skein of brittle stalks, this dormant vine
Yet expressed
White, opaque flesh and the socketed pistil,
The six joined petals and sevenfold spears.
Alas, they say
The one inimitable scene
May now be feigned with bitter almonds,
Tonquil beans, vanilla, that we need
No longer travel to China in our dreams.
And yet I feel with each new efflorescence
My interest in earth is permanent,
A current lack of love
Easily compensated in another life.
Nudeleaf, yellow jasmine,
Pale haunters of the winter, potted primula,
Cold cyclamen, the yellow bush that Fortune
Fetched from the heights of lost Yunnan,
Fruitless cherry and the paeony's frilled drumsticks
Promise, promise, when the year is early,
And as the dog-day comes and the parched leaf
Curls on the tree, with fifteen fingers
Lupin promises (in the anxious palm
A drop of dew like quicksilver).
Promises a late wind.
Tossing the ripe corn to the flying clouds,
And last before there comes an aconite
This ice-bound music crying to be loosed
Promises. Promise all, beyond performance
Unless it be, O Father, by your leave.

Bibliography

CRIME HISTORY

A Little Pattern of French Crime, Hamish Hamilton, 1969.
French Crime in the Romantic Age, Hamish Hamilton, 1970.
Bluebeard and After, Peter Owen, 1972.
The Sex War and Others, Peter Owen, 1973.
Reflections on the Newgate Calendar, W. H. Allen, 1975.
Tales from the Newgate Calendar, Constable, 1981.

CRITICISM

Middleton Murry: A Study in Excellent Normality, Jonathan Cape, 1934.
Apology for Dancing Faber & Faber, 1936.
The Double Image, Secker & Warburg, 1947.
Leon Bloy, Bowes & Bowes, Cambridge, 1954.
The Fourfold Tradition, Barrie & Rockliff, 1962.
Raymond Roussel: A Critical Guide, Calder & Boyars, 1966.

MEMOIRS

Four Absentees, Barrie & Rockliff, 1960.
The Intellectual Part, Barrie & Rockliff, 1963.
Portrait of the Artist as a Professional Man, Peter Owen, 1969.
(*My Bit of Dylan Thomas* was printed for private circulation
     [80 copies] in 1957.)

NOVELS

The Blaze of Noon, Secker & Warburg, 1939; Alliance Book Cor-
     poration, 1940; Barrie & Rockliff, 1962; Sphere (paperback),
     1962; Allison & Busby (hardback and paperback), 1980.
Saturnine, Secker & Warburg, 1943.
The Lesser Infortune, Jonathan Cape, 1953.
The Greater Infortune (a revision of *Saturnine*), Peter Owen, 1960,
     and "Red Riband" paperback 1961.

The Woodshed, Barrie & Rockliff, 1962; Calder & Boyars (paperback), 1968.
The Connecting Door, Barrie & Rockliff, 1962.
The Shearers, Hamish Hamilton, 1969.
Two Moons, Allison & Busby (hardback and paperback), 1977.
The Pier, Allison & Busby, 1986.

POETRY

Patina (reproduced from typewriting), Literary Guild, 1932.
First Poems, Heinemann, 1935.
Sebastian, Dent, 1937.
Blind Men's Flowers are Green, Secker & Warburg, 1940.
Poems 1933-1945, Secker & Warburg, 1946.

TRANSLATIONS FROM THE FRENCH

Atala and *René* (Chateaubriand), Oxford University Press, 1963.
Impressions of Africa (Roussel), with Lindy Foord, Calder & Boyars, 1969.
A Harlot High and Low (Balzac), Penguin (hardback and paperback), 1970.
When Justice Falters (Floriot), Harrap, 1972.

MISCELLANEOUS

Three Tales of Hamlet (with Michael Innes), Gollancz, 1950.

Rayner Heppenstall also contributed essays, stories, etc. to a number of books.

Index

271

272